ENCOUNTERS WITH TROUBLED PASTS IN CONTEMPORARY DUTCH AND GREEK HISTORIOGRAPHY

ENCOUNTERS WITH TROUBLED PASTS IN CONTEMPORARY DUTCH AND GREEK HISTORIOGRAPHY

EDITED BY
PHILIP CARABOTT & WILLEM W. LEDEBOER

PUBLICATIONS OF THE
NETHERLANDS INSTITUTE AT ATHENS VIII

© 2023 Individual authors

Published by Sidestone Press, Leiden
www.sidestone.com

Publications of the Netherlands Institute at Athens VIII

Lay-out & cover design: Sidestone Press
Photograph cover: SuriyaPhoto | Stock.adobe.com

ISBN 978-94-6426-176-9 (softcover)
ISBN 978-94-6426-177-6 (hardcover)
ISBN 978-94-6426-178-3 (PDF e-book)

DOI 10.59641/sip493jk

Contents

Preface — 7

Notes on Contributors — 9

An Undigested Past. The Netherlands and Its Colonial History — 13
  Frank van Vree

Pride, Shame, Responsibility. New Historical and Heritage Studies on the Holocaust and Slavery — 25
  Dienke Hondius

The Other Side of the "Catastrophe". Greek Army Atrocities During the Asia Minor Campaign (1919-1922) — 33
  Tasos Kostopoulos

An Unclaimed Past. The Shoah in Athens — 41
  Philip Carabott

The Silent Tree. Collaborationism, Political Power and Collective Guilt. A Dutch-Greek Case Study in Memory — 53
  Riki Van Boeschoten

A Ticket of Re-Admission into Dutch Society. The Controversy on Amsterdam's Monument of Jewish Gratitude (1950) — 63
  Roel Hijink & Bart Wallet

Persecution Through Demonisation, Condemnation Through Silence. Reflecting on Left-Wing Violence in 1940s Greece — 73
  Iason Chandrinos

The "Morality Narrative" on Jewish Rescue in Greece. Commemorative Practices and Representations — 83
  Anna Maria Droumpouki

"Narratives Don't Burn". Understanding Oral Testimonies and Conceptions of Loyalty Among Exiled Greek Minorities in Central Asia After the Stalinist Repressions — 91
  Eftihia Voutira

Narratives Competing for the Public Space in Post-Soviet Russia. A Case Study in Challenges to Transitional Justice — 99
  Nanci Adler

The Narratives of the Survivors of Srebrenica — 109
  Selma Leydesdorff

Preface

The volume in hand throws light on historical encounters with troubled pasts in contemporary Dutch and Greek historiography. Contributors, experts in their respective research fields with a wide range of scholarly publications, eschew dominant national accounts, deconstruct top-down narratives, and situate the historical subject(s) at the centre of the analysis. Troubled pasts are the outcome of local, national and international conflicts, of the continuous quest for growth and dominance, of Colonialism and Great Power rivalry, of ideologically-motivated purges, of Genocide, of National Liberation Struggles, and of Civil Wars. They go hand-in-hand with a great deal of human suffering and horrendous atrocities against civilians on ethnic, religious, racial and political grounds. The examination of troubled pasts and their accompanying imagery raise enduring questions: Whose past is remembered? How is the past appropriated and memorialised? Which pasts are at best neglected, at worse silenced – and why? *Encounters with Trouble Pasts* addresses such issues by reference to Dutch Colonialism in the New World and South East Asia, the Greek campaign in Asia Minor, the Shoah and its aftermath in Greece and the Netherlands, the Greek Civil War of the 1940s, Transitional Justice in Post-Soviet Russia, and the Massacre of Srebrenica. It will be of interest to postgraduate students and academics working on Colonialism, the Shoah, modern Dutch and Greek History, Memory, and on Oral History.

Seven of the volume's chapters were first delivered at the workshop "History Unwanted: Testimonies, silence and public memory", which was held at the Netherlands Institute at Athens (NIA) in September 2016. As many scholarly accounts on troubled pasts are only discussed in publications in Dutch and Greek, the aim of the workshop was to bring together scholars from Greece and the Netherlands in a Greek-Dutch academic setting to present their current research on troubled pasts in English. For reasons beyond our control, some of the workshop's papers have not been integrated here. This "unwanted" outcome has been offset by the inclusion of four commissioned chapters (Carabott, Hijink & Wallet, Hondius, van Vree).

As the third volume in the publication series of the NIA with Sidestone Press, *Encounters with Troubled Pasts* highlights the dynamism of the Institute's activities. Ranging from Ancient History and Classical Studies to Contemporary History and Social Anthropology, they have cemented close and fruitful research ties among Dutch, Greek and other European scholars in what have been undoubtedly difficult times.

Many thanks to Henriette-Rika Benveniste, Anna Maria Droumpouki, Pothiti Hantzaroula, and Riki Van Boeschoten for their help in the planning of the 2016 workshop; to Selma Leydesdorff, Winfred van de Put and Bart Wallet for their profitable suggestions and overall support on the NIA's Greek-Dutch workshops and seminar series since 2016; and, of course, to the volume's contributors for their patience and courteous understanding.

Philip Carabott & Willem Ledeboer
December 2022

Notes on Contributors

Nanci Adler (n.Adler@niod.knaw.nl) is Professor of Memory, History and Transitional Justice at the NIOD Institute for War, Holocaust, and Genocide Studies (Royal Netherlands Academy of Arts and Sciences) and the University of Amsterdam. Inter alia, she has authored *Keeping Faith with the Party: Communist Believers Return from the Gulag* (Indiana University Press, 2012), *The Gulag Survivor: Beyond the Soviet System* (Transaction Publishers, 2002), *Understanding the Age of Transitional Justice: Courts, Crimes, Commissions and Chronicling* (Rutgers University Press, 2018), co-edited (with A. Weiss-Wendt) *The Future of the Soviet Past: the Politics of Memory in Putin's Russia* (Indiana University Press, 2021), and published numerous scholarly articles on political rehabilitations and the consequences of Stalinism. Her current research focuses on transitional justice and the legacy of Communism.

Philip Carabott (philip.carabott@kcl.ac.uk) is Research Associate of King's College London, where he taught modern and contemporary Greek history from 1990 to 2011; CEO of the Civil Non-Profit Company "Workshop on the Study of the Jews of Greece" (Athens, 2016-); and Commissioned Researcher of the Jewish Community of Athens. He has published widely on politics, society and minorities in Greece of the modern era. Currently, he is completing a monograph on the Shoah in Athens, and is Principal Investigator at the project "Hiding and rescue in German-occupied Athens, 1943-1944: Jewish persecutees and Greek compatriots", which is financially supported by the German-Greek Future Fund of the German Federal Foreign Office.

Iason Chandrinos (jahandrinos@yahoo.gr) was born in Athens in 1984. He studied modern history and received his PhD from the University of Athens in 2015. From 2007 to 2015 he worked as a special researcher for the Jewish Museum of Greece. He is a founding member of the Civil Non-Profit Company "Workshop on the Study of the Jews of Greece" (Athens, 2016-). From 2016 to 2018, he worked at the Greek-German project "Memories of the Occupation in Greece" (Free University of Berlin). In March 2022, he completed his habilitation thesis on "Internment, forced labour, labour migration: Greeks in the Third Reich, 1939-1945" at the Chair of Modern European History of the University of Regensburg with funding from the Deutsche Forschungsgemeinschaft (DFG). He has authored (in Greek) *The People's Punishing Arm: The Activities of ELAS and OPLA in Occupied Athens, 1942-1944* (Athens, 2012); *Cities at War: European Urban Centres Under Nazi Occupation, 1939-1945* (Athens, 2018); *Making It Through the Night: An Oral History of the Athens Polytechnic Uprising* (Athens, 2019); *Brothers in Arms: The National Liberation Front and the Jews of Greece* (Salonika, 2020). Currently, he is Researcher at the project "Hiding and rescue in German-occupied Athens, 1943-1944: Jewish persecutees and Greek compatriots", which is financially supported by the German-Greek Future Fund of the German Federal Foreign Office.

Anna Maria Droumpouki (anna.droumpouki@lrz.uni-muenchen.de) holds a BA in History and Archaeology, an MA in Museology and a PhD in Contemporary Greek and European History (all from the University of Athens). She was Visiting Research Scholar at the Institute for Jewish History and Culture – Simon Dubnow (Leipzig, 2009); Postdoctoral Fellow at the Research Centre for Modern History (Panteion University of Social and Political Sciences, Athens, 2014-2016); Scientific Coordinator of the Greek-German project "Memories of the Occupation in Greece" (Free University of Berlin, 2016-2018); and Research Fellow of the Gerda Henkel Foundation (2019-2021). She is a founding member of the Civil Non-Profit Company "Workshop on the Study of the Jews of Greece" (Athens, 2016-). She has authored (in Greek): *Monuments of Oblivion. Traces of the Second World War in Greece and Europe* (Athens, 2014); *Endless Negotiations: The Reconstruction of the Jewish Communities of Greece and German Reparations, 1945-1961* (Athens, 2019); and co-edited (with Agiatis Benardou) the volume *Difficult Heritage and Immersive Experiences* (Routledge, 2022). At present, she is Scientific Coordinator of the project "Tales from Block 15 – A virtual journey to a grim past", financed by the German Federal Foreign Office, and Research Assistant at the History Department of the Ludwig Maximilian University of Munich, working on the Deutsche Forschungsgemeinschaft-funded project "The worst times are not yet over: Jewish life in post-war Greece, 1944-1949".

Roel Hijink is an independent art historian, specialising in the material and immaterial heritage of the Second World War and colonialism in the Netherlands.

Dienke Hondius (d.g.hondius@vu.nl; https://research.vu.nl/admin/workspace/personal/overview/) is Assistant Professor of Contemporary and Political History at Vrije Universiteit Amsterdam, Faculty of Humanities; Staff member at the Anne Frank House; Co-chair of the Oral History Commission, Huizinga Instituut of Humanities Research (Utrecht); Member of the Jewish Studies Commission of the Menasse Ben Israel Institute (Amsterdam); and Ida E. King Distinguished Visiting Professor of Holocaust Studies at Stockton University, Galloway (New Jersey). At the Anne Frank House, she helped to establish the international department by making international travelling exhibits in many countries. She combines teaching and research and is also active in the field of Oral History and Memory Studies. In her research project "Mapping Hiding Places", Hondius has build maps with information about locations where Jews hid during the Shoah in Europe. This international research initiative has stimulated a new focus on the history of Jews in hiding during World War II – e.g., student research projects on hiding places in Amsterdam, international grant proposals and presentations on international comparative studies, in particular on urban histories of hiding in the Netherlands, Jerusalem (Yad Vashem), Paris, Athens, New York, and in New Jersey. In 2012, she initiated the research project "Mapping Slavery" at Vrije Universiteit. In cooperation with the United States Holocaust Memorial Museum's Oral History department, she has directed the oral history project "Bystander Memories" with interviews of non-Jewish eyewitnesses of the Holocaust. Hondius has published extensively in the broad field of Holocaust Studies and anti-Semitism, and on race, racism and Slavery Studies. She has authored *Absent: Herinneringen aan het Joods Lyceum in Amsterdam, 1941-1943* [Absent: Memories of the Jewish Lyceum in Amsterdam, 1941-1943] (Amsterdam, 2001); *"Oorlogslessen": Onderwijs over de oorlog sinds 1945* ["War Lessons": Education on the War since 1945] (Amsterdam, 2010); *Return: Holocaust Survivors and Dutch Anti-Semitism* (Westport, 2004); *Blackness in Western Europe: Racial Patterns of Paternalism and Exclusion* (New Brunswick, 2014); *Amsterdam Slavery Heritage Guide* (Arnhem, 2014); (co-author) *Dutch New York Histories: Connecting African, Native American and Slavery Heritage* (Washington DC, 2017); (co-author) *Netherlands Slavery Heritage Guide / Gids Slavernijverleden Nederland* (Edam, 2019).

Tasos Kostopoulos (tkostop1965@gmail.com; https://independent.academia.edu/tasoskostopoulos) is post-doctoral researcher at the Institute for Mediterranean Studies (Rethymo). A long-time journalist by profession, he obtained his PhD in Modern History from the Department of Social Anthropology and History, University of the Aegean, with his thesis (in Greek) on "National parties and early Macedonism. The social and political dimension of national strife in late Ottoman Macedonia" (2018). He has authored (in Greek) *The Prohibited Language. State Repression of Slavic Dialects in Greek Macedonia* (Athens, 2000); *Self-Censored Memory. The Security Battalions in WWII and Post-War Greek "National Correctness"* (Athens, 2005); *War and Ethnic Cleansing. The Forgotten Aspect of a Ten-Year National Campaign, 1912-1922* (Athens, 2007); *A "Macedonian Question" in Thrace: State Policies Concerning the Pomak Population, 1956-2008* (Athens, 2009); *Red December. On the Question of Revolutionary Violence* (Athens, 2016); *Police and "Extremism" in the Metapolitefsi. The Ghikas Report and Other Documents* (Athens, 2017).

Selma Leydesdorff (s.leydesdorff@uva.nl) is Professor Emerita of Oral History and Culture at the University of Amsterdam, and a well known author in national and international debates. Her career is part of the transformation of oral history from mostly a fact-finding method – adding to and criticising traditional historical narratives – to research on the ways memory is framed and modified over time. Her work has always been influenced by women's history. She moved from gender studies to a position where she could promote oral history by extensive teaching. She has also participated in the discussion on interconnectivity between the many existing audio-visual websites. In 2002, she started a project with survivors of Srebrenica, which brought her major international attention as an oral historian of trauma. The book, detailing the Srebrenica story, was published first in Dutch, then in Bosnian and English. The American edition got major public attention and the book appeared in paperback in 2015. She has lectured widely in the USA and participated in several publication projects. Her chapter "When all is lost: Metanarrative in the oral history of Hanifa, survivor of Srebrenica", in Mark Cave & Stephen Sloane & (eds), *Listening on the Edge: Oral History in the Aftermath of Crisis* (Oxford 2014), is part of a collection that got the prize of the American Oral History Society in 2015. She is the author of *Sasha Pechersky: Holocaust Hero, Sobibor Resistance Leader, and Hostage of History* (New York 2017), a life story based on oral sources. Since 2008, she has recorded life stories around the trial of John Demjanjuk in Munich, including survivors of Sobibor and co-plaintiffs in the trial. The last years she has worked as co-editor of the Rutledge series "Memory and Narratives". Currently, she is working on a "Handbook of Global Oral History".

Riki Van Boeschoten (rvboes@gmail.com) is Emerita Professor of Oral History and Social Anthropology at the University of Thessaly and Chair of the Greek Oral History Association. Her research interests include ethnicity, migration, war and civil war, and memory. Her latest publication is *Children of the Greek Civil War: Refugees and the Politics of Memory* (co-authored with Loring Danforth, Chicago 2012).

Eftihia Voutira (effievoutira@gmail.com) is Emerita Professor of the Anthropology of Forced Migration at the Department of Balkan, Slavonic and Oriental Studies, University of Macedonia, Thessaloniki. She has done fieldwork and published extensively on the Greek Diaspora in the former Soviet Union, and on refugee issues and the political economy of humanitarian assistance in Africa, the Middle East and the Balkans. She is the author of *Conflict Resolution: A Cautionary Tale* (with Shaun A. Whishaw Brown; Uppsala 1995); *Anthropology in International Humanitarian Emergencies* (with Jean Benoist; Brussels 1994); *Between Past and Present. Ethnographies of the Post Socialist World* (in Greek, Athens, 2007); and *The "Right to Return" and the Meaning of "Home". A Post Soviet Greek Diaspora Becoming European?* (Zurich & Berlin 2011).

Frank van Vree (F.P.I.M.vanVree@uva.nl) is director of the Amsterdam-based NIOD Institute for War, Holocaust and Genocide Studies of the Royal Academy of Arts and Sciences, and Professor of History of War, Conflict and Memory Studies at the University of Amsterdam. Previously he was Dean of the Faculty of Humanities and Professor of Media Studies at the University of Amsterdam, Professor of Media History at the Erasmus University (Rotterdam) and visiting scholar at various institutes abroad, e.g. New York University. He studied modern history and philosophy at the University of Groningen and received his PhD from the University of Leiden. Van Vree works mainly in the fields of history and memory, cultural and intellectual history as well as media studies. His publications include various books, essays and articles – in scholarly journals as well as newspapers and weeklies – in the field of memory studies (particularly regarding the Second World War), historical culture, and cultural history, as well as the history of Dutch media and journalism. He has co-edited *History of Concepts: Comparative Perspectives* (Amsterdam 1998); *Feit & Fictie*, a journal on the history of representation; *Performing the Past, Memory, History, and Identity in Modern Europe* (with Jay Winter and Karin Tilmans, Amsterdam 2010); and *Site of Deportation, Site of Memory. The Amsterdam Hollandsche Schouwburg and the Holocaust* (with David Duindam & Hetty Berg, Amsterdam 2017).

Bart Wallet (b.t.wallet@uva.nl) is Professor of Early Modern and Modern Jewish History at the University of Amsterdam. His field of specialisation is the history and culture of Dutch Jewry, on which he has authored a range of publications. In his PhD dissertation (2012), he analysed a corpus of eighteenth-century Yiddish historiography written in Amsterdam, whereas other studies dealt with the integration of Jews in Dutch society, the relations between the House of Orange and the Jews, and the reconstruction of the Jewish community after the Second World War. He is one of the authors and editors of the authoritative *Reappraising the History of the Jews in the Netherlands* (Littman Library of Jewish Civilization, 2021). Wallet is the editor of the much acclaimed war diary of Rotterdam Jewish girl Carry Ulreich, which was published in Dutch and translated into Hebrew, German, Spanish, Portuguese and Italian. He is co-editor-in-chief of *Studia Rosenthaliana. Journal of the History, Culture and Heritage of the Jews in the Netherlands*, and editor of the *European Journal of Jewish Studies*. He is also a member of the steering committee of the Digital Forum of the European Association of Jewish Studies.

An Undigested Past

The Netherlands and Its Colonial History

Frank van Vree

Abstract

The history of the Netherlands and its predecessor, the Republic of the Seven United Netherlands, is permeated with violence, looting and inequality, both in the country itself and on the world stage. In that respect, the history of the Netherlands differs little from that of other countries – although for many years, the country was able to play a role that was disproportionate to its geographical and demographic size.

In the sixteenth and seventeenth centuries, the Republic's semi-public companies built up a powerful trading empire stretching from Japan to South Africa and North America. This empire, which took the form of a network of controlled trade routes, including the transatlantic slave trade, rested primarily on treaties, fortifications and military interventions. Until the end of the eighteenth century, the establishment of settlements such as those in New Amsterdam, Cape Town and Batavia, was secondary, albeit sometimes instrumental. This changed only after the Napoleonic era, when the state took a leading role in the Netherlands too. At that time, the most important goal was the subjugation of the enormous archipelago in South East Asia, the "Dutch East Indies"; a process of colonisation accompanied by extreme violence; just as decolonisation in 1945-1949 would go hand in hand with systematic violence.

It is precisely these pages of the national past that have proved resistant to becoming part of the dominant historical image, and thus also the self-image of the Netherlands. In the chapter, I address this problematic relationship with history: Dutch colonialism, especially in South East Asia, as an unassimilated past.

"Our tortured bride"

Somewhere in the Eastern Netherlands, in the woody region on the outskirts of Arnhem, lies the country estate of Bronbeek: a stately building surrounded by a garden full of monuments, which accommodates both a home for elderly soldiers and a museum. The name of the estate, Bronbeek, is closely intertwined with Dutch colonial history. For decades, it was home to disabled and retired soldiers from the colonies, whilst the museum is dedicated to the history of the Dutch East Indies. As the country's only "real" colonial museum, unlike the general anthropological and ethnological museums in the west of the country, the marginal geographical location of Bronbeek perhaps says much about the relationship between the Netherlands and its colonial past: one that is difficult and uncomfortable, fraught with ambiguities and denial.

This problematic relationship with colonial history is also evident in the museum itself. *The Story of the East Indies*, the permanent national retrospective that opened in 2010, is a compromise between recognising the fundamental inequality and violent

Figure 1. *Colonialism as a marriage*, Museum Bronbeek. © Frank van Vree.

character of colonialism on the one hand and, on the other, the idea of the East Indies as a country of longing – the Emerald Belt – that simultaneously evokes memories of traumatic experiences caused by Japanese violence during the Second World War and the inevitable Indonesian independence. In other words, the exhibition is critical and problematises all kinds of representations, but at the same time, it also succumbs to ambivalence.

A good illustration of this ambiguity is the four-poster bed that has been placed in one of the rooms, accompanied by the following text:

> The relationship between the Netherlands and the archipelago has been described as a marriage. The question is whether the two partners shared the colonial bed with equal pleasure. The bride was never really asked for her hand, and there was no romantic courtship before the marriage. The groom seemed mainly interested in her possessions.

This image – the white bed with the accompanying text – is ambiguous and problematic in every respect. This starts with the four-poster bed itself, which can be seen as a symbolic object, loaded with romantic and exotic, not to say erotic, connotations. Colonialism is subsequently depicted as a marriage, be it one between unequal partners, who nevertheless "share the bed"; whereby Indonesia is ascribed the role of the woman and the Netherlands that of the man. Admittedly, the tone of the accompanying text can be read as lightly ironic, but even then the representation of colonialism as a marriage and Indonesia as the bride would still *grate*; something that is further reinforced by the posing of the euphemistic question of whether the two partners shared the bed "with equal pleasure." To put it bluntly: for the hundreds of thousands of victims of the colonial wars, this relationship was far from one of good-natured irony.

Nevertheless, something else could have been made of this motif of the colonial marriage-bed. For it so happens that the image of Indonesia as the bride of the Netherlands had been used before, in the very first poem by the painter and writer Lucebert (Lubertus Jacobus Swaanswijk), the interpreter *par excellence* of "art with a burned face". *Minnebrief aan onze gemartelde bruid Indonesia* [Love letter to our tortured bride Indonesia] was the title of this debut, written on 19 December 1948; the day that the Netherlands took up arms against the new republic for a second time. For Lucebert, it was clear that in the wake of the horrors of the German occupation, the Dutch were deploying similar methods in Indonesia. The curtains of the four-poster bed – symbolising concealment – were ripped away with a single tug.

We might see these conflicting depictions, built from the same imagery, as counterpoints in the culture of remembrance surrounding the colonial past following the demise of the Dutch empire. As it is impossible to describe and analyse this culture of remembrance and its development fully in a chapter of this length, I will limit myself here to several main themes and prominent questions. I begin with some recent developments, whence I travel back in time.

Theatres of memory

The state of flux in the postcolonial culture of remembrance was recently revealed during a very heated meeting at the Pakhuis de Zwijger debating venue in Amsterdam. The meeting, held on 13 September 2018, was organised by three academic institutes. Funded by the Dutch government and in cooperation with Indonesian historians, these institutes were in the middle of a research programme on the violent decolonisation process in Indonesia that took place between 1945 and 1950.[1] The purpose of the evening was to discuss the direction of the research programme, the terminology, and the different perspectives on this painful history. The institutes deliberately sought public debate on this socially explosive theme. For this reason, critics of the research programme were also invited, including Jeffry Pondaag, chair of the Comité Nederlandse Ereschulden (Committee of Dutch Debts of Honour), which campaigns for financial compensation for victims of Dutch violence in the colonial war of re-conquest between 1946 and 1949.

What followed that evening was a stimulating, emotional confrontation in a packed hall between representatives of diverse social groups, each with their own connections to the colonial past, either personally or via their parents or grandparents, as well as a number of spokespeople for anti-colonial campaign groups. A panel of grandchildren of Dutch and Indonesian soldiers discussed their relationship with this history, whilst a theatre group, Delta Dua, acted out a number of moving scenes from a play about conflicting loyalties among Moluccans, who then made up a considerable share of the Royal Netherlands East India Army (KNIL).

There were also speakers, including the Indonesian historian Bonnie Triyana, whose work deals with the links between the Netherlands and Indonesia, focusing on the actions and emotions of individuals, such as the writer Multatuli (Eduard Douwes Dekker) and the leader of the Republicans, Sukarno. Jeffry Pondaag, in turn, was critical of the fact that not only Indonesia's basic right to independence, but also the fundamentally violent character of colonialism have yet to be recognised in the Netherlands, not even by the pertinent research institutes. A second panel held a discussion on the need to decolonise thoroughly the picture presented by Dutch history, not only in educational institutions, but also in museums and politics.

The debate evening in Amsterdam – a unique "theatre of memory", to quote Raphael Samuel,[2] – saw a clash of opinions and emotions. The speeches, discussions and performances – and, not to forget, the sometimes forceful interruptions from the hall – brought an arsenal of views and feelings to light. In other words, that evening, Pakhuis de Zwijger provided a stage for extremely diverse communities of remembrance in the Netherlands. What unfolded was the beginning of what is known in German as *Vergangenheitsbewältigung*: a process of "coming to terms with the past".

Whereas at that discussion evening noisy expression was given to clashing views and feelings about Dutch colonialism, especially in relation to the period between 1945 and 1949, by contrast, the permanent exhibition in Museum Bronbeek is an attempt to tone down what are often conflicting memories. *The Story of the East Indies* is a compromise between on the one hand recognition of the violent nature of colonialism and the inevitability of the war of independence and, on the other, the idea of the East Indies as a lost country, laden with both nostalgic sentiments and memories of traumatic events.

A striking illustration of this is the third exhibition room, entitled *The Empire, 1919-1942*. One wall is covered with massive photo-montages of plantations, with white owners, overseers and coolies – symbolising modernisation and exploitation in rural areas – next to a monochrome-

---

1 As the director of the NIOD Institute for War, Holocaust and Genocide Studies, I have been the principal coordinator of the programme "Independence, decolonisation, violence and war in Indonesia, 1945-1950". This was a four-year research programme carried out by the Royal Netherlands Institute of Southeast Asian and Caribbean Studies (KITLV), the Netherlands Institute of Military History (NIMH) and NIOD. See now *Over de grens: Nederlands extreem geweld in de Indonesische onafhankelijkheidsoorlog, 1945-1949* [Over the Border: Dutch Extreme Violence in the Indonesian War of Independence, 1945-1949], Amsterdam 2022.

2 *Theatres of Memory: Past and Present in Contemporary Culture*, London 1994.

toned collage of idyllic landscapes. The opposite wall shows an iconic urban street scene, referring to the countless, endlessly-recycled photographs and films that function as symbols of the Netherlands of the tropics, worldly and relaxed. In short, the exhibition is critical and shows many clichés to be problematic, but at the same time it also partly elaborates on them, and thereby lacks a critical edge, as shown by the story with the four-poster-bed.

We should not be surprised by this ambiguity. On the one hand, the museum – whose original collection had the principal purpose of showing visitors that "something great" was being established overseas and that Dutch rule was superior – is unmistakably a product of colonialism in its purest form. On the other hand, the museum forms part of the Bronbeek country estate, which for many years functioned as *the* port of call for the East Indian community in the Netherlands, partly due to the presence of the East Indies Memorial Centre, which also co-produced the permanent exhibition. With *The Story of the East Indies*, the museum is thus attempting to serve diverse communities of remembrance in the Netherlands, starting with that of former soldiers, mainly those from the KNIL (especially the Moluccan veterans), Indo-Europeans – the children of ethnically mixed couples – and Indonesians, who chose the side of the colonial power, and, of course, their children and grandchildren.

Seen as such, we can hardly be surprised that the creators of the exhibition in Bronbeek avoided taking a hard line. In doing so, one might add, they were joining a long tradition. The presence of so many communities with diverse, often incompatible memories of the colonial past – or, to use Aleida Assmann's terminology, handed-down "social memories"[3] – has always exercised considerable influence on how this past has been addressed. This not only concerned the above-mentioned groups, but also, for instance, Dutch conscripts and professional soldiers, conscientious objectors, repatriated colonial Europeans ("totoks") and Dutch of Chinese-East-Indian origin – to limit ourselves to the most significant groups. All in all, at present, it is estimated that more than 1.5 million Dutch – one in ten of the population – have direct familial links to the history of the Dutch East Indies.

All of these groups fostered their own memories, shaped by the forced farewell to what was for many their native land, and by earlier experiences, such as the violence during and after the Second World War, including in Japanese prison camps, and the Dutch conflict with the Republic. Until the turn of the century, these memories were deeply divergent and sometimes diametrically opposed – and, to an extent, this remains the case today. For decades, there prevailed among Dutch of East Indian origin an unmistakably nostalgic longing on the one hand for the period known as the *tempoe doeloe*, the "good old days"; and, on the other, a deep sense of misunderstanding for the misery they had suffered during the Japanese occupation, the violent period that followed and the cool welcome they received upon arriving in the Netherlands.[4] Far on the other side were the soldiers who had waged – and lost – a war on the wrong side of history, and who also felt misunderstood, haunted as they were by the never-ceasing fear of being blamed for the colonial violence.

In this way, the idea of the Dutch East Indies as a lost paradise, which dominated the traditional representations, found an unexpected but complementary counterpart in the implicit but powerful suggestion that the Dutch, Dutch East Indians and other groups connected to the colonial power were above all also *victims* – first of the Japanese occupying forces, then of the Indonesian revolutionaries, and finally of their own Dutch government, which had deployed conscripts and professional soldiers in what would later prove to have been a "dirty war".

A "national secret"

For more than half a century, all of these emotions shaped the way in which colonialism and the war against the Republic were regarded in the public sphere. What is more, for many years, a large part of the population was not – or hardly – interested in this history. Partly this was the outcome of the silence lingering in politics, the media and the school. But that was not all. If the Dutch East Indies had always been distant for the great majority of the population, after 1950, this gulf only widened; whilst there were countless references to the colonial past, from restaurants and street names to the presence of a sizeable East Indian community, the East Indies were simultaneously far away in time and space.[5] However, this distance was also *sought*, consciously or unconsciously, because a past of oppression and violence sat – and sits – uncomfortably with the Dutch self-image, which is suffused with a sense of moral superiority.[6] Politicians

---

3   "Re-framing memory: Between individual and collective forms of constructing the past", in Karin Tilmans, Frank van Vree & Jay Winter (eds), *Performing the Past: Memory, History, and Identity in Modern Europe*, Amsterdam 2010, p. 35-50.

4   Elsbeth Locher-Scholten, "Land van ooit, land van nu. Koloniale herinneringen in Nederland 1980-2001" [Land of ever, land of now. Colonial memories in the Netherlands from 1980 to 2001], *Ons Erfdeel* 45 (2002): 661-671; Pamela Pattynama, *Bitterzoet Indië. Herinnering en nostalgie in literatuur, foto's en film* [Bittersweet India. Memory and Nostalgia in Literature, Photos and Film], Amsterdam 2014.

5   Locher-Scholten, *op. cit.*

6   See, for example, Abram de Swaan, "Postkoloniale absences" [Postcolonial absences], *De Groene Amsterdammer* (10 May 2017); special issue "Nederland als gidsland" [The Netherlands as an exemplary country], *De Gids* 160 (1997): 7/8. Cf. Wim van Noort and Rob Wiche, *Nederland als voorbeeldige natie* [The Netherlands as an Exemplary Nation], Hilversum 2006.

Figure 2. *Karbau (De Buffel) School chart of the Dutch East Indies*. Whole generations in the Netherlands were raised with idyllic images such as these at primary school. © E. Nijland (Utrecht 1897).

and soldiers thus had their own motives for ignoring this painful history.

The impact of this systematic lack of reflection – or, in the words of the leading sociologist Abram de Swaan, the repeated covering-up of this "national secret" – is unmistakable.[7]

> One still senses a propensity to downplay the sharp sides of Dutch colonialism and retain as much as possible of the exoticism and romanticism attached to this long episode in national history,

argued the historian Gert Oostindie in 2002, in response to the relatively uncritical celebrations of the 400th anniversary of the Dutch East India Company (VOC). And he concluded:

> The Dutch still have a hard time incorporating colonialism into their version of the nation and in a sense therefore, they still have not completed the decolonization process.[8]

Oostindie was certainly not alone in holding this opinion. Two years earlier, the political philosopher Jos de Beus had opined that the public memory of the Dutch East Indies had become imprisoned in a labyrinth of predominating moralism, in which universal ethical values competed with a strong need for justification, solidarity with veterans, returned emigrants and camp survivors, as well as shame and nostalgia for a lost paradise. Nor had historiography, De Beus argued, managed to escape these patterns, although most historians had distanced themselves radically from

---

7   "Postcolonial absences", *op. cit.*

8   Gert Oostindie, 'Squaring the circle; Commemorating the VOC after 400 years', *Bijdragen tot de Taal- Land- en Volkenkunde* 159 (2003): 141, 158.

colonialism on moral grounds.⁹ What they still lacked was an adequate analytical framework for writing the mutually intertwined history of the Netherlands and Indonesia. Moreover, they had allowed themselves to be guided by "the experiences of a thin, mostly white upper layer in the colony."¹⁰ Like many social and cultural scientists, historians have failed to reflect, or have hardly reflected, on what Edward Said called the "cultural archive", by which he meant the intellectual, aesthetic and even emotional repertoire that is rooted in the imperial culture of the nineteenth century, founded on euro-centrism and (racial) inequality.¹¹

The historical picture, in short, had remained biased and one-sided for decades, with a strong Dutch-centric slant. Although the Netherlands is not alone in this, as historian Remco Raben has observed:

> In a country such as France or in the Anglo-Saxon world, the tone of the debate is no less moralising. Moralism is never far away in colonial history, precisely because in so many respects, colonial history exists in a strained relationship with the ideals and standards of the mother country. Slavery, the denial of civil rights to indigenous peoples and large-scale violence are just a few examples of the dissonance between the rules of the game for the mother country and colonial practice.¹²

This continuing difficult relationship with colonial history is also, of course, of great importance to the self-perception of the modern Netherlands as a postcolonial society and its position in the world. In contrast to the strongly-felt and repeatedly-articulated awareness of continuity between the Second World War in particular and modern Dutch society, politics and culture, the place of the colonial past stands out sharply in the national consciousness. In the words of Elleke Boehmer and Frances Gouda:

The status of the Netherlands as an ex-colonial power remains unproblematised, and consequently the manner in which the history of colonialism might link up with the formation of contemporary national and migrant identities is left insufficiently examined.¹³

None of which is to say, however, that the colonial past remains unaddressed. On the contrary, the "national secret" has been divulged time and again, always with the same public commotion, as De Swaan and others have shown. In this context, cultural scholar Paul Bijl has introduced the term "emerging memories" to describe memories that, paradoxically enough, have always been visible and yet perceived as absent – such as the horrific photographs of the mass killings in Aceh in 1904, which "regularly emerge and submerge and are therefore time and again semanticized as forgotten."¹⁴ We should note that this is a phenomenon that occurs not only in relation to the colonial past, but also in relation to other episodes and affairs that sit unhappily with the idealised national identity, such as collaboration, slavery or war crimes – which is the case for other countries, of course, just as much as for the Netherlands.

Each time that such shocking facts – in the form of reports, photographs, diaries or academic studies – are revealed or rediscovered, there is a commotion, bewilderment and indignation, after which it is not unusual for a more detailed investigation to be established. And this is precisely the background to the above-mentioned research programme, "Independence, decolonisation, violence and war in Indonesia, 1945-1950", to which the Dutch government gave a grant of over four million euro at the end of 2016.

Burning kampongs

The immediate reason for deciding to fund this extensive programme on the violent decolonisation process was the publication of a study, as voluminous as it is thorough, by the young Swiss-Dutch historian Rémy Limpach, on the Dutch conduct of war in Indonesia between 1945 and 1949.¹⁵ Based on an overwhelming quantity of archival material and countless candid testimonies by veterans, Limpach concluded that soldiers in Dutch service had resorted to extreme violence during the Indonesian war of independence. This he defined as

---

9   "God dekoloniseert niet. Een kritiek op de Nederlandse geschiedschrijving over de neergang van Nederlands-Indië en Nederlands Suriname" [God is not decolonising. A criticism of Dutch historiography about the decline of the Dutch East Indies and Dutch Surinam], *Bijdragen en Mededelingen betreffende de Geschiedenis der Nederlanden* 116/3 (2001): 307-324, with responses from Elsbeth Locher-Scholten, Joop de Jong and H.W. van den Doel.

10 Remco Raben, "Wie spreekt voor het koloniale verleden? Een pleidooi voor transkolonialisme" [Who speaks for the colonial past? A plea for trans-colonialism], inaugural lecture, University of Amsterdam, 28 September 2016, p. 8, https://uu.academia.edu/RemcoRaben.

11 *Culture and Imperialism*, New York 1994, p. xxi; cf. Gloria Wekker, *White Innocence: Paradoxes of Colonialism and Race*, Durham 2016.

12 "De lange sporen van overzee. Nieuwe koloniale geschiedenis in Nederland en eromheen" [The long traces of overseas. New colonial history in the Netherlands and around it], *De Gids* 170 (2007): 1222.

13 "Postcolonial studies in the context of the 'diasporic' Netherlands", in M. Keown, D. Murphy & J. Procter (eds), *Comparing Postcolonial Diasporas*, Houndmills Basingstoke 2009, p. 39; cf. Ulbe Bosma, "Why is there no post-colonial debate in the Netherlands?", in Ulbe Bosma, Jan Lucassen & Gert Oostindie (eds), *Postcolonial Migrants and Identity Politics*, New York 2012, p. 193-212.

14 *Emerging Memory. Photographs of Colonial Atrocity in Dutch Cultural Remembrance*, Amsterdam 2015; cf. Raben, *op. cit.*, p. 1220.

15 *De Brandende Kampongs van Generaal Spoor* [The Burning Kampongs of General Spoor], Amsterdam 2016.

"physical violence that is mainly used outside regular combat situations against non-combatants and against combatants after their surrender or capture, usually in the absence of direct military necessity or without clear-cut military purposes," such as torture and the summary executions of prisoners of war, mass internment, and the burning down or destruction of kampongs with artillery, euphemistically described as "technical violence".

According to Limpach, the violence was not only extreme, but it was also *structural* in nature: the army, led by chief commander General Spoor, used extreme violence on a large scale as a weapon, resulting in large numbers of civilian casualties. This was, in short, a "dirty war", which was covered up by "broad coalitions" of soldiers of all ranks and officials within the judiciary and the civilian administration. In the words of the historian Peter Romijn:

> Military leaders, the judicial authorities and the administrative machinery overseas attempted to keep the affair as quiet as possible, to dismiss it as incidents and excesses, and largely to refrain from criminal prosecutions. This was accepted de facto by political leaders in The Hague, whilst whistle-blowers were discredited and dissident voices were disparaged as unpatriotic. The politicians involved thereby assumed a heavy responsibility; a legacy that can still be felt today.[16]

The choice of this violent strategy was a direct consequence of the character of the war: it was an *asymmetrical* war, in which the Netherlands, with its conventional army, was fighting a revolutionary movement that used very different tactics and methods, and in which it was difficult to distinguish between combatants and innocent civilians. The Dutch troops were utterly unprepared for such a war and could not cope with it. Violations of the laws of war on both sides, in the form of mass, excessive and unacceptable violence, were thus ingrained in the very nature of the conflict – although Limpach states that the majority of Dutch soldiers overseas were not directly involved in this.

With his conclusions, Limpach drew a thick line through what had been the official position of the Dutch government since 1969: the claim that, aside from the acts of violence by intelligence units and the commandos of Captain Westerling, only occasional excesses had been committed in the former Dutch East Indies. What Limpach revealed could no longer be construed as "incidents" or "lapses"; it was deliberate, systematic violence, with the aim of breaking and intimidating the population, and thereby undermining support for the independence movement. On this basis, Prime Minister Rutte's cabinet, supported by the Dutch House of Representatives, concluded a few months later that there was a need for a broader and deeper historical investigation, which should address all aspects of this decolonisation history.

"War crimes" vs. "Excesses"

The official government position that the Rutte cabinet had cited was based on the *Excessennota* (memorandum on excesses), a research report drafted in 1969 at the request of the then De Jong cabinet. The latter was thereby responding to the commotion that arose in the wake of a revealing television interview with a former conscript soldier, J.E. Hueting, in the popular progressive current affairs programme *Achter het Nieuws*.[17] Hueting, now a psycho-physiologist, had defended his doctoral thesis a month earlier, in which he had included a statement on Dutch actions in Indonesia:

> One might wonder why, in the Netherlands, we have yet to make a start on an investigation into the legal, historical, sociological and psychological aspects of the war crimes committed by soldiers in the service of this country between 1945 and 1950; in contrast to the attention paid by a number of other countries to the perpetration of war crimes by soldiers in their service.[18]

This striking statement caught the attention of the leftist daily newspaper *De Volkskrant*, which decided to interview Hueting on 19 December 1968, exactly twenty years after the start of the *Tweede Politionele Actie* (Second Police Action), the name which was given to the second military offensive against the Indonesian Republic. This interview subsequently led to the television interview in

---

16 Peter Romijn at the presentation of *De Brandende Kampongs van Generaal Spoor*, The Hague, 30 September 2016, https://www.ind45-50.org/lezing-peter-romijn-bij-presentatie-de-brandende-kampongs-van-generaal-spoor (accessed 6 October 2018).

17 On the Hueting affair and the *Excessennota*, see in particular Jan Bank, "Inleiding bij de heruitgave van de Excessennota" [Introduction to the reissue of the memorandum on excesses], *De excessennota; nota betreffende het archiefonderzoek naar de gegevens omtrent excessen in Indonesië begaan door Nederlandse militairen in de periode 1945-1950* [Memorandum on Excesses: Note Concerning Archival Research into the Data on Excesses Committed in Indonesia by Dutch Soldiers in the Period 1945-1950], The Hague; Mirjam Prenger, *Televisiejournalistiek in de jaren vijftig en zestig. Achter het nieuws en de geboorte van de actualiteitenrubriek* [Television Journalism in the Fifties and Sixties. Behind the News and the Birth of the Current Affairs Section], Diemen 2014; Stef Scagliola, *Last van de oorlog: de Nederlandse oorlogsmisdaden in Indonesië en hun verwerking* [The Burden of War: Dutch War Crimes in Indonesia and their processing], Amsterdam 2002.

18 Statement 9, doctoral thesis by J.E. Hueting, *Psychofysiologisch onderzoek van lichamelijke arbeid* [Psychophysiological Examination of Physical Labour], Assen 1968.

Figure 3. Joop Hueting in conversation with journalist Herman Wigbold about the war in Indonesia in the TV programme *Achter het Nieuws*, 17 January 1969. Still from the program © Beeld & Geluid, Hilversum.

early January 1969. The timing was not accidental. In the preceding year, the war in Vietnam had provoked fierce protests, including in the Netherlands, especially when it became known that the American army had repeatedly resorted to extreme violence. In other words: whilst Hueting had tried in vain in the preceding years to draw attention to his story, the Vietnam War seems to have prepared the ground for his revelations in the Netherlands.[19]

The first images of the television broadcast were symbolic of the "great silence" that the programme wished to break: the familiar idyllic, happy scenes from the colonial East Indies, taken from cinema newsreels.[20] Hueting subsequently explained how the Dutch soldiers had operated, and gave examples of actions that he characterised as "war crimes": torture with the aid of electric shocks, the shooting of excess or burdensome prisoners of war, the killing of farmers who happened to be passing, the senseless shooting of kampong dwellers.[21]

The programme came like a bombshell. "Meaningless and nauseating," wrote the editor-in-chief of the national-conservative newspaper *De Telegraaf*; many Dutch were said to be "deeply aggrieved."[22] Veterans' organisations struggled to find the words to express their indignation, whilst "Father Drees", the universally-respected former Prime Minister and Social Democrat, declared that he could recall "only two concrete cases of crimes" in those years when he governed.[23] Not only the television company, but also the newspapers were flooded with letters and phone calls. These fell into two camps: on the one hand, Hueting was accused of lies and treason and, on the other, he was praised for his courage and, more importantly, he received

---

19   Prenger, *op. cit.*, p. 270.
20   *Ibid*, p. 273-274.
21   *Ibid*, p. 269.
22   *De Telegraaf* (21 January 1969).
23   *Het Parool* (20 January 1969).

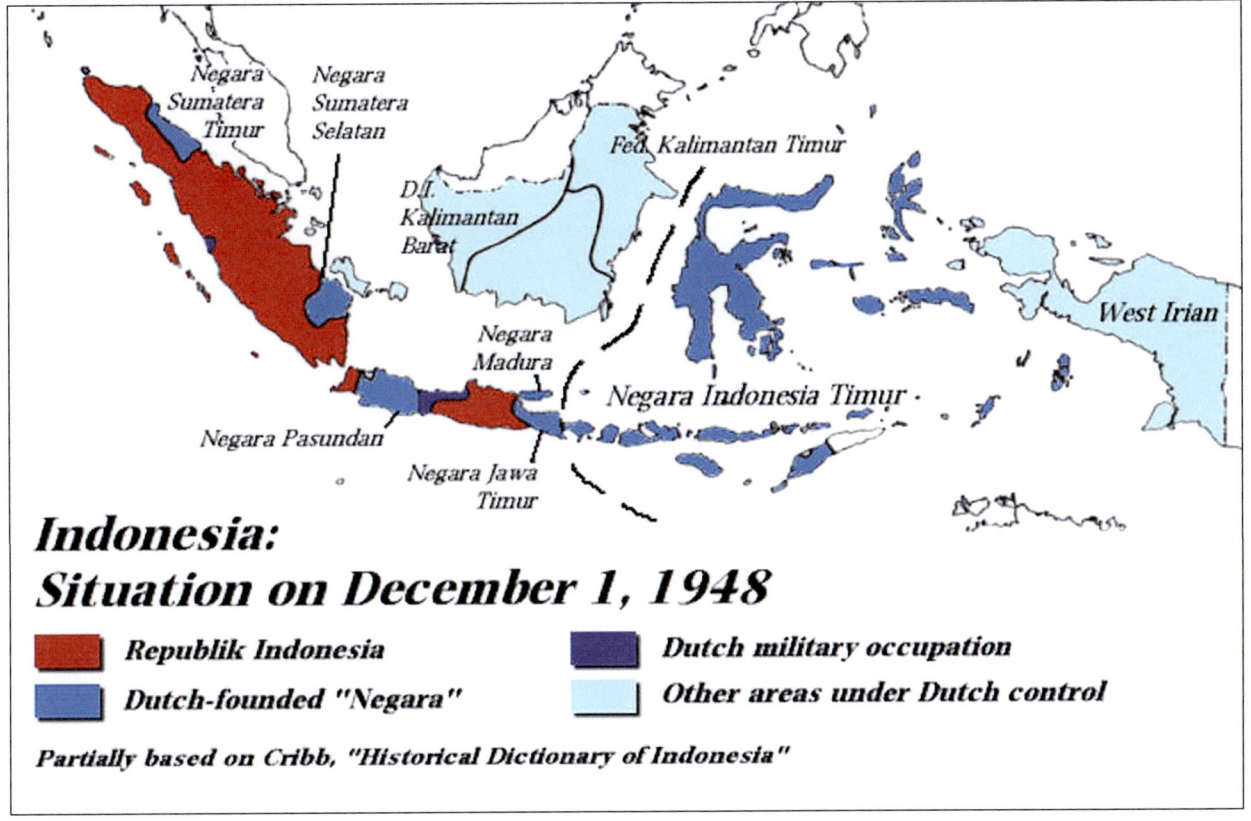

Figure 4. Source: https://www.globalsecurity.org/jhtml/jframe.html#https://www.globalsecurity.org/military/world/indonesia/images/map-1948-dec-01.jpg.

the support of other former soldiers. Hueting himself and his family had to go into hiding in a hotel.[24]

The many responses led in turn to new TV broadcasts and newspaper articles. *Achter het Nieuws* also produced two additional programmes, which not only gave the floor to new witnesses, but also examined the question of why this history had been hushed up for so long. A former Dutch pastor in Indonesia, Rev. Hildering, did have an answer to this:

The Netherlands was deaf and blind to the reality and truth of the situation. The Netherlands didn't want to understand that what the Dutch had yearned for during the years of the occupation, namely freedom, was precisely the same as *merdeka* [independence, freedom] for the Indonesians.[25]

It immediately became clear that the affair would have political consequences. This was also what the programme's makers were seeking: at the end of the first broadcast, Herman Wigbold, the programme's leftist anchorman, called for a parliamentary inquiry. Less than four days later, the leader of the opposition, the Social Democrat and later Prime Minister Joop den Uyl, submitted a motion calling on the government to publish a memo providing clarity on possible wrong-doings committed by Dutch troops. This motion was adopted, whereupon the government – led by the Catholic Prime Minister P.J. de Jong, a former submarine captain – promised an investigation. Within a month, a steering committee had been appointed, consisting of the most senior civil servants from six ministries, whilst the actual work was done by a smaller group led by a young civil servant, lawyer and historian, Cees Fasseur.

Less than four months later, on 3 June 1969, the committee published its results, set out in the *Excessennota*. Based on the archives they had studied – all 1,814 metres of them – the committee had concluded that the Dutch army had generally behaved "correctly" in Indonesia, and that there had been no "systematic atrocities". About seventy excesses had occurred, however, the nadir being the actions of the Special Forces under Captain Raymond Westerling in

---

24 Prenger, *op. cit.*, p. 273; Liesbeth Stam & Ben Manschot, "'De Hueting affaire'. Analyse van reakties op t.v.-uitzendingen over oorlogsmisdaden in het voormalig Nederlands-Indië tijdens de politionele akties" [Analysis of responses to TV broadcasts about war crimes in the former Dutch East Indies during police actions], *Massacommunicatie* 1/1 (1972): 3-16.

25 *Achter het Nieuws* (25 January 1969), cited in Prenger, *op. cit.*, p. 276. On the letters from veterans, see Limpach, *op. cit.*, p. 22 ff.

South Sulawesi. The intelligence services were also said to have been guilty of this. The memo was based exclusively on archives; nobody had been interviewed.

The report, which would quickly become known as the *Excessennota*, was published as the government's position – but not before the government had modified the original text, in the deepest secrecy, to firm up its claims in a positive sense.[26] The three pages of concluding observations were written by Prime Minister De Jong himself, with the clear intention of downplaying the matter.[27] In general, there was praise for the swift and open manner of reporting, but at the same time, there was shock at the findings in the media, especially the passage on the extreme violence deployed in South Sulawesi. In the debate in the House of Representatives, the opposition therefore called for an inquiry into the administrative and political responsibility for the terror in South Sulawesi, but this motion was not adopted.

In the immediate aftermath of the *Excessennota*, however, doubts grew as to whether the report had been comprehensive enough, and whether the term "war crimes" was not appropriate here. The sociologists J.J.A. van Doorn and W. Hendrix, who had both fought as conscripts in the Dutch East Indies and had gathered material there at the time, believed that the memo gave an "utterly incomplete picture." They also voiced a more critical opinion in a study they published the following year.[28] Their study did not have a great impact, however. First, their historical-sociological analysis was inadequate in a number of respects and too complicated to make an impression; and second, the commotion about this episode in colonial history had already died down substantially in 1970. The *Excessennota* thus proved to be an effective cover-up, which spared the interests of almost everyone involved, starting with the veterans and the politicians themselves.[29]

"Mild colonialism"

And so things would continue in the following decades. Time and again, whenever wrongdoings were revealed, indignation at the colonial past – and with it, shame – would temporarily flare up once more.[30] Publications such as Willem IJzereef's 1984 book on Captain Westerling, who had in fact been given *carte blanche* for his "pacification campaign" in South Sulawesi and who carried out at least 6,500 executions, drew relatively little attention.[31]

Three years later, though, a commotion was provoked by a draft text by Loe de Jong, author of a 14-volume general history – in 28 parts – on the history of the Netherlands and its colonies during the Second World War (*Het Koninkrijk der Nederlanden in de Tweede Wereldoorlog* [The Kingdom of the Netherlands in the Second World War]), commissioned by the government immediately after the war. In a leaked manuscript of the epilogue, De Jong had devoted a separate chapter to the military violence during the colonial war of re-conquest, in which he stated that this had involved "war crimes" that in no way differed from the methods used by the German occupying forces in the Netherlands. After angry protests from veterans and various political groups – and strong criticism of the basis of his argument by his committee of readers – De Jong changed his text. Given De Jong's almost unassailable position as the "conscience of the nation'" in relation to the war, this was not insignificant; moreover, it revealed much about the power of interest groups.[32]

Thus, in the decades following the *Excessennota*, there was no fundamental debate about the colonial past and the actions of the Dutch armed forces in the war against the republic. By contrast, the victims of the Japanese occupation and the veterans who had fought in Indonesia could count on greater recognition in the 1980s. This not only resulted in financial settlements, but also in the erection of two monuments. August 1988 saw the unveiling of the national Indies Monument in The Hague to commemorate all Dutch citizens and soldiers who had fallen victim during the Second World War to the Japanese occupation of Indonesia, in combat, during forced labour or in the camps. A month later in the southern city of Roermond, the National Indies Monument 1945-1962 was unveiled, in memory of more than 6,200 Dutch soldiers who had perished in the Dutch East Indies and New Guinea between 1941 and 1963.

As stated earlier in this chapter, until the turn of the century, the culture of remembrance in relation to the Dutch East Indies was dominated by the themes of nostalgia and victimhood; a pattern that is also reflected in films and television programmes of the time. Although there was unmistakably critical reflection and fierce controversy from the 1960s onward, many sensitive themes in colonial history remained virtually unmentioned. Not only was

---

26   For example, the committee stated that its research had not yielded any facts that undermined the "impression" that the army had generally behaved correctly; the government changed this into a positive statement, which confirmed its view that the army had generally behaved correctly – as though this had been a conclusion of the research. The government's modifications were only revealed much later; Bank, *op. cit.*, p. 12.

27   For a critical analysis, see Scagliola, *op. cit.* and Limpach, *op. cit.*

28   *Ontsporing van geweld. Over het Nederlands/Indisch/ Indonesisch conflict* [Derailment of Violence. About the Dutch/Indian/ Indonesian Conflict], Rotterdam 1970.

29   C.f. Scagliola, *op. cit.*.

30   Locher-Scholten, *op. cit.*, p. 668.

31   *De Zuid-Celebesaffaire. Kapitein Westerling en de standrechtelijke executies* [The South Sulawesi Affair. Captain Westerling and the Summary Executions], Dieren 1984.

32   "Historici kraken De Jong" [Historians break De Jong], *De Telegraaf* (18 November 1987): 1. On this affair, see J.TH.M. Bank & P. Romijn (eds), *Het Koninkrijk der Nederlanden in de Tweede Wereldoorlog. Deel 14/2. Reacties* [The Kingdom of the Netherlands in the Second World War. Part 14/2. Reactions], The Hague 1991, p. 900-918.

there a stubborn adherence to the Dutch perspective, but there was also a continuous – albeit occasionally veiled – romanticising of the colonial past and a depoliticising of the historical picture.

Many films and documentaries of these decades open with familiar romantic images of paddy fields, a town scene, an image of a family surrounded by East Indian staff, taking tea in the garden; idyllic scenes that are cruelly interrupted by images of the attack on Pearl Harbour, which marks the beginning of the misery; in other words, the East Indies as a lost paradise. It is, in short, a history that recognises only victims, including the soldiers who fought a lost war, but one that is effectively stripped, by this very perspective, of its sensitive political dimensions at the same time.[33]

The films and documentaries exhibit a seemingly indestructible, relativising sense of self-justification; something that is also reflected in the scholarly literature based on the underlying notion that Dutch colonialism was a "mild form of rule" – less bad and less heartless, at any rate, than French, British, Portuguese or Belgian colonialism. The hollow nature of the idyllic and harmonious images of colonial society is seldom exposed, as Rudy Kousbroek once argued, whilst the majority of the Dutch have never been truly interested in the Indonesian people.[34]

The "black book" of colonialism

The reason why the focus on war crimes during the colonial wars waned time and again after new revelations were made was also partly due to the fact that the perpetrators could no longer be prosecuted. In 1971, acts of violence committed by Dutch troops were legally proscribed from the category of "war crimes" and "crimes against humanity"; a category, it was declared, that was no longer subject to the statute of limitations. Thus, crimes committed by the Dutch during the colonial war in Indonesia could no longer be brought to justice. In politics, there was little enthusiasm for changing this situation.

A true shift occurred only in December 2011, when, in a civil lawsuit, the Dutch state agreed to pay individual compensation to nine widows of men who had been executed by soldiers in the village of Rawagede on 9 December 1947. They had formed part of a group of 431 youths and men aged between fifteen and sixty, each and every one of whom had been killed by a Dutch battalion of one hundred conscripts. The unit had been ordered to "cleanse" the village, because a republican fighter was said to be hiding there. The *Excessennota* had mentioned Rawagede as a place where twenty men had reportedly been executed – as well as 130 Indonesian men, who were said to have "perished".

The matter had arisen several years beforehand, after a television programme in late 2007 had once again rescued history from oblivion, and questions had been raised on the matter in parliament. A claim for compensation had been declared inadmissible by the State Attorney, however, because the case was subject to the statute of limitations, even though it concerned war crimes. That it nevertheless came to a lawsuit was largely thanks to the Committee of Dutch Debts of Honour, led by Jeffry Pondaag, and its lawyer, Liesbeth Zegveld, who decided to take the case forward in a civil action, despite the State Attorney's position. This eventually resulted in an emotive lawsuit at the district court of The Hague in the summer of 2011, in the presence of a number of the widows. This was followed on 14 September by a ruling in which the judge qualified the state's appeal to the statute of limitations as "unacceptable in view of standards of reasonableness and fairness." The court also drew a comparison with other claims that were also linked to a history "yet to be settled," such as claims relating to the restitution of artworks looted by the Nazis and other reparations.[35] The state did not appeal. On 10 December 2011, the obligation to pay compensation was recognised; several months later, the Dutch ambassador in Indonesia would travel to Rawagede to offer his apologies to the people, in front of the world's press, for the "tragedy" on 9 December 1947. It was clear that with this compensation and expression of regret, the Netherlands hoped to close this chapter of history.[36]

---

33 Frank van Vree, "'Onze gemartelde bruid'. De Japanse bezetting van Indonesië in Nederlandse films en documentaires" [Our tortured bride. The Japanese occupation of Indonesia in Dutch films and documentaries], in Remco Raben (ed.), *Beelden van de Japanse bezetting van Indonesië. Persoonlijke getuigenissen en publieke beeldvorming in Indonesië, Japan en Nederland* [Images of the Japanese Occupation of Indonesia. Personal Testimonies and Public Perception in Indonesia, Japan and the Netherlands], Amsterdam 1999, p. 202-217; cf. Pattynama, *op. cit.*

34 Rudy Kousbroek in *Het meer der herinnering* [The Lake of Memory], a 1994 documentary that takes a different line from the mainstream of programmes and films. A radically different approach can be found in the 1995 documentary *Moeder Dao, de schildpadgelijkende* [Mother Dao, the Turtlelike], a fascinating compilation of "found footage" from 1931-1932, made by Vincent Monnikendam. See also Paul Bijl, "Colonial memory and forgetting in the Netherlands and Indonesia", *Journal of Genocide Research* 14/3-4 (2012): 441-461.

35 Chris Lorenz, "De Nederlandse koloniale herinnering en de universele mensenrechten" [The Dutch colonial memory and universal human rights], *Tijdschrift voor Geschiedenis* 128/1 (2015): 109-130; W. Veraart, "Uitzondering of precedent? De historische dubbelzinnigheid van de Rawagede-uitspraak" [Exception or precedent? The historical ambiguity of the Rawagede ruling], *Ars Aequi* 4 (2012): p. 251-259. On the lawsuit, see: https://www.recht.nl/rechtspraak/uitspraak/?ecli=ECLI:NL:RBSGR:2011:BS8793.

36 "Excuses voor tragedie Rawagede. Nederland hoopt met schadevergoeding en spijtbetuiging hoofdstuk af te sluiten" [Apologies for the Rawagede tragedy. The Netherlands hopes to close the chapter with compensation and regrets], *Trouw* (10 December 2011).

But the opposite would prove to be the case. It seems that the storm that broke with Rawagede can no longer be contained. Words such as those of the ambassador were insufficient, just like the hesitant apologies that the Minister of Foreign Affairs, Ben Bot, had offered to Indonesia in 2005, by stating that the Netherlands had waged a war "on the wrong side of history." More claims and lawsuits followed, new photos emerged – including more of Rawagede – and more critical studies were published, including Gert Oostindie's *Soldaat in Indonesië*[37] and Limpach's *Brandende Kampongs* – in addition to more academic publications, such as the special issue of the *Journal of Genocide Research* (2012), to name but one example.

By now, it has long been the case that the critical voices are not limited to the years of decolonisation. Also in relation to earlier periods, there has been a toppling of the image, whereby the picture of "mild rule" has been smashed for good. One striking example of this was the publication of the voluminous study *Koloniale oorlogen in Indonesië: Vijf eeuwen verzet tegen vreemde overheersing*[38] by the journalist Piet Hagen. It is an account of 500 military campaigns, expeditions and wars on land and on sea, not all conducted by the Dutch but also by other European countries and Japan, primarily to exploit the country's resources – and thereby contributing to the Dutch edition of the *livre noir du colonialisme*, the "black book" of colonialism, which clearly shows that inequality, violence and oppression were the be-all and end-all of colonialism. Although the full impact has yet to be felt, in schoolbooks for example,[39] there seems to have been a tentative change in thinking on a wide range of subjects relating to the history of colonialism and slavery.

The passing of time and the disappearance of the generation that lived through this history have undoubtedly contributed to this, but other developments seem to have played a more decisive role, such as increasing pluralism in society and political and cultural globalisation. Greater mutual dependence, both within society and in international relations, requires *inclusiveness*, allowing justice to be done to a wide range of viewpoints and values.

This does not occur without resistance, in the Netherlands or elsewhere. Countering the powerful trend in the direction of inclusiveness is the unmistakable rise of neo-nationalism in Europe, the US and other parts of the world. The question, however, is whether we can imagine a stable, peaceful world without mutual recognition. Martine Gosselink, Head of the Department of History at the Rijksmuseum, was thus right when she spoke of an urgent need to recast history: "There is not one history. There are many voices."[40] Recognising the historical perspective of the other is the first step in being truly able to digest the history of colonialism.

November 2018

---

37 *Soldaat in Indonesië, 1945-1950. Getuigenissen van een oorlog aan de verkeerde kant van de geschiedenis* [Soldier in Indonesia, 1945-1950. Testimonies of a War on the Wrong Side of History], Amsterdam 2015.

38 [Colonial Wars in Indonesia: Five Centuries of Resistance to Foreign Rule], The Netherlands 2018.

39 Marc van Berkel, *Welk verhaal telt? De oorlogen in Nederlands-Indië/Indonesië 1942-1949 in het geschiedenisonderwijs* [Which Story Counts? The Wars in the Dutch East Indies/Indonesia 1942-1949 in History Education], Amsterdam 2017.

40 *NRC-Handelsblad* (22 September 2017).

Pride, Shame, Responsibility

New Historical and Heritage Studies on the Holocaust and Slavery

Dienke Hondius

Abstract

In History and Heritage Studies, past and present are connected. Present day remnants of buildings, street names, monuments, parks and country estates can be used as starting points for a study. We can look at what was preserved and what was destroyed, reconstructing crucial events, decisions and developments. Places and traces still visible today are the remnants of what has for some reason been kept as it was regarded sufficiently "valuable" and "worthwhile" to renovate or to maintain. Similarly we can look at what was destroyed, where, when, by who and with which narratives.[1] The inspiration for this chapter comes from learning about the destruction of the city of Salonika, particularly of Jewish property and community buildings, graveyards and other heritage, during the Holocaust.[2] What happened in Salonika made me aware of comparative developments in Amsterdam's city centre during and after the Second World War. A second thread of the chapter is the traces of Amsterdam's involvement in colonial history, in the slave trade and in slavery (towards and within the West Indies and the East Indies). Both the history and memory of the Second World War and of slavery are today sensitive topics in education, in the media and in commemorative culture. These developments are recent and ongoing. While looking at what is still standing today, we can look back at what was considered fit for destruction; both give insight in the value attached to elements and aspects of local, national, institutional, urban and family histories. The chapter observes turning points in postwar histories and memory culture: narratives about "the war" and the "Golden Age", about victims, perpetrators, bystanders, about resistance and collaboration.

Introduction

In the first decades after the Second World War, city planning and city renovation took a sharp turn, and proposals to radically change the face of Amsterdam's city centre were made without much initial resistance. The area that was most affected by this atmosphere of radical change was the former poorest Jewish city centre area, popularly called the

---

1   The chapter is based on my presentation at the Netherlands Institute at Athens in September 2018, and on my chapter "Naar een complexer en completer beeld van Peter Stuyvesant: Ontwikkelingen in New York en Nederland" [Towards a more complex and complete picture of Peter Stuyvesant: Developments in New York and the Netherlands], in Fred van Lieburg (ed.), *Geschiedenis aan de Zuidas: Essays van VU-historici* [History at Zuidas. Essays by VU Historians], Amsterdam 2018, p. 91-100.
2   See Dirk A. Moses & Giorgos Antoniou (eds), *The Holocaust in Greece*, Cambridge 2018.

Jodenbuurt (Jewish Quarter), between Amstel River and IJ River, including the Waterlooplein, Weesperstraat, Valkenburgerstraat and Rapenburgerstraat areas and the city "island" Marken in between. Looking back, it is painful to realise the destruction, in the early 1960s, of Amsterdam's old Jewish quarter. It was almost entirely destroyed. Today this area is dominated by an eight lane highway directly cutting through Amsterdam East right into the IJ-tunnel, a traffic tunnel to Amsterdam Noord that was opened in 1968. By that time and in the following years, in the early 1970s, a movement for restoration gained strength. Since then, no other parts of the city have been similarly destroyed.[3] To people in Amsterdam today, a similar city "renovation" is inconceivable and unthinkable. In the immediate postwar period, however, it was presented and accepted as necessary step for modernisation and sanitation, as inevitable, and as progress. The radical changes we see in thinking about urban heritage and the value of historical buildings are remarkable. They show that value, historical worth and heritage status are attached selectively; some buildings are worthwhile to preserve, whereas many other are destroyed.

In Amsterdam, the old Jewish quarter was part of the oldest areas in the city centre. Not only "Jewish" apartments were destroyed, but also a large area that contained an assortment of buildings dating back to at least four centuries. Significantly, however, some buildings were preserved; they were regarded as too significant and valuable to destroy. These buildings survived a postwar radical wave of urban renewal. On the corner of the eight lane highway, where the cars enter and exit the IJ-tunnel, a set of two seventeenth-century pepper warehouses of the VOC (Dutch East India Company), still stands today. It is not a museum or a site one can visit, but a preserved building with two shops on a noisy corner. These were the warehouses of the old seventeenth-century Amsterdam merchant companies. The East India Company's pepper warehouses, the West India Company's headquarters and warehouses for beaver pelts and spices, as well as the Amsterdam Admiralty's warehouses were preserved as historical landmarks. Everything else in the old Jewish quarter was mercilessly destroyed. Apparently, the colonial warehouses were considered historically relevant and fit to preserve. These hard facts show that the history of the Holocaust had not yet significantly entered public and political consciousness and awareness to realise the value of what was destroyed and lost forever. By contrast, they illustrate that the idea of the history of the seventeenth century as a "Golden Age" dominated the narrative. What was associated with that "golden" age continued to merit preservation, as heritage referring to a proud and valuable period in Amsterdam's history, well into the postwar period. Simultaneously, the history of slavery remained entirely unmentioned and unaddressed, whereas the much more recent history of the Holocaust was ignored as well.

From the late 1950s onwards, and particularly in the 1960s and 1970s, an active critical social movement grew against the destruction of the city centre. On Prinsengracht, in a different part of Amsterdam city centre, the former hiding place of Anne Frank and her family was up for destruction until groups of concerned Amsterdam citizens fought successfully to keep the house intact.[4] The house of one of the colonial and slave-owning families, De Pinto, became a symbol of the struggle to keep the city centre more intact and to stop destruction.[5] Yet, in this movement and struggle, the older colonial and slavery history connections were not yet mentioned. In the decade after the De Pinto house was saved from destruction there were fierce struggles between squatters and the police to keep housing blocks in the neighbourhood intact. The protests succeeded partially. In the Nieuwmarkt neighbourhood, many small streets and canals remained intact and small blocks of affordable housing replaced

---

3 For a summary of these developments, see Boris van der Lugt, "Victims of modernity. The sanitation and redevelopment of the old Jewish neighbourhood and Nieuwmarktbuurt (1901-1978)", unpublished BA dissertation, Vrije Universiteit Amsterdam 2021. For a moving 1964 song by Rika Jansen about how Amsterdam's city centre changed after the war, see https://www.youtube.com/watch?v=pr4erUiuWYM&list=RDpr4erUiuWYM&t=164 (accessed on 22 December 2021). In a 2006 interview, the singer explained her personal connection with the topic as her mother was arrested for resistance work, including helping Jews in hiding; cited in *Het Parool* (21 January 2016).

4 The painter Anton Witsel was among the activists. He made drawings and paintings from inside the former hiding place that helped to convince the city council. For Anton Witsel at work and an overview of his work, see https://www.nationaalarchief.nl/onderzoeken/fotocollectie/ae289d92-d0b4-102d-bcf8-0030489 76d84 and http://antonwitsel.com/ (accessed on 22 December 2021), respectively.

5 See, for example, Herman De Liagre Böhl, *Amsterdam op de helling. De strijd om de stadsvernieuwing* [Amsterdam on the Slope. The Battle on Urban Renewal], Amsterdam 2010; Virginie Mamadouh, *De stad in eigen hand. Provo's, kabouters en krakers als stedelijke sociale beweging* [The City in Your Own Hands. Provo's, Gnomes and Squatters as an Urban Social Movement], Amsterdam 1992; Walther Schoonenberg, "Hoe de Nieuwmarktbuurt werd gered" [How the Nieuwmarkt neighbourhood was saved", *Maandblad Amstelodamum* 100 (2013): 3-23; Karel Davids, "Sporen in de stad. De metro en de strijd om de ruimtelijke ordening in Amsterdam" [Tracks in the city. The metro and the battle for spatial planning in Amsterdam], *Historisch tijdschrift Holland. Werken aan een open Amsterdam* 32 (2000): 157-182; Tim Verlaan, "Dreading the future: Ambivalence and doubt in the Dutch urban renewal order", *Contemporary European History* 24/4 (2015): 537-553; Louis Schoewert, "De ontstaansgeschiedenis van de IJ-tunnel" [The history of the IJ-tunnel], *Jaarboek Amstelodamum* 89 (1997): 127-150.

what was destroyed. In other parts of the neighbourhood, particularly the area between IJ-tunnel, Prins Hendrikkade and Waterlooplein, massive destruction of houses took place. By 1978, the Waterlooplein was almost entirely destroyed except for a small market area. The rest of the large square along the Amstel River became the place of a new city council building and the new opera house.[6]

Moral geography

In his masterful 1987 study on the cultural history of the Netherlands in the seventeenth century, English historian Simon Schama writes about what he calls the dominant "moral geography" in Dutch culture – that is, the many ways in which water influenced Dutch society. Controlling the water flows, keeping the sea and river water out of houses and the city limits required significant effort and cooperation and, thus, to some extent influenced the mentality of the Dutch, according to Schama. Fear of flooding, of large waves, fear of drowning influenced policy within the dikes and ditches. Strange large sea creatures, like stranded whales on Dutch beaches, were regarded as bad omen and possible punishment by God, while at the very same time the promise of international trade and profit led to enormous investments in shipbuilding, resulting in hundreds of ships that sailed away from the dikes.[7]

Schama's book became a bestseller but provoked some criticism here and there. Susan Buck-Morss of Cornell University, for example, pointed out that it lacked any reference to slavery history and the slave trade.[8] This is significant as the *Embarrassment of Riches* was published only some thirty years ago. Schama had good contacts with the Netherlands research communities, with archives and libraries, and used an impressive amount of very different and beautiful source material. How could he have missed this aspect of Dutch history? Apparently, nobody mentioned this at the time – it was overlooked. It shows that only so recently it was perfectly possible to ignore this topic. Let me clarify that this was not the result of Schama's personal decision; he did not consciously exclude the topic. Twenty years later, slavery and abolition in the British Empire became one of his main topics of research and publication.[9] Times were changing. In particular the bicentennial commemoration of the prohibition of the slave trade in the British Empire (1807-2007) was a year full of active forms of recognition, activities, publications and exhibitions across the United Kingdom. Ignoring and overlooking slavery history and heritage was not only a British or Dutch phenomenon either. Across Western Europe silence ruled over this topic well into the twenty-first century. In the course of the commemoration events for the 400th anniversary of the establishment of the Dutch East India Company and the ties between Ghana and the Netherlands in 2002, the theme of slavery history and heritage remained almost entirely unmentioned. A decade later, Afro-Surinamese groups were successful in a movement for change, for recognition of slavery history and the commemoration of the abolition of slavery. Step by step, confrontations and interventions began to change research agendas, the media, public debate, as well as museum culture, heritage studies and education.[10]

There is now a movement to include slavery heritage in the moral geography of the Netherlands and into national, regional, urban and family histories. Not just in the larger port cities, but across the Netherlands, families and firms were directly involved in co-financing the slave trade and slavery. As knowledge about this spreads, a certain uneasiness grows – think of Schama's title word "embarrassment"; fitting here too, because it concerns an uneasy, bitter aspect of the past. For a long time, slavery history was ignored, and a collective choice was made – also by historians – for an easier digestible historical narrative, that of the "Golden Age" and the proud seafaring nation. Because of this long dominant narrative, the integration and acknowledgment of slavery history is sometimes met with disbelief and rejection. There is a need for pride about a history we regard as "our own", a need found in families as well as cities, provinces and countries, institutions and companies. Slavery history and heritage by contrast denote a much less proud, more uneasy, more shameful narrative. The Netherlands is known as a nation that attaches strong value to consensus and common ground. The new critical narrative currently leads to an active search for a new balance in which the involvement in slavery and the slave trade is recognised – up to a point.[11]

---

6   For photographs recording the changes in the area, see http://www.mokums.nl/waterloopleinmarkt-vroeger.html (accessed on 22 December 2021).
7   *The Embarrassment of Riches. An Interpretation of Dutch Culture in the Golden Age*, New York 1987.
8   "Hegel and Haiti", *Critical Inquiry* 26/4 (2000): 821-865.
9   Simon Schama, *Rough Crossings: Britain, the Slaves and the American Revolution*, London 2005.
10 See www.mappingslavery.nl and two publications by Dienke Hondius, Nancy Jouwe, Dineke Stam, Jennifer Tosch & Annemarie de Wildt: *Amsterdam Slavery Heritage Guide*, Arnhem 2014, and *Dutch New York Histories: Connecting African, Native American and Slavery Heritage*, Volendam 2017. Also see the special issue of *Slavery & Abolition* 42/1 (2021): "Europe and slavery: Revisiting the impact of slave-based activities on European economies, 1500-1850", edited by Tamira Combrink & Matthias van Rossum.
11 See, for example, the exhibitions "Slavernij/Slavery" at the Netherlands national gallery Rijksmuseum (2021), and "Aan de Surinaamse Grachten/Along the Surinamese Canals" at the Museum van Loon (2019). The National Maritime Museum, the National Museum of World Cultures, the Amsterdam Museum, and many more museums are going through significant changes.

Cultural nationalism

The quest for a proud national past is not new. During the nineteenth century, national heroes were searched for, found and admired all over Europe. National folk songs, hymns, laudatory poems, national histories and very many monuments and statues were created at the time.[12] Looking back at earlier centuries was part of this search for heroes. In the Netherlands the focus was especially on seventeenth-century ancestors, forefathers and examples; from then on, this time was called the "Golden Age" (*Gouden Eeuw*). An impressive overview of these developments is made by the Amsterdam historian Joep Leerssen in his research project on cultural nationalism in Europe and its attendant growing database. Nationalism, according to Joep Leerssen, is a feeling, a sentiment, a secular religion; it provides an anchor, a grip in a modernising world. Pride is crucial in nationalist movements, but mistrust is also part of nationalism; the feeling of a threatened "we" is never far away.[13] That is why European nationalisms also contain an assignment to every citizen to propagate, express, maintain and protect what is "ours". It is not coincidental that many national heroes are war heroes and artists who expressed heroism. For example, among the Dutch men of whom statues and monuments were erected at the time were, from the seventeenth century, the poets Jacob Cats and Joost van den Vondel, the maritime conquerors Michiel de Ruyter and Piet Heyn, the legal scholar Hugo de Groot, the colonial conqueror Jan Pietersz Coen and the painters Frans Hals and Rembrandt van Rijn. Significantly, all the "conquerors" mentioned here are now controversial, as they were also directly or indirectly involved in structural violence, slave trading and enslavement.

The contrast of pride and shame, noise and silence in national narratives about the past can be studied in several branches of European history: In colonial history, in slavery heritage and in the history of the Second World War and the Holocaust (Shoah). In my view this is a field of connected histories.

Pieter Stuyvesant in Dutch New York

In what follows, I want to describe these developments on the backdrop of the case of a seventeenth-century figure, by and large unknown at the time, and the remarkable development concerning his imagery. How and why did his image change? Unmentioned in the database on European cultural nationalism, Pieter (Petrus/Peter) Stuyvesant (1612-1672) was the director-general of the Caribbean island of Curaçao (1642-1644) and then of Nieuw Amsterdam (1647-1664), later New York. He was ordered by the West India Company in Amsterdam to protect Dutch interests in Curaçao and the colony of New Netherland (Nieuw-Nederland), now covering large areas of New York State, which later was taken over by the British. A handful of statues of Stuyvesant can be found in New York, Curaçao, New Jersey, Friesland and in Amsterdam, but all are fairly recent, erected in the twentieth and early twenty-first century. In addition, both during the Great War, and the Second World War and its aftermath streets and parks were named after him. It appears that he was made into a hero quite belatedly. References to the history of the transatlantic slave trade, to slavery and slavery heritage are few and far between in this movement to name and celebrate Stuyvesant. In the twenty-first century historian Jaap Jacobs was the first to write something different about Stuyvesant: "He was a slave driver, who introduced the trade in human beings on Curaçao, and later had no problems in selling Negro slaves in North America."[14]

This phenomenon of leaving slavery history unmentioned is a much broader phenomenon across Europe. The Netherlands is a country that likes to remember and celebrate the fact that New York was one of its first colonies, from 1609 onwards, when Henry Hudson, who was sent by the Dutch VOC, somewhat lost his way and accidentally "discovered" the area. During the large programme of celebrations and commemorations for the 400th anniversary of the ties between the Netherlands and New York in 2009, slavery heritage was virtually absent.[15] In its aftermath, there was an opportunity to address this gap and to offer a different historical narrative to the existing one. Our research project "Mapping Slavery" contributed to this with a new guide about Dutch New York locations and histories that included slavery history and heritage.

Early empire

American historians have become more interested in the history of slavery in Dutch New York. The longer British presence in New York had turned New York's slavery history into an almost entirely British-American history, not least because the British continued and expanded

---

12 Dienke Hondius, "Naar een complexer en completer beeld van Peter Stuyvesant: Ontwikkelingen in New York en Nederland" [Towards a more complex and complete picture of Peter Stuyvesant: Developments in New York and the Netherlands], in Fred van Lieburg (ed.), *Geschiedenis aan de Zuidas* [History at the Zuidas], Amsterdam 2018.

13 *Nationalisme* [Nationalism], Amsterdam 2015. See also Joep Leerssen (ed.), *Encyclopedia of Romantic Nationalism in Europe*, Amsterdam 2018.

14 *Petrus Stuyvesant, een levensschets* [Petrus Stuyvesant, a Life Sketch], Amsterdam 2009.

15 http://www.henryhudson400.com/home.php (accessed on 16 November 2021). In a travel guide published in 2012, some locations were first mentioned in connection with slavery; Gajus Scheltema & Heleen esterhuijs (ed.), *Nederlands New York. Een reisgids naar het erfgoed van Nieuw Nederland* [Dutch New York. A Travel Guide to the Heritage of Nieuw Nederland], Haarlem 2012.

slavery as a system. This created the impression that slavery during the earlier period of Dutch rule in New York had been limited, trouble-free and mild. This impression and image deserve to change. Everywhere in archives both in the Netherlands and in New York City and throughout the State of New York we can find examples of the Dutch as slave traders and slave owners.[16] Peter Stuyvesant was one of the most important among them. In 1660 he had forty enslaved men and women working on his farm. No other larger slave owners at that time have been found to-date. Slavery in New Netherland was smaller in scale than in the large plantation colonies, like Guyana or Suriname, in the north of Latin America. There, particularly in Suriname, many large sugar and coffee plantations were initiated directly from Amsterdam. Dozens of merchant families and networks organised co-ownership as shareholders of plantations in what is now called crowd funding; everyone co-invested. In similar ways, shipbuilding was organised. This is not how slavery was organised in early Dutch New York; there were no massive investments from Amsterdamian families. In New Amsterdam and New Netherland we see more pioneer work, a trial period, in which the Dutch look at what is possible and what works. This trying out is typical to this period of *Early Empire*. Stuyvesant was one of the pioneers who saw a larger scale slave trading and plantation agriculture with slave labour as a possibility and sought to set it up. Similar enterprises were carried out at the time in the Dutch East Indies, for example on the Banda Islands (now the Moluccas, part of Indonesia), in Madagascar, in the Cape Colony, in Brazil, in West African coast castles, like Fort Elmina. In New Netherland and New Amsterdam, these were initially supported and facilitated by the West India Company (WIC) before being taken over by private merchants and families.[17]

The first Dutch colonists in North America were not yet used to enslaving Africans. It took a while and some improvisation to establish this organised dehumanisation. It was a new phenomenon in New Netherland's small villages and communities, a small scale process of enslaving African and Asian men and women in Dutch houses and on Dutch farms. However, for Peter Stuyvesant slavery was not new at all. He was experienced and had worked in the system of slave trading and enslavement in Curaçao. This experience formed the background of his own involvement in the slave trade, his attempts to stimulate it between Curaçao and New Netherland, and his plans for building plantations. He was a slave owner himself and convinced that many more Africans and Asians could be brought to New Netherland from Curaçao. Indeed, he wrote about the organisation of a slave auction in New Amsterdam in 1666. Apart from this, he was also active in enslaving indigenous American men and women, an aspect about which the American historian Nicole Saffold Maskiell presents a lot of new information and sources.[18]

There is no reason to assume that the Dutch white colonists' conduct towards the enslaved men and women was less violent and less dehumanising than that of the English. Here the religious aspect of Stuyvesant is important as well. The religious networks of the Dutch in New Amsterdam were also networks of slave owners. The West India Company selected Dutch protestant preachers and paid them. Born as the son of a Frisian Protestant minister, Stuyvesant brought this branch of strict Protestantism with him to North America.

Inventing a proud narrative

Both Stuyvesant's year of birth and his year of death are uncertain. The year 1672 appears on his grave, but there are American documents that give 1682 as his year of death. He was born in 1611 or 1612 in Peperga, a village in Friesland, and his parents came from Dokkum.[19] In Friesland, in Amsterdam, and in New York City and New Jersey his first name does not appear on monuments. In the Frisian towns of Wolvega, Scherpenzeel and Peperga a Stuyvesant Festival was organised in the summer of 1955. Ten years after Liberation there was a strong atmosphere of national pride and a search for heroes to celebrate as inspiring examples for the new generation. In Wolvega, a large new statue of Stuyvesant was unveiled by the Dutch Minister for Overseas Territories, Professor Kernkamp. There was an exhibition and a festival booklet about the works of Stuyvesant. All texts take pride in Stuyvesant's life and work. His manliness, his Dutchness, his many virtues are stressed: "Stuyvesant was a man. He was a man who knew what duty and calling demanded of him and who viewed his task as having been laid upon him by God."[20] Not a word here about his involvement in

---

16 See Dienke Hondius et al., *Dutch New York Histories*, op. cit.
17 See Pepijn Brandon, Guno Jones, Nancy Jouwe & Matthias van Rossum (eds), *Slavernij in Oost en West: Het Amsterdam onderzoek* [Slavery in East and West: The Amsterdam Research], Amsterdam 2020.
18 I would like to thank Nicole Saffold Maskiell and Andrea C. Mosterman for insights in their pathbreaking work. See Andrea C. Mosterman, *Spaces of Enslavement. A History of Slavery and Resistance in Dutch New York*, New York 2021; Nicole Saffold Maskiell, *Bound by Bondage: Slavery and the Creation of a Northern Gentry*, New York 2022; Dennis J. Maika, "To 'experiment with a parcel of Negros'. Incentive, collaboration, and competition in New Amsterdam's slave trade", *Journal of Early American History* 10 (2020): 33-69.
19 Barbara Henkes, *Sporen van het Slavernijverleden in Fryslân* [Traces of Slavery in Fryslân], Groningen 2021, p. 86-96.
20 Martha Eerdmans, *Pieter Stuyvesant. An Historical Documentation*, New York 1957.

slavery or the slave trade. Yet, in some of the original texts written by Stuyvesant himself we find indirect references. For example, he reports that he has to be present at the departure of some merchants that are leaving Curaçao to work together with the English, who are busy "looking for Negroes." The book also mentions the presence of "Red Indians", with whom the Dutch were trading goods – *worthless trinkets* for *valuable beavers*. This shows the well known but historically misleading image of the smart Dutch traders who exchange "beads and mirrors" for valuable goods with "ignorant" Native Americans and Africans.

Old and new monuments

The island of Curaçao is also mentioned in the festival booklet in the context of a report about the opening of a new school, the Pieter Stuyvesant College, by Queen Juliana in 1954, on a site where a statue of Stuyvesant had been erected in 1941. The school is still there today, but has been renamed. The monument was removed in 2011. This was also the case with a Stuyvesant statue in New Jersey, standing next to a school building near Bergen Square. A monument of Stuyvesant in Manhattan, in the garden of St. Marks Church, close to where he lived, is now a source of heated debate. The statue was unveiled on 5 December 1915 on behalf of the Dutch government and Queen Wilhelmina (Juliana's mother). A window in the church shows Stuyvesant with a sword in one hand and the Bible in the other. In the family grave cellar 82 descendants have been buried together with Pieter; the last one, a certain Catherine Stuyvesant, in 1924. In 2017 the Mayor of New York City ordered that a list of potentially controversial monuments was compiled, following the rightwing extremist march in Charlottesville at the monument of Confederate General Robert E. Lee. Stuyvesant is now controversial; one reason being his refusal to allow Jews to settle in New Amsterdam, as well as his measures against Lutherans and Quakers. The Manhattan monument is on the list. Sites and schools named after Stuyvesant, like the currently quite popular Brooklyn area Bedford-Stuyvesant (*Bed-Stuy*), as well as one of the most expensive private schools in downtown Manhattan, *Stuyvesant High School*, have so far remained intact. *Stuyvesant Avenue* in Brooklyn was renamed recently by the well-known filmmaker Spike Lee – it is now called *Do The Right Thing Avenue*.

A complete turnaround in imagery

The Netherlands continued to attempt to promote Stuyvesant's name and fame after 1955. In one instance, we see the most remarkable and surprising turnaround in imagery. In 1962, the Stedelijk Museum Amsterdam held an exhibition of artworks from the Peter Stuyvesant (Modern Art) Collection.[21] Until 2006 at least, the seventeenth-century director-general would no longer be openly mentioned. It seems that the image of the Frisian Calvinist with his wooden leg had lost its appeal. It was replaced by a completely anti-Calvinist image. The association of Stuyvesant with Modern Art, with glitz and glamour, with the fast and hip life of New York constituted a dominant image in the 1970s and 1980s. Thus, *De wereld van Peter Stuyvesant* (The world of Peter Stuyvesant) became the slogan of a series of cigarette advertisements. Eye-catching television commercials invited the viewer to smoke Peter Stuyvesant cigarettes. The "world of Stuyvesant" was a hedonist spectacle; enjoying luxury, fancy expensive clothing, fast cars, windsurfing, flying to New York for a weekend spent in nightclubs, always smoking Peter Stuyvesant cigarettes. These commercials carried similar messages with those of the James Bond films. Many of the clips can be found on YouTube. The cigarette brand was sold in many countries. It was the director of the Turmac cigarette factory, Alexander Orlow, who started this new campaign and approach. He was an art lover and ordered large format modern art paintings to be made and "exhibited" in the tobacco factory at Zevenaar. His successors continued his work, building a modern art collection, with many exhibitions held at the Stedelijk Museum Amsterdam.

The association of Stuyvesant with tobacco and Art became dominant in subsequent decades. In the aftermath of a 2002 law, which banned commercials with cigarette brand names, the old imagery of Pieter returned. In 2006, a new small bronze statue of him, with a fountain, was placed behind the gables of the West India House, the former headquarters of the Company at Herenmarkt/Haarlemmerstraat, in Amsterdam's city centre. This statue was offered as a "gift" by the Turmac Tobacco BV on the occasion of the 60th anniversary of the company's establishment. Very few were noticing the silences and gaps in the imagery of Peter Stuyvesant; nobody mentioned slavery and the slave trade, not even in the commemorative year 2009. However, things were changing by then.

Commemorating slavery and emancipation

On 1 July 2002, Queen Beatrix unveiled at Oosterpark, at a park next to Tropenmuseum (the former colonial institute), a new national monument to commemorate slavery heritage. An earlier suggestion that the monument be erected next to Pieter Stuyvesant's statue at the historically very relevant West India Company House on Herenmarkt

---

21 Arnold Witte, "The myth of corporate art: The start of the Peter Stuyvesant Collection and its alignment with public arts policy in the Netherlands, 1950-1960", *International Journal of Cultural Policy* 27/3 (2021): 347.

unfortunately did not carry the day.²² In its wake, the Nationaal Instituut Nederlands Slavernijverleden en Erfenis (National Institute for the Study of Dutch Slavery and Its Heritage), which is housed next to the park where the monument is, set about organising research projects, debates, educational projects and a permanent exhibition. Afro-Surinamese and Antillean Dutch guides take through the exhibition school groups and adult visitors and enter in meaningful discussions and reflections. Since 2002, a government representative gives a speech at the national annual commemoration on the abolition of slavery on 1 July. In the United Kingdom, large commemorative projects across the country took place in 2007 on the bicentenary of the abolition of slave trade in 1807. More changes were on the horizon. In 2008 Barack Obama was elected president of the United States. One of his first measures was the explicit acknowledgment of the slavery past of the USA and the decision to make education about it mandatory in American schools.

Dutch debate about "Black Pete" and racism

In the Netherlands a fierce debate about slavery heritage, race and racism broke out from 2011 onwards. It started around the figure of Zwarte Piet (Black Pete), a blackface character that is part of the very popular feast that takes place annually on 5 December, where everyone gives each other, and especially children, presents and sweets. Black Pete's racist imagery was exposed and attacked by activists, provoking a period of controversy, debate and slow change. Issues like whiteness, white privilege, slavery, and institutional racism, the history of imagery, the Dutch cultural archive, colonial history and heritage were and still are discussed.²³ The debate signifies the process of the emancipation of postcolonial and other black Dutch communities with a growing group of white Dutch in solidarity. In the context of this debate, many began to wonder how this early colonial history began. Did Black Pete have direct connections to slavery history or were there very different explanations? Remarkably, research has shown that the invention of Black Pete as a black figure was first introduced in a children's book written by an Amsterdam school teacher, Jan Schenkman, in 1850. He also invented a Jewish figure, the cowardly soldier Levie Mozes Zadok, in a series of humorously intended short stories written to read out aloud in groups of family or friends. The Dutch historian Ewoud Sanders has recently pointed out the similarities he discovered in these anti-Jewish and anti-Black forms of "funny" popular stereotypes in books and stories that became bestsellers.²⁴

New directions in heritage education on location

Education and research about slavery history and heritage are encouraged and growing. Visible markers – like statues, monuments, gable stones on houses, inscriptions, names of houses, streets, bridges, ships, parks and tunnels – are becoming controversial, forming starting points for discussion. It is time for a more complete image and history of slavery heritage in the Netherlands. In this history, Peter Stuyvesant was directly involved, as a slave owner in his capacity as director-general of one of the first Dutch colonies. It is understandable that his name, his statues and monuments are now becoming more controversial as this knowledge about him is spreading. In light of these changes, it is remarkable that as late as 2006 a new statue of Stuyvesant was erected, in the backyard of the West India House (the former headquarters of the West India Company), without any reference to this historical context. Even more remarkable is the fact that until 2020 the motto of the West India House, leisure centre by now, was "A Matter of Taste", while the wine bar on the busy Haarlemmerstraat was called Stuyvesant. Following some publications, today it is called Nieuw Amsterdam.

The West India House, the East India Warehouses, the stock exchange and the banks, the churches, synagogues and many canal houses and gable stones are still standing, visible reminders of the city's past. Names of former heroes become more contested. As long as a more complete and multifaceted history is told on location, in my view it is unnecessary to remove all "unwanted" reminders of local histories. Older monuments and statues may be regarded as obsolete, and provoke rejection, but they can still work as good conversation starters. A plaque with additional text can work well in many cases. Including the voices of eyewitnesses or descendants of painful and controversial histories in education is an option chosen more often today. Multigenerational memory discussions, well prepared, can be important eye-openers for participants and students. Crucially, in the course of walks, tours and educational projects, new heritage education and public history initiatives are now being tried out, using a reframed narrative that includes both proud and shameful aspects of local history.²⁵

---

22 Today the West India House, whose direct links to slavery history pass unmentioned, is a leisure centre where, *inter alia*, wedding receptions take place.

23 See Elisabeth Koning, "Zwarte Piet, een blackface-personage" [Zwarte Piet, a blackface character], *Tijdschrift voor Geschiedenis* 131/4 (2018): 551-575.

24 *Lachen om Levie. Komisch bedoeld antisemitisme 1830-1930* [Laughing at Levi. Comically intended anti-Semitism, 1830-1930], Zutphen 2020; see the review by Dienke Hondius in *Studia Rosenthaliana* 47/2 (2021): 226-228.

25 See Dienke Hondius, "Nieuwe Aandacht voor oorlog en slavernij: Uitdagingen voor erfgoedstudies, geschiedschrijving en onderwijs" [New attention for war and slavery: Challenges for Heritage Studies, Historical Studies and Education), *Tijdschrift voor Geschiedenis* 132/4 (2020): 637-655.

The Other Side of the "Catastrophe"

Greek Army Atrocities During the Asia Minor Campaign (1919-1922)

Tasos Kostopoulos

Abstract

The 1922 collapse of the Greek Army in the Asia Minor front, itself the culmination of a bloody three-year war in Anatolia and a decade of warfare in an array of Balkan or far-away battlefields, has been elevated into a milestone of the nation's modern history. As a consequence of defeat, the violent uprooting of more than one million Greek Orthodox Christians from Anatolia not only put an end to eight decades of Greek irredentism but also deeply transformed the social fabric of mainland Greece. "The Catastrophe", as it is usually called in both everyday language and official discourse, is a story that every Greek learns from his childhood; not only (nor even mostly) in school, but also through various channels of socialization, identity building and ideological formation: Family members, media, established literature, political groups, local associations and even football teams, whose followers' imagined community is often based on their founding fathers' "1922 refugee" status. While "the Catastrophe" has rightfully gained such a pre-eminence in the Greek national narrative, this has not at all been the case with the war that led to it. Even less known is today the darkest side of the story: The atrocities perpetrated by the Greek occupation forces in the Anatolian hinterland during those three bloody years. Although never a state secret, these atrocities are rarely evoked in the public discourse and even more rarely discussed as such. The chapter deals with this repressed social memory, providing a counter-narrative based mostly on first-hand published accounts by Asia Minor War participants that both mainstream scholarly and nationalist public history usually ignore or even refuse to take into account.

Introduction

War atrocities are not easily acknowledged by those who carry them out. Even the deeds of the Wehrmacht during the Second World War, although common knowledge across the formerly occupied Europe, provoked a storm of protests by veteran and other far-right groups in Germany during the 1990s, when they were openly brought to mind by a special exhibition focusing on the issue of war crimes perpetrated not by special Nazi units but by the "regular" German military.[1] Even more difficult has been the public acknowledgment of similar misdeeds perpetrated during more controversial endeavours – such as colonial

---

1   Hannes Heer et al. (eds), *The Discursive Construction of History. Remembering the Wehrmacht's War of Annihilation*, New York 2008.

ventures, nationalist strife or wars of national liberation. Recent public debates in France and the Netherlands on the respective armies' criminal record during the suppression of anti-colonial liberation movements in Algeria, Madagascar, Indochina and Indonesia, and the absence (to the best of my knowledge) of any similar reflection in Britain constitute convincing examples of the difficulties inherent in such an undertaking of collective self-criticism.[2] In the Balkans, where a century-old tradition of nationalist in-fight between neighbouring populations goes hand in hand with an even older tradition of collective resistance to foreign invasion and/or domination, speaking about the dark side of what has been commonly perceived as a succession of heroic – albeit often unfortunate – struggles is an equally disturbing enterprise. Those who undertake it are confronted not only with the reflexes of self-defence by those social groups that feel threatened by such revelations (i.e. war veterans, nationalist politicians and propagandists or mainstream scholars), but also with a long tradition that perceives the respective national past as a trail of collective expiation through repeated martyrdom.

The war between the Greek Kingdom and the Turkish national movement led by Kemal Ataturk of 1919-1922, a conflict widely known in Greece as the "Asia Minor Campaign" and in Turkey as the "War of [Turkish] Independence", constitutes a clear-cut paradigm of such collective amnesia. In Turkey, the atrocities perpetrated by Kemalist troops against the local Christian population have been usually suppressed by both a long tradition of state censorship and a national liberation narrative that emphasises indigenous sacrifices in the face of a foreign invasion sponsored by western imperialism. The most emblematic case of this self-censorship is the collective silence over the destruction of Smyrna/Izmir, a city with a population of circa 300,000 in 1922, inhabited by a clear majority of Christians and therefore nicknamed *Gavur Izmir* (Infidel Smyrna).[3] Started and rekindled by Kemalist troops, the great fire that engulfed most Christian neighbourhoods (including those inhabited by the highly protected Levantine community) has been officially attributed to the city's former Christian inhabitants. Nevertheless, as an excellent recent study by a modern Turkish historian has aptly demonstrated, "the way in which the fire is deliberately overlooked" in most subsequent narratives "implies the presence of an offence, violence, and the concerted effort spent to forget it speaks of an attempt of [self-] amnesty."[4]

Needless to say that in Greece this same event is elevated to a symbol *par excellence* of the "Catastrophe" – as the war's outcome and the subsequent uprooting of more than one million Greek Orthodox refugees from Anatolia has been designated in both everyday language and official discourse. This Catastrophe is a story whose main traits every Greek with an elementary knowledge of history learns from childhood onwards; not only (nor even mostly) in school, but also through various channels of socialisation, identity building and ideological formation: Family members, mass media, mainstream literature, political groups, local associations and even football teams, whose followers' imagined community is often based on their founding fathers' 1922 refugee status. In fact, at least one fifth of Greece's population today derives from one or both parents of Anatolian descent.[5]

While the Catastrophe has rightfully gained such a pre-eminence in the Greek national narrative, this is not at all the case with the war that led to it. For some decades the object of bilateral recriminations between the political heirs of the rival factions (i.e. Royalists and

---

2 Yves Benot, *Massacres coloniaux. 1944-1950: La IVe République et la mise au pas des colonies françaises*, Paris 1994; Mohammed Harbi & Benjamin Stora (eds), *La guerre d'Algérie, 1954-2004: La fin de l'amnésie*, Paris 2008; Stef Scagliola, "Cleo's 'unfinished business': Coming to terms with Dutch war crimes in Indonesia's War of Independence", *Journal of Genocide Research* 14/3-4 (2012): 419-439.

3 According to local Ottoman registers, in 1919 Smyrna had a population of 260,971: 48.8% were Orthodox Greeks, 30.4% were Muslims, 9.3% were Jews, 5.7% were "foreign nationals (almost all of them Christians), 4.6% were Armenians, and 1% belonged to other Christian denominations. The head of the Greek Administration's Political Section, on the other hand, estimated that in late 1919 the Greater Smyrna Area had a population of 330,592 (64.55% Orthodox Greeks) – an obvious over-estimation, given that the local bishopric recorded its flock at around 140,000 in the city proper, plus 15,500 in the outskirts.

Between 1919 and 1922, Smyrna also harboured an unspecified number of internal refugees, both Orthodox Greeks and Muslims, who had been displaced from the war-torn hinterland; see Michalis Notaras, Εις την Ιωνίαν, Αιολίαν και Λυδίαν πριν πενήντα χρόνια [In Ionia, Aeolis and Lydia Fifty Years Ago], Athens 1972, p. 19-20.

4 Biray Kolluoğlu Kırlı, "Forgetting the Smyrna fire", *History Workshop Journal* 60 (2005), p. 41. The best account of Izmir's destruction, although somehow tainted by an obvious anti-Turkish bias, is Marjorie Housepian, *Smyrna 1922. The Destruction of a City*, New York 1971; see also Hervé Georgelin, *La fin de Smyrne*, Paris 2005. For first-hand accounts by former Greek inhabitants who survived the slaughter, see Kentro Mikrasiatikon Spoudon, Η έξοδος [The Exodus], 2 vols, Athens 1980 & 1982, vol. I: p. 7-12, 26, 28-29, 31-39, 42-43, 58-59, 64, 100-101, 116-117, 120-122, 126-128, 159-160, 182-183, 204-205, 354-357.

5 According to the 1928 census, 13.66% of the country's population were refugees of Anatolian origin. This was clearly an underestimation, as a number of refugee communities were not recorded by the census-takers as such; Tasos Kostopoulos, Πόλεμος και εθνοκάθαρση. Η ξεχασμένη πλευρά μιας δεκαετούς εθνικής εξόρμησης, 1912-1922 [War and Ethnic Cleansing. The Forgotten Aspect of a Ten-Year National Drive, 1912-1922], Athens 2007, p. 264-265. Taking into consideration the initial endogamy of the refugees and their later extensive intermarriage with the rest of the Greek population, my estimation of one fifth of at least partially Anatolian descent may be too conservative.

Republicans)⁶ that waged them and put the blame on each other for the final defeat, the conduct of the Greek military campaigns has stopped long ago being at stake in both public history and professional historiography. An even more comprehensive silence has covered the atrocities perpetrated by the Greek occupation forces in the Anatolian hinterland during these three bloody years. Although never a state secret, these atrocities are rarely evoked in the public discourse and even more rarely discussed as such.

From "colonial" policing to inferno

We may discern three different phases of Greek Army atrocities during the Asia Minor campaign. Each one was more widespread and indiscriminate than the previous, as a result of the interplay of various factors: The expansion of the Greek occupation zone beyond the areas inhabited by substantial Greek Orthodox populations; the gradual barbarisation of war-worn fighters, who could not see any "light at the end of the tunnel"; and, last but not least, the replacement of the earlier military command, linked to a Liberal government more or less conscious of the limits of its mandate, by an openly racist leadership around King Constantine, whose irredentism was based on the completely irrational concept of a Christian crusade aiming at the enforced "return" of all Muslim Turks *"into the interior of Asia whence they came [from]."*⁷

The first phase began in May 1919 with the landing of a Greek expeditionary force in Smyrna as a police force under Allied command, and lasted until the early days of 1921 when its leadership was taken over by the staff of the recently reinstated King Constantine. Meanwhile, in June 1920, the zone occupied by the Greek troops had expanded eastwards to include a buffer zone destined to protect the flanks of the British troops positioned across occupied Istanbul.⁸ Although presented as an enterprise of national liberation, this campaign was nevertheless waged in an area that contained at least as many enemies as unredeemed brethren. According to official Greek statistics, the population of the Smyrna Occupation zone ceded to Greece by the Treaty of Sèvres (10 August 1920), on an allegedly provisional basis, comprised 46.3% Orthodox Greeks and 46.8% Muslims.⁹ The secret statistics compiled by the Greek Administration sketched an even less favourable correlation of forces, the Orthodox Greeks numbering less than 40% of the total population.¹⁰ As a consequence, the expeditionary force found itself from the very beginning in an awkward position, in the face of a growing resistance put up by Turkish nationalists. As the Greek soldiers quickly discovered, the latter were supported by a considerable part, if not the absolute majority, of the local Muslim element.¹¹

In order to suppress this resistance movement, under the supervision of the Allied Command and in the context of "taking exams" in front of the Colonial Powers on its own ability to dominate "inferior races",¹² the Greek Army resorted to the classical patterns of colonial counterinsurgency: Search and destroy sweep operations, use of torture to extract information about the guerrillas' whereabouts, bloody reprisals for any attack on its troops, and destruction of settlements that resisted its advance. As a rule, pressure was also put on the local Muslim population in order to dissociate itself from the "bandits", so that the rebel "fish" would be devoid of its vital "water".¹³ Although not on schedule, such a policy allowed also some room for individual transgressions, like plundering and/ or rape; the former constituted quite a common and more or less tolerated practice, in order to remedy the chronic

---

6   The "National Schism" of 1915-1922 began as a confrontation between the pro-Entente Liberals led by Venizelos (representing the social alliance between the reform-oriented local and Diaspora bourgeoisie with the landless peasants of Thessaly) and pro-German "neutralists" around King Constantine (representing the bulk of the traditional petite-bourgeoisie and small peasantry, under the leadership of the traditional Athenian elite and entrepreunial land owners). It progressively assumed the character of a clash between Royalists and Republicans. It has been especially perceived as such since 1924, when the monarchy was abolished by Venizelist radicals.
7   King Constantine to Princess of Saxe-Weimar Paola (Kutahya, 9 August 1921), in King Constantine, *A King's Private Letters. Being Letters Written by King Constantine of Greece to Paola Princess of Saxe-Weimar During the Years 1912 to 1923*, London 1925, p. 191 (emphasis added).
8   Michael Llewellyn Smith, *Ionian Vision. Greece in Asia Minor 1919-1922*, London 1973, p. 125-126.
9   *Documents on British Foreign Policy, 1919-1939*, London 1967, 1ˢᵗ series, vol. XV, p. 182-188.
10 Notaras, *op. cit.*, p. 87-115.
11 For pertinent accounts in diaries and memoirs of Greek soldiers, see Stylianos Gonatas, Απομνημονεύματα, 1897-1957 [Memoirs, 1897-1957], Athens 1958, p. 180; Spryos Vlachos, Απομνημονεύματα [Memoirs], Athens 1975, vol. I, p. 115, 209-210; Christos Karayannis, Το Ημερολόγιον, 1918-1922 [The Diary, 1918-1922], Athens 1976, p. 228-230; Ioannis Yalirakis, Αναμνήσεις από τη Μικρασιατική εκστρατεία [Reminiscences from the Asia Minor Campaign], Athens 1985, p. 24-25, 28; Dimitrios Kefaloyannis, Οδοιπορικό. Σμύρνη, Ιούνιος 1920 – Νικομήδεια, Ιανουάριος 1921 [Travelogue. Smyrna, June 1920 – Nicomedia, January 1921], Athens 2005, p. 98. The massive support of the Turkish population to the anti-Greek resistance, immediately after the 1919 landing of the expeditionary force, is also openly admitted by the Greek Directorate of Army History; Diefthynsis Istorias Stratou, Η εκστρατεία εις την Μικράν Ασίαν [The Campaign in Asia Minor], Athens 1957, vol. I, p. 107-108.
12 As the Greek High Commissioner of Smyrna, Aristidis Stergiadis, used to say: "We are taking exams and, if we fail, then we have lost Smyrna"; Stamatis Chatzibays, Μια ζωή γεμάτη αγώνες [A Life Full of Struggles], Athens 1965, p. 62.
13 For a description of such practices, as narrated in the memoirs of former Greek combatants, see Kostopoulos, *op. cit.*, p. 101-107.

deficiencies of military logistics, whereas the latter was always considered a crime to be punished.

Two factors that strongly affected the conduct of Greek soldiers during this phase were the atrocities committed by Turkish guerrillas against both their military captives and local Christian civilians, and the attitude of the local Christian population towards their Muslim neighbours, after the landing of Greek forces. In the first case, the Greek Army faced a classic feature of guerrilla warfare: Confronted with its own inability to wage a frontal attack on the occupation forces, guerrillas tried to intimidate them (and their civilian supporters) through sporadic acts of barbarity against individual targets. The repressive reactions instigated by such actions set in motion a vicious circle of violence that isolated completely the occupation troops from the population under enemy control. In the second case, a mixture of revenge for earlier sufferings (during the 1914 anti-Christian pogrom and First World War mass deportations) and individual grabbing of what was perceived as a window of opportunity for personal advancement led to a multitude of violent local incidents that the Greek expeditionary force was called to pacify. As it was to be expected, its intervention was usually carried out at the expense of local Muslims, who were perceived as an alien population that should be curtailed. Just after the Greek landing in May 1919, the convergence of these two factors led to an array of bloody massacres at Smyrna/Izmir, Menemen and – worst of all – at Aydin, massacres that seriously compromised any plans for a peaceful colonial rule.[14]

The second phase began with the Greek offensive of March 1921 and culminated in the advance of the Greek Army to the outskirts of Ankara during the summer. In the event, after its retreat to a line of defence that was to be held until August 1922, the Greek occupation zone comprised 100,000 km², an area seven times larger than that ceded to Greece on a provisional basis by the 1920 Treaty of Sèvres and circa 70% of the size of the independent Greek Kingdom.[15] As already mentioned, colonial policing now gave place to a war of annihilation targeting not only the enemy military but also the local population per se. Muslim villages along the lines of advance or retreat of the Greek Army were systematically plundered and burned down, a measure ordered by the Greek General Staff[16] as part of a scorched earth policy that aimed to deprive the enemy of any local resources. When the advancing forces met with popular resistance, the destruction of villages was accompanied by sporadic wholesale massacres.[17] This attitude was exacerbated by the fact that, in contrast to the mixed ethnological composition of the coastal zone, the Anatolian hinterland had an almost exclusively Turkish character, its sparse Christian minorities already deported or annihilated by the Kemalist forces. Marching through a terrain inhabited by a foreign and more or less openly hostile population, which *"only the archaeological skills of the Greek journalists could prove not only that it had been Greek but still was Greek"*, as a Marxist intellectual of the time put it,[18] the average soldier lived by the day, waging his own personal war against all odds, and local communities had to pay the bill.

Two specific events, which unfolded under peculiar circumstances, add to the general picture described above. The first was the systematic ethnic cleansing of the Izmid region, on the seashore across Istanbul, carried out during the first half of 1921. It is amply documented by foreign eyewitnesses such as Arnold Toynbee,[19] an Inter-Allied Commission dispatched to the scene,[20] and the envoy of the International Red Cross that accompanied it.[21] According to the commission's findings, the main motive behind the systematic violence applied by the Greek Army and paramilitary units against the local Muslim population between April and June 1921 had been the proposal of the Allied Council on 25 February for an "impartial investigation into the facts respecting the population of Eastern Thrace and Smyrna" as a precondition for the arbitration by the Great Powers on the final status of both regions.[22] Although unanimously rejected by the Greek Parliament three days later,[23] it alarmed Greek nationalists, who decided to ethnically cleanse a strategic area that bordered on both the

---

14 *Documents on British Foreign Policy, 1919-1939*, London 1948, 1st series, vol. II, p. 237-258; Llewellyn Smith, *op. cit.*, p. 89-91; Michael Rodas, *Η Ελλάδα στη Μικράν Ασία (1918-1922)* [Greece in Asia Minor, 1918-1922], Athens 1950, p. 69-79, 87-111, 146-164; Arnold Toynbee, *The Western Question in Greece and Turkey*, London 1922, p. 270-274, 390-405; Kostopoulos, *op. cit.*, p. 98-105. For a vivid first-hand account of the events in Aydın, see Karayannis, *op. cit.*, 132-138.

15 Speech of Prime Minister Dimitrios Gounaris on 2 October 1921 in *Εφημερίς των Συζητήσεων της Γ´ Εν Αθήναις Συντακτικής των Ελλήνων Συνελεύσεως* [Proceedings of the Third Constituent National Assembly], Athens 1932, p. 123.

16 Nikos Vassilikos, *Ημερολόγιο μικρασιατικής εκστρατείας* [Diary of the Asia Minor Campaign], Athens 1992, p. 109.

17 Kostopoulos, *op. cit.*, p. 108-113, based mostly on Greek soldiers' accounts.

18 Serafim Maximos, *Κοινοβούλιο ή Δικτατορία* [Parliamentarism or Dictatorship], Athens 1975 (first published in 1930), p. 19 (emphasis added).

19 Toynbee, *op. cit.*, p. 274-319.

20 Inter-Allied Commission, *Reports on Atrocities in the Districts of Yalova and Guemlek and in the Ismid Peninsula*, London 1921; also see *Documents on British Foreign Policy, 1919-1939*, London 1970, 1st Series, vol. XVII, p. 177, 295-296.

21 Maurice Gehri, "Mission d'enquête en Anatolie (12-22 mai 1921)", *Revue Internationale de la Croix Rouge* 31 (1921): 721-735.

22 *Documents on British Foreign Policy* (1967), *op. cit.*, p. 193-203.

23 Proceedings of the Third Constituent National Assembly, *op. cit.*, p. 225-250.

coveted Ottoman capital and the backwater irredenta of the (Western) Pontus.[24] The cleansing was set in motion by the semi-private agency of local paramilitaries and finished off by the conventional forces of the Greek Army and Navy in a bloodbath similar – though on a much smaller scale – to the one that would follow a year later at the waterfront of Smyrna/Izmir.[25] Such was the level of violence unleashed, however, that it provoked a double backlash. The Greek administration was seriously compromised in the eyes of a – not so favourable anymore – Western audience, whereas the ethnic cleansing project completely backfired as the local Christian population, already tormented by the Kemalist bands and fearing a new wave of deadly reprisals,[26] also left their homes on a massive scale under the protection of Greek battleships.[27]

The second event concerned the harsh suppression of a peasant armed revolt that erupted during the spring of 1922 in the mountainous area of Simav, behind the frontline. Instigated by excessive confiscations enforced on the local peasant economy by Greek military logistics and organised by guerrilla bands already active in the field, the revolt began with the atrocious massacre of a Greek military convoy by the rebels and was put down by fire and axe, every mountain village burned to the ground, its inhabitants subject to slaughter and/or rape.[28] Contrary to what was the case with the overexposed Izmid peninsula, this time there were no external witnesses to the carnage.

The third phase of Greek Army atrocities was radically different from the earlier two, as it was carried out in a setting of total collapse of military discipline, after the Kemalist break through the Greek defences on 15 August 1922. Motivated in part by the collective refusal of Greek soldiers to fight anymore for what they perceived as a lost cause, the massive desertion of the frontline troops, described by many first-hand accounts as a *απεργία πολέμου* (strike of war),[29] took the form of a mayhem of plunder, arson and wanton murder that afflicted Muslim and Christian settlements alike, which were considered as both a legitimate booty and the reason for the soldiers' ordeal. Not only small villages and provincial towns but also fair-sized cities (e.g. Afyonkarahisar, Uşak, Filadelfeia/Alaşehir, Kaşaba, Manisa, Panormos/Bandırma) were targeted by the retreating troops, the only notable exceptions being Ak-Hissar and Smyrna/Izmir itself.[30] The latter was also destroyed a little bit later, this time by the Kemalist victors who were prone to get rid not only of an unwanted Christian outpost, but also of an emblematic breeding ground of Western-instigated comprador capitalism.

From oblivion to mnemonic revival

During the Asia Minor campaign, the Greek public was subjected to a barrage of war propaganda that emphasised Turkish atrocities against Greek Orthodox civilians. Greek troops, on the other hand, were praised as the bearers of Western civilisation in the Anatolian hinterland.[31] In the quite rare cases of explicit reference, the physical destruction of Turkish villages was usually portrayed as collateral damage, the burned down localities being considered hideouts or ramparts of Kemalist guerrillas.[32] Patriotic self-censorship notwithstanding, any attempt to inform newspaper readers about what actually happened at the frontline (and behind it) was frustrated by pre-emptive Press censorship, whose traces (in the form of various spaces intentionally left void) are still visible in the extant Athenian or provincial dailies of those

---

24　Gehri, *op. cit.*, p. 724.
25　Toynbee, *op. cit.*, p. 287-311; Gehri, *op. cit.*, p. 732-735; *Documents on British Foreign Policy* (1970), *op. cit.*, p. 282, 295-296.
26　Toynbee, *op. cit.*, p. 275; Inter-Allied Commission, *op. cit.*, p. 11; Kentro Mikrasiatikon Spoudon, *op. cit.*, vol. I, p. 300-302, 325-333; Vasilis Kouligas, *Κίος 1912-1922. Αναμνήσεις ενός Μικρασιάτη* [Kios 1912-1922. Reminiscences of a Man from Asia Minor], Athens 1988, p. 172-173; Kostas Faltaits, *Αυτοί είναι οι Τούρκοι. Αφηγήματα των σφαγών της Νικομηδείας* [These are the Turks. Tales from the Nicomedia massacres], Athens 1921; Patriarcat Œcuménique, *Les atrocités kémalistes dans les régions du Pont et dans le reste de l'Anatolie*, Constantinople 1922, p. 77-100.
27　*Documents on British Foreign Policy, 1919-1939* (1970), op. cit., p. 282; Toynbee, *op. cit.*, p. 297.
28　For an eloquent first-hand account by a Greek trooper, see Karayannis, *op. cit.*, p. 290-293. Even the Greek Directorate of Army acknowledges at this point that the local population "went through the mill" during the suppression of its revolt; Diefthynsis Istorias Stratou, *op. cit.*, p. 133.
29　For some cases of use of the "strike" metaphor by former soldiers and officers of a very diverse spectrum of attitudes towards the events, see Vlachos, *op. cit.*, p. 207, 278; Kostas Doulas, *Ένας φαντάρος θυμάται (το Μικρασιατικό Πόλεμο)* [A Soldier Remembers the Asia Minor War], Athens 1976, p. 50; Dimitrios Arvanitis, *Εκστρατεία Μικράς Ασίας. Λεύκωμα προσφιλών αναμνήσεων, Ημερολόγιον μαχών κλπ. Ιούνιος 1919 – Σεπτέμβριος 1922* [Asia Minor Campaign. Album of Favoutite Memories, Diary of Battles etc., June 1919 – September 1922], Athens 2006, p. 54; Eleftherios Stavridis, *Τα παρασκήνια του ΚΚΕ* [The Communist Party of Greece Behind the Scenes], Athens 1988, p. 81, 88. For a detailed narrative of the mental process that led to this collective decision, see Konstantinos Glendis, *Αναμνήσεις από την Μικρασιατικήν εκστρατείαν*, [Reminiscences from the Asia Minor Campaign], Athens 1971, p. 105-110.
30　Kostopoulos, *op. cit.*, p. 125-135.
31　Indicatively see Faltaïts, *op. cit.*; *Empros* (23 August 1919): 1; *Empros* (21 November 1920): 3; *Empros* (12 September 1921): 3; *Kathimerini* (3 July 1921): 1; *Skrip* (30 December 1921): 3.
32　*Kathimerini* (8 July 1921): 3; *Kathimerini* (9 July 1921): 1; *Patris* (29 August 1921): 1; *Skrip* (21 April 1921): 4.

days.³³ Turkish propaganda of course made a big story out of Greek atrocities,³⁴ but its claims could be easily dismissed as an enemy fabrication. More or less, the same applied also to Western European news items and to the reports compiled by Inter-Allied Commissions on the events of 1919 and 1921. Any criticism therein was usually attributed to diplomatic machinations aiming to undermine the Greek occupation.³⁵

After the Catastrophe, issues such as Greek atrocities were of course sidelined by the highly visible ordeal of hundreds of thousands of refugees, who flooded Greece with their own stories of tremendous suffering at the hands of the victorious Kemalist troops. Then followed the repatriation of Greek prisoners of war, who had survived the deadly mix of death marches, forced labour and widespread starvation that decimated a good percentage of their comrades in arms. Once more, there was no room for discussion of what had taken place before their capture. Confronted with appalling living conditions, everyday racism and the struggle to survive in a social environment less affluent than their places of origin, the refugees themselves were not of course in a position (and in most cases did not bother, either) to challenge the dominant discourse on the events that led to their uprooting.³⁶

However, Greek war crimes in Asia Minor were officially recognised at the highest possible level, i.e. the Treaty of Lausanne, which brought to an end the confrontation between Turkey and the Entente Powers. According to article 59, Greece acknowledged in a symbolic way "its duty to repair the destructions caused in Anatolia by the Greek army and administration against the laws of war," while Turkey, "taking into consideration the economic situation of Greece" and the heavy burden imposed on the latter by the task of refugee rehabilitation, "definitely renounced" all of its claims of indemnity arising from this recognition.³⁷ It was a save-facing formula that allowed Greece to overcome the prospect of heavy indemnities such as those imposed on the countries defeated in the recent Great War, while at the same time satisfying the Kemalists' need of a moral victory that left no room for being incriminated for the widespread massacres of Christian Ottoman civilians that crowned their victory. Moreover, due to its lack of concrete legal consequences, this formula left no trace at all on the collective consciousness of interwar Greeks.

On the other hand, although antiwar literature thrived in interwar Greece, as it did in the rest of Europe, it tended to bypass or minimise the question of Greek army atrocities against Muslim civilians in Asia Minor. The genre's masterpieces focused mainly on the soldiers' experiences from the trenches of the Great War or on the ordeal of POWs after the 1922 defeat. Most writers were content with some off-hand allusions of what preceded the Muslim civilians' barbarity towards captured Greek soldiers. More precise incidents, like the short but graphic reference to the horrible killings by torture perpetrated

---

33 Indicatively see the void spaces filled with humoristic figures either gagged or brandishing a huge pair of scissors in the pages of the communist daily *Rizospastis* (10 April 1919, 4 May 1919, 6 May 1919, 20 May 1919, 12 June 1919, 17 June 1919, 29 August 1921, 31 August 1921). In many other instances, one finds only blank spaces where the censored articles or cartoons once stood (e.g. 1 August 1920, 30 August 1921, 22 November 1921). War censorship affected all newspapers, both anti- and pro-government; indicatively see the Venizelist *Kairoi* (2 July 1919, 10 August 1919) and *Patris* (6 September 1920, 8 September 1921), as well as the Antivenizelist *Empros* (11 July 1921) and *Kathimerini* (2 July 1920, 7 July 1921). For explicit references to the censorship in place, see the editorial comments of *Kathimerini* (21 & 29 June 1921).

34 Ligue pour la défense des droits des Ottomans, *Atrocités grecques dans le Vilayet de Smyrne*, Geneva 1919; Permanent Bureau of the Turkish Congress in Lausanne, *Greek Atrocities in the Vilayet of Smyrna*, Lausanne 1919; Ministry of Interior – Department of Refugees, *Greek Atrocities in Turkey*, Constantinople 1921; Anonymous, *Atrocités grecques à Eski-Chéhir. Relation d'un témoin oculaire de la débâcle des armées helléniques*, Constantinople 1922.

35 *Empros* (23 August 1919): 1; *Empros* (26 June 1921): 3; *Kathimerini* (1 July 1921): 1; *Patris* (30 August 1921): 1. Even in the rare instances where such accusations were acknowledged as being at least partially true, their effect was immediately undermined (and implicitly justified) by the description of far more horrible Kemalist atrocities, e.g. *Patris* (30 August 1921).

36 There is a rich (and ever-growing) literature on native hostility towards the Anatolian refugees in the post-1922 period. Indicatively, George Mavrogordatos, *Stillborn Republic. Social Coalitions and Party Strategies, 1922-1936*, Berkeley 1983, p. 201-206; Idem, *Μετά το 1922. Η παράταση του Διχασμού* [After 1922. The Prolongation of the Schism],

Athens 2017, p. 171-181; Stephen Salamone, *In the Shadow of the Holy Mountain. The Genesis of a Rural Greek Community and its Refugee Heritage*, New York 1987, p. 100-103; Alkis Rigos, *Η Β' Ελληνική Δημοκρατία, 1924-1935. Κοινωνικές διαστάσεις της πολιτικής σκηνής* [The Second Greek Republic, 1924-1935. Social Dimensions of the Political Scene], Athens 1988, p. 223-231; Takis Salkitzoglou, *Η Σύλλη του Ικονίου. Μια ελληνική κωμόπολη στην καρδιά της Μικράς Ασίας* [Sille of Konya. A Greek Town in the Heart of Asia Minor], Athens 2005, p. 177-179; Spyridon Mouratidis, *Πρόσφυγες της Μικράς Ασίας, Πόντου και Ανατολικής Θράκης στην Κέρκυρα (1922-1932)* [Refugees from Asia Minor, the Pontus and Eastern Thrace in Corfu, 1922-1932], Athens 2005, p. 162-184; Maria Sorou, *Πρόσφυγες στο Μεραμπέλο* [Refugees at Merabelo], Ayios Nikolaos 2008, p. 152-159, 169; Dimitris Konstandaras-Statharas, *Μικρασιάτες Πρόσφυγες στη Μαγνησία* [Asia Minor Refugees in Magnesia], Nea Ionia 2008, p. 94-102; Achilles Kyriakou-Kondostathis, *Η Νέα Ερυθραία στη χαραυγή της ζωής της* [Nea Erythrea at the Dawn of Its Existence], Nea Erythrea 2013, p. 69, 131-132, 160-162. For pertinent oral testimonies of the refugees themselves, see Kentro Mikrasiatikon Spoudon, *op. cit.*, passim. As is usually the case with racism, the underlying causes for native enmity were often purely material (professional antagonism, housing shortages, rivalry for the same pieces of available land, etc), but at the end of the day anti-refugee prejudice was expressed on the basis of a "cultural" or overtly "racial" argumentation.

37 *Treaty of Peace with Turkey and Other Instruments Signed at Lausanne on July 24, 1923*, London 1923, p. 48-51.

by a Greek Army "reprisal squad" in Bergama in 1919, were thus overshadowed by the author's infinitely more detailed description of the sufferings of Greek POWs and Greek Orthodox civilians during the death marches that crowned the "Catastrophe".[38] In another case of antiwar literature, the gang rape and atrocious murder of a Muslim girl by Greek soldiers in Bergama is blurred by the author's reluctance to disclose the nationality of either the victim or the perpetrators, in sharp contrast to similar atrocities that are clearly attributed to Kemalist guerrillas or soldiers.[39] Last but not least, even the rare references to Greek atrocities were later subjected to self-censorship, as the authors' initial antimilitarist zeal had in the meantime been moderated by social advancement, cooptation by state nationalism after 1936 and/or the positive re-evaluation of Greek nationalism through their association with various forms of the antifascist resistance during the Axis occupation (1941-1944).[40] As the post-war national security state did not allow much space for Resistance literature focusing on the struggle against the Axis occupation, which had been carried out mostly by communist-led forces that were outlawed after 1947, the collective need for a heroic narrative was mostly satisfied by an imaginary return to the days of the struggle against the Turks. In this context, the perennial "enemy" was used as a convenient substitute for the German occupation troops, whose local collaborators were actually running the post-war anticommunist Greek state.[41]

During the interwar period, the only notable exception was provided by communist literature. Greek communists had denounced the Asia Minor campaign from the beginning and had promoted antiwar actions in both the front and the mainland.[42] Therefore, they had no inhibition about discussing the atrocities perpetrated by Greek soldiery against local civilians. The *Rizospastis* gave to former soldiers the opportunity to describe their own experiences, openly denouncing what for the mainstream Press constituted an epic event. Such narratives appeared mainly over the summer months, during the "antimilitarist days" commemorating the Great War all over Europe, or in moments of tension between the Greek state and its neighbours, when readers had to be reminded of the dangers inherent in a nationalist mobilisation.[43] Naming names and usually in a very eloquent manner, these testimonies constitute a rare source of alternative discourse on the Asia Minor war from below; one that has mostly evaded the attention of professional historians.

The transformation of communist strategy in the mid-1930s, with a shift from proletarian antimilitarism to antifascist patriotism, and the subsequent experience of armed resistance during the Axis occupation, when former Venizelist officers formed the backbone of the communist-led Greek People's Liberation Army (ELAS), radically transformed the perception of earlier national adventures by the post-war Greek Left. The most popular narrative on the ordeal of Asia Minor Greeks, a documentary novel composed by Dido Sotiriou on the basis of a narrative provided to her by a male refugee by the name of Manolis Axiotis, did not avoid mentioning Greek army atrocities, but these were presented in the light of – and partially justified as a reaction to – the far worse crimes perpetrated by the Kemalist forces against Greek Orthodox civilians.[44] The personal memoirs of Axiotis were published in 1976 and have been totally ignored by the public, in part because of the book's misleading title.[45] Axiotis is far more critical to the conduct of the Greek soldiers (including the narrator himself), openly comparing the Greek occupation of Asia Minor with the German occupation of Greece – a real sacrilege in the eyes of mainstream Greek nationalists of both Right and Left.[46]

---

38 Elias Venezis, *Το νούμερο 31328* [Number 31328], Athens 1931, p. 63 (for the "reprisal squad") & *passim*.

39 Stratis Myrivilis, *Η δασκάλα με τα χρυσά μάτια* [The Schoolmistress with Golden Eyes], Athens ²1934, p. 6-7 (murderous gang rape in Bergama), 93 (similar atrocity by Kemalist guerrillas against two Greek Orthodox girls in Papazli). The passages in case were not edited in subsequent editions of the novel.

40 Angela Kastrinaki, "Το 1922 και οι λογοτεχνικές αναθεωρήσεις" [1922 and Literary Revisions], in A. Argyriou et al (eds), *Ο ελληνικός κόσμος ανάμεσα στην Ανατολή και τη Δύση, 1453-1981* [The Greek World Between East and West, 1453-1981], Athens 1999, vol. I, p. 165, 169-170.

41 *Ibid*, p. 172-174.

42 Communist Party of Greece, *Επίσημα κείμενα* [Official Texts], Bucharest 1964, vol. I, p. 114-116, 151-153, 170-173, 176-179, 250-255; Philip Carabott, "The Greek 'Communists' and the Asia Minor campaign", *Deltio Kentrou Mikrasiatikon Spoudon* 9 (1992): 99-118.

43 Indicatively see Kostas Tsalaras, "Το αίμα που χύσαμε εμείς ας γίνει παράδειγμα για σας. Γράμμα παλαιού πολεμιστή" [Let the blood we shed be an example for you. A letter by an old warrior], *Rizospastis* (2 August 1934): 3; A. Dimitriou, "Απ' τη φρίκη του πολέμου. Φωτιά και αίμα" [From the horror of war. Fire and blood], *Rizospastis* (31 August 1934): 3; G.D., "Απ' τα χαρακώματα στη Σωτηρία" [From the trenches to the Sotiria consumptive hospital], *Rizospastis* (16 November 1934): 3.

44 *Ματωμένα χώματα* [Bloody Earth], Athens ⁹³1983, p. 219-227. More than 400,000 copies have been sold in half a century, corresponding to a readership of circa 10 to 12 million. In 2007 it was also given gratis to primary school pupils by the Ministry of Education, as a moderate counterbalance to the "unpatriotic" lack of reference to the Kemalist atrocities in a new sixth-grade textbook.

45 Manolis Axiotis, *Ενωμένα Βαλκάνια* [United Balkans], Piraeus 1976, p. 115-116. It was recently re-published, together with some other works of the author, under the more attractive title *Εγώ, ο Μανόλης Αξιώτης* [I, Manolis Axiotis], Athens 2016.

46 For a comparison between the two narratives, see Tasos Kostopoulos, "'Εγώ, ο Μανόλης Αξιώτης'. Τα αυθεντικά 'Ματωμένα χώματα'" [I, Manolis Axiotis. The authentic Bloody Earth], *Eleftherotypia* (4 January 2009): 33-35.

On a different scale, a precious collection of refugee testimonies, which were commissioned during the 1950s and 1960s by the private Centre of Asia Minor Studies set up by Melpo Merlier, preserved a lot of information long suppressed by nationalist narratives on both sides of the Aegean. Although the emphasis is on the refugees' ordeal, they contain also many references to the atrocities perpetrated by Greek Army units or paramilitary formations against the local Muslim element.[47]

However, the main source of information about Greek Army atrocities is provided by the former soldiers themselves, in an array of war diaries and memoirs that have been published during the last decades. In my book, which appeared in 2007 and deals mostly with atrocities perpetrated by all sides during the decade of successive wars between 1912 and 1922, I have used 37 such testimonies from the Asia Minor front. Many more have since been published. Their treatment of Greek atrocities is of course highly disproportionate, differing from one account to the other as a result principally of personal ideology and class origin. There is a former soldier, later a high-ranking official in the Ministry of Justice, who insists that he saw no atrocities at all during the 1922 retreat, although his route was identical with that of his colleagues who bore testimony to many of these.[48] Another high-ranking officer explicitly declared that he decided to bypass any "destruction, arson or other ugly things" he saw, in order not to tarnish the reputation of the Army and the nation.[49] In most cases, however, the extent of what has been recorded was determined by objective factors.

Middle class intellectuals, who served in the "aristocratic" Signal Corps and Artillery units and composed most of the available narratives, can provide us with interesting details about the chain of command responses but were usually less exposed to frontline "ugliness". On the other hand, those who bore the brunt of the fight and witnessed (or perpetrated) the worst atrocities, were usually illiterate privates who left no written records of their experience. The case of a former private from Boeotia, a shepherd by profession who had no schooling at all but was taught how to write by the schoolboys of his village, can be considered as a notable exception that confirms the rule.[50]

Although clearly revealing the darkest aspects of the Asia Minor war, all these narratives have however failed to inscribe themselves into the collective memory of modern Greek society. This phenomenon can be partially explained by a stubborn reluctance to call into question the fundamental narrative that is widely considered as a pillar of social cohesion keeping together the nation's imagined community. Another reason is the obvious absence of a social agent who could promote the agenda of an alternative history, demystifying the dominant discourse. If during the 1990s a nationalist discourse (with openly fascist overtones) focusing on the Macedonian Question met with a quite broad resistance that brought together activists of both the Left and (to a lesser extent) the Liberal Centre-Right, who converged on a minimum agenda defending democratic values and minority rights,[51] challenging the righteousness of past Greek irredentism has proved to be a far more difficult – and lonely – affair.

---

47 Kentro Mikrasiatikon Spoudon, *op. cit.* Three more volumes have been published recently (2013, 2015 and 2016) with testimonies from the Pontus.
48 Charalampos Triantafyllidis, *Η Μικρασιατική Εκστρατεία και το ημερολόγιον ενός οπλίτου* [The Asia Minor Campaign and a Soldier's Diary], Athens 1982, vol. II, p. 624.
49 Petros Demestihas, *Αναμνήσεις* [Reminiscences], Athens 2002, p. 104.

50 Karayannis, *op. cit.*
51 Athéna Skoulariki, "Au nom de la nation. Le discours public en Grèce sur la question macédonienne et le rôle des médias (1991-1995)", unpublished PhD thesis, Université Paris II, 2005; Erik Sjöberg, *Battlefields of Memory. The Macedonian Conflict and Greek Historical Culture*, Umeå 2011, p. 173-273.

An Unclaimed Past

The Shoah in Athens

Philip Carabott

In memory of Matilda Jacob Mionis (Athens 1935 – Tel Aviv 2019) & Elias Moses Koen (Athens 1927 – Haifa 2021)

Abstract

Much of the literature on the Shoah in Greece focuses on the destruction of the *Madre d'Israel*, Salonika. By contrast, save brief mentions in general works, the history of the persecution and deportation, of the hiding and rescue of the Jews in the Greater Athens Area by and large constitutes *terra incognita*. This short chapter, part of a book-length monograph and several digital spin-offs, constitutes a first attempt to redress this lacuna. It offers a concise chronicle of the Shoah in the capital; discusses narratives on the gamut of survival strategies; and presents quantitative data on those Athenian Jews who were arrested in the Greater Athens Area, deported to Auschwitz in three consignments (April, June and August 1944) and murdered. Last but not least, it makes the case for the urgent need to reclaim the past of those murdered innocent souls.

A community in ascent

On the eve of Greece's entry into the Second World War in October 1940, the Jews of the Greater Athens Area (GAA) numbered circa 3,500 souls. Though small both in comparison to Salonika's circa 50,000 strong and as a percentage of the overall total population of the Athens municipality (a meagre 0.72%), the Jewish Community of Athens (JCA), the second largest of its kind in Greece at the time, enjoyed all the formal trappings of a self-sustained legal entity governed by public law: A council, whose members were elected, rather than appointed by the dictatorial regime of the time – as was the case with that of Salonika; two synagogues on Melidoni Street near the Temple of Hephaestus, one under construction, and one make-shift in Piraeus, officiated by Sephardic and Romaniote rabbis born in Salonika and Yannina; a communal cemetery, adjacent to the principal Greek-Orthodox necropolis; an active Zionist association; a Refugee Relief Committee (*Ahnassath Orehim*), which played a vital role in the safe passage via Greece of more than a thousand fleeing Jews from Germany and central Europe to Mandatory Palestine; and a Jewish primary school in Petralona, where pupils followed, in addition to the curriculum set by the Ministry of Religions and National Education, free of charge classes in Hebrew and Judaism that were taught by a community employee, whose salary was in part paid by the ministry.¹

Data derived from the JCA's electoral register of 1938 show that its members came from all walks of life. Indeed, gone were the days when the Jews of Athens were mostly peddlers. Out of a total of 761 identified male heads of families, 29% were merchants, 22% white-collar workers, 20.50% peddlers, 12.50% commission and insurance agents, 9% blue-collar workers, 4% professionals, 1.70% industrialists, and 1.30% unemployed. Likewise, whereas until the late 1910s Psiri constituted the par excellence run-down neighbourhood where most Jews resided, two decades later we find them living in rented lodgings in working-class neighbourhoods (Gazi, Metaxourgio and Petralona), but also in owned accommodation in upcoming localities (Sepolia, Patisia and Kypseli). Such upward social mobility, if only as a trend, is also evinced by the number of pupils who attended the primary school in Petralona. For example, only 76 families enrolled their children (boys and girls) for the school year 1939-40. The schooling of the majority was carried out either at state-run or at private schools. In at least two of the latter, the community paid for the salary of a teacher of Hebrew for the needs of Jewish pupils. Yet, the fact that the majority received a non-Jewish schooling can also be read as evidence of upward social mobility and social acculturation to the prevailing Greek culture and societal norms.²

Acculturation went hand-in-hand with integration. In Article I of its last pre-war statutes, one reads that the JCA's principal aims included the "support of any beneficial initiative seeking to serve national needs." Such a goal, prior to the imposition of the Fourth of August Regime that compelled all Jewish communities to conform to its *Weltanschauung*, does not appear in the statuses of the Jewish Community of Salonika (JCS). Crucially, it is highly suggestive of the JCA's desire on the one hand to underscore the national credentials of an entity that was projected not as an ethnic minority but as a hetero-religious group, and on the other to construct an identity as the "respectable" face of Jewry in Greece. It drew on a narrative that the JCA had constantly sought to publicly articulate, and display, ever since its establishment in 1890. For, unlike other Jewish communities, the JCA was an entity with no past. Post-1912 Salonikan Jewry, to state the obvious, had indeed one to boast of; as did the Jews of Halkida, Yannina, Larissa, Volos, Hania, etc. Not so the Jews of Athens, who settled in the capital as entrepreneurs from Central Europe and as economic migrants from parts of Greece and the Ottoman Empire from the 1830s onwards, and from Asia Minor, Constantinople and Egypt in the 1920s. Indicatively, less than two percent of those who appear in the 1938 electoral register were born in Athens. Likewise, of the nine-member community board, only one was a native of the capital. In this respect, Athenian Jewry was the mirror image of the Jews of Greece as a whole, albeit one that lacked a past steeped in history. On the other hand, the early post Shoah attestation of the historian and prominent member of the JCS Joseph Nehama that on the eve of the Second World War the JCA "végète dans la médiocrité" is simply not borne out by the facts.³

Newcomers, refugees, escapees

In the context of Greece's tripartite occupation by the Axis powers (Germany, Italy and Bulgaria) in late spring 1941, the GAA fell under Italian control. This did not mean that the JCA did not fall prey to the activities of the Rosenberg Sonderkommando. Part of its archives were confiscated, individuals were "interrogated", their premises and those of Jewish organisations were searched for "incriminating material", while four prominent members of the community were arrested in May 1941. Following a month's incarceration at Averoff Prison, three of them were released after considerable ransom payments to the "Gestapo", which in the case of one of the arrestees amounted to 1,500 gold sovereigns.⁴

After this targeted show of strength, in August 1941 the Germans "appointed" the Rabbi of Athens Eliyahu Pinhas

---

* Many thanks to Aliki Arouh, Chief Archivist of the Historical Archive of the Jewish Community of Thessaloniki, for her kind assistance in the identification of the murdered and survived Salonikan victims of the Shoah in Athens, and to Sophie Costi, whose father survived the death camps, for unearthing pertinent sources and testimonies in Hebrew and for translating them.

1 United States Holocaust Memorial Museum (USHMM), RG-11.001M.0758: Rabbi Barzilay to Ministry of the Interior (3 November 1938); Philip Carabott, "The Fourth of August Regime and the Jews of Salonika: From mobilization and manipulation to social isolationism", unpublished paper; Central Zionist Archives (CZA), file Z4/30487; Jewish Museum of Greece (JMG), Archive of the Jewish School in Athens (AISA), various files.

2 USHMM/RG-11.001M.0759: Electoral register of the JCA (1938); Philip Carabott, "Η Ισραηλιτική Αδελφότης Αθηνών (1890-93)" [The Jewish Brotherhood of Athens (1890-93)], in K. Aroni-Tsichli et al. (eds), *Η Ελλάδα της νεωτερικότητας* [Greece of Modernity], Athens 2014, p. 113-142; JMG/AISA, file 4; USHMM/RG-11.001M.0758: Director of Moschandreou private school to JCA (14 October 1939).

3 *Government Gazette* 1/118 (4 April 1935); Philip Carabott, "Έλληνες Εβραίοι πολίτες στα τέλη του 19ου – αρχές 20ού αιώνα" [Greek Jewish citizens, late 19th – early 20th century], *Archeiotaxio* 19 (2017): 43-62; USHMM/RG-11.001M.0758: List of the JCA's Board members (10 January 1939); Michael Molho & Joseph Nehama, *In memoriam. Hommage aux victimes juives des Nazis en Grèce*, Salonika ²1973, p. 165.

4 Bundesarchiv: "Abschlußbericht über die Tätigkeit des Sonderkommandos Rosenberg in Griechenland, 15 November 1941" (many thanks to Iason Chandrinos for providing me with a copy of this report); Non-catalogued Archives of the Jewish Community of Athens (AJCA): Certification by Rabbi Barzilai (14 April 1950); Author's Archive (AA): Research files on each of the four arrestees.

Barzilai (b. Salonika 1891) as president of the community. All this was partly in line with their policy of instilling a degree of fear, of forcing into submission the elected lay elements of Jewish communities and of entrusting with figurative powers either non-entities or rabbis, whom they believed to hold more sway over their flock. It certainly served well their interests as regards the persecution and deportation of Salonikan Jewry, much less so in the case of the Jews in Athens. Knowledge of what had befallen their brethren in Salonika and much of northern Greece in the first half of 1943 played into the persecutees' hands. And whereas by early March 1943, the Germans had, with Chief Rabbi Koretz's complicity, a more or less precise record on all their victims in Salonika, in Athens they were on the dark, so to speak. The material confiscated by the Rosenberg Sonderkommando did not include the JCA's registers; these were kept by its director Victor Josef Eliezer (b. Corfu 1892). When in February 1942 Eliezer and his family fled Athens and went into hiding in western Greece, he seemingly either destroyed or hid them so as to "avoid providing data to the German occupation authorities".[5]

The "vanishing" of the registers aside, by the time the Germans assumed full control over the whole of Greece following the Italian capitulation in early September 1943, the Jewish presence in the capital had been significantly augmented. In fact, this new wave of newcomers to Athens, a city that traditionally had served as the melting pot for Jews (and Christians), began in earnest in the wake of the outbreak of the Greco-Italian War. For example, Asher Yeshua Amaraggi (b. 1906), owner of an ironworks shop in his native Salonika, moved with his wife and their two-year old boy to Athens in November 1940 to escape the Italian bombings. He was soon joined by his brother Leon, who however decided to return to *Madre d'Israel* a couple of months later, only to be deported and murdered, whereas Asher's family survived by "hiding in different places."[6]

Many more Salonikan Jews left in the wake of Black Sabbath at Liberty Square on 11 July 1942. As before, most of these had the financial means to undertake such a venture and find shelter in the Greek-Christian milieu of the capital where they would not "stand out." As the Italian Consul General in Salonika noted in late July, "almost all rich Jews have left for various locations occupied by Italian troops, some with false documents and some by other means." Although fleeing to Athens was a much riskier choice for the not so well-off, such were the dynamics of individual Jewish agency that some did not hesitate to take the plunge. Defying the German order to appear at Liberty Square and register for hard labour, and against his father's wishes that he stay put, the unemployed Rofel Solomon Arouh (b. 1913) fled by train in mid July with the assistance of a Christian gendarme, with whom he had served at the Greco-Italian front. The latter also facilitated the safe passage of Rofel's fiancée Allegra Avraam Levi (b. 1919) two weeks later, receiving for his "services" the not inconsiderable sum of thirty gold sovereigns. In Athens they got married on 9 December in a ceremony officiated by Rabbi Barzilai. The staged photo from their wedding shows them not merely as passive victims, but as active agents; they themselves chose the place and the occasion they wished to mark and celebrate, to remember and memorialise. There is nothing in the shot indicating or even suggesting a condition overstepping the mark or having the potential to be something other than a still of the formally recognised union of two people. In late September 1943 Rofel, Allegra and their newly born baby-boy found shelter in the mountains of central Greece that was under the control of the left-wing resistance movement.[7]

A new wave of escapees began to reach Athens in parallel with the intensification of the persecution, the aryanisation, the ghettoisation and the deportation of Salonikan Jewry from mid-February 1943 onwards. Although the vast majority was deported and eventually murdered in the death camps, for some it was possible to override familial concerns and responsibilities because the exigencies of the times were so demanding and the exogenous factors so crucial. The selfless assistance of a Christian fellow-undergraduate at the Law School played a pivotal role in the decision of Dora Leon Segoura (b. 1922) to leave behind her parents and younger sister and escape from the ghetto, as did the presence of relatives in the host city. Any lingering doubts as to the wisdom of fleeing she naturally might have had, given that the Germans had decreed that the relatives of any Jew who was known to have "escaped" would be executed, were wiped out by Antonis' simple, albeit potent, reasoning:

> You must leave immediately, now! We'll go together to Athens. The Germans are also after me. In Athens the Jews are not persecuted. Nobody knows you there. If you take off the star, who would know you are Jewish. We'll run away tomorrow, early in the evening!

---

5   Archives of the Central Board of Jewish Communities in Greece (ACBJCG), file 154: Testimony of Barzilai in the trial of Isaac Kampeli (19 September 1946); AJCA: Certification by Rabbi Barzilai (6 June 1945).
6   Personal communication by Maurice Amaraggi (31 May 2021).
7   University of South California, Shoah Foundation, Visual History Archive (VHA) 44944: Solomon Paparos (1 June 1998); Daniel Carpi (ed.), *Italian Diplomatic Documents on the History of the Holocaust in Greece (1941-1943)*, Tel Aviv 1999, p. 83-85; R.S. Arouh family archive, (courtesy of Aliki Arouh); Philip Carabott, "Group portraits of hope on the way to starting a new life", paper delivered at the international workshop "Readings of the Visual: Holocaust Photography and Education in the Digital Era", Netherlands Institute at Athens (19 October 2018).

Figure 1. *The wedding of Rofel and Allegra.* © Aliki Arouh.

Some two years later, Benjamin Haim Capon (b. 1928) would refer to the point of no return and describe the difficulties inherent in such daring endeavours thus:

> A Christian friend of my uncle advises us to try to escape to Athens by hook or by crook. A friend of my cousin informs us that that the first train with deportees has already departed. It has been decided! We should leave by any possible means! But it isn't so easy. The escape must be done with the help of Christian guides who ask for exorbitant sums of money. The first [guides] took the deposit and disappeared. We're getting ready to flee but we keep coming back. All this secretly in case someone sniffs us out and betrays us.

In the event, both Dora and Benjamin made it to Athens, surviving the Shoah in conditions that could have been penned by a novelist. Less onerous were the circumstances of the journey to Athens for circa 180 Salonikan Jews of Spanish nationality (159 were deported to Bergen-Belsen on 2 April 1944), as well as 217 of Italian nationality and 92 designated as *protetti italiani*, who arrived with an Italian *tradotta* (troop train) on 19 July 1943. Initially, the properties of the "Spaniards" were not confiscated, while the "Italians" were allowed to take with them much more of their movable property than was the case with the fugitive "Greeks" of the ghetto, whose staple kit consisted of the clothes they were wearing, a small suitcase at the most and carefully concealed jewellery and gold sovereigns.[8]

Escapees to the capital did not come solely from Salonika, though naturally these constituted by far the largest group. Hundreds of Jews from other cities took the decision to "disappear" from their native neighbourhoods and "get lost in the big city," albeit one that was "deeply wounded, with its inhabitants exhausted, frightened and starving." Most, like their Salonikan counterparts who moved to Athens in 1941-42, had the financial means to undertake such an enterprise and/or had relatives and business acquaintances in the host city. Crucially, knowledge of what was transpiring in Salonika, even in the form of rumours, was a determining factor in the strategies of survival that an increasing number of Jews began to resort to by 1943. Moses Jacob Nahmias (b. 1901) owned a fabric shop with his three brothers in their city of birth, when the 1st Mountain Division of the Wehrmacht set its base at Yannina in early summer 1943. During the Occupation, he frequently visited the capital to procure merchandise. In late August, while recuperating from an operation in a hospital in downtown Athens, he was paid a visit by a Salonikan friend, one of the thousands of fugitives from *Madre d'Israel*. "Like a prophet of doom,"

---

8 Dora Se[goura], *Γη μας, αγάπη!* [Our Land, Affection!], Athens 1970, p. 42-47; Yannis Karatzoglou, *Το ημερολόγιο Κατοχής του Βενιαμίν Χαΐμ Καπόν: 1446 μέρες αγωνίας* [The Occupation Diary of Benjamin Haim Capon: 1446 Days of Anguish], Salonika 2018, p. 158-160; International Tracing Services (ITS), Bad Arolsen, 3394231; Carpi, *op. cit.*, p. 256-272; Shlomo Venezia, *Inside the Gas Chambers. Eight months in the Sonderkommando of Auschwitz*, Cambridge 2009, p. 17.

he told him: "What are you waiting for! Send a letter and tell Anna and the children to come to Athens." Moses' daughter recalls:

> This warning about the imminent danger reached him while he was far from the narrow world of our city; and thus he had the opportunity to judge it, to evaluate it objectively and, finally, make the best of it in order to save us, and himself. He didn't hesitate for a moment. Years later, I realized from my mother's words how grateful she was to him for saving us. But she didn't realize how much she herself contributed in her own way to this salvation. For, if nothing else, it was she who packed up and brought us to Athens as soon as he asked her to, without hesitation, leaving everything and everybody behind.[9]

The number of all these newcomers and fugitives in the capital on the eve of the Italian capitulation remains a matter of conjecture, with estimates ranging from 3,000 (from Salonika alone) to more than 7,000. Either way, the influx continued even after the Germans took over. Leon Elias Levy (b. Halkida 1937) writes that in early 1944 his father, fearing that the Germans would soon discover their hideout in Amarinthos, some 20 km south of his city of birth, concluded that Athens, "with its bustling crowds, could absorb us. Besides, we had good friends there who would help us." What is certain is that as a result of this on-going influx the Jewish element in the GAA had (nearly?) doubled since the late 1930s.[10]

This is plainly evident in two extant records on "Greek survivors" in Athens. Based on the census that the Central Board of Jewish Communities in Greece (CBJCG) carried out in late November 1944, the first record tabulates 4,878 survivors by "age and sex". The second is a name list, with place of residence before the persecution, which was forwarded to the American Jewish Joint Distribution Committee (Joint) in spring 1945. It does not include escapees to the Middle East, deportees from Athens who survived the death camps, those who had already returned to the cities where they resided in 1940, and circa 20 survivors, mostly natives of Athens, whom the British had interned at the El Daba camp in Egypt as "communists" in early January 1945. Out of 4,323 souls who had survived the Shoah – by hiding (principally in the GAA but also in the Peloponnese and Central Greece), by escaping from the labour camps in Karya and Thebes or by joining the resistance movement -, 1,845 (42.68%) did not reside in the capital before 1940. If one adds the circa 500 former refugees who had returned home, then the number rises to 2,345 (48%).[11]

The Shoah in German-occupied Athens

The Italian capitulation on 8 September 1943 and the immediate advent of direct German rule brought home the gravity of the imminent persecution for natives, newcomers, refugees and fugitives alike, after two and half years of relatively benign rule under the Italians. In the beginning, SS Dieter Wisliceny ordered Barzilai to provide him with the names of all Jews in the capital. This came to nothing, as the rabbi stalled for time, maintaining in the course of two meetings with the "executioner" that all community records had been stolen and that he could not compile new lists at such short notice. In-between, according to his 1954 testimony, he made it abundantly clear to all Jews that "they had to abandon their houses at once, save whatever they could save, and [make certain] that neither the Germans nor the Greeks knew of their hideouts." Shortly thereafter he fled (or was abducted by the left-wing resistance movement, as the case might be) to the mountains of free Greece.[12]

The German response was to issue an order (dated 3 October), which partly ran thus:

1. All Jews within the area of German administration are to go immediately to their permanent residences, where they were living on June 1, 1943.
2. Jews are forbidden to abandon their permanent residence or to change residence.
3. Jews in Athens and the suburbs are required to report within five days to the Jewish Religious Community of Athens and to register in the records there. During registration, they must declare their permanent residence.
4. Jews not obeying these orders will be shot. Non-Jews, who hide Jews, afford them a hiding place or help them to escape, will be deported to concentration camps, if a heavier penalty is not imposed on them.

---

9   Iosif Venturas, *Ibbur: Οι Εβραίοι της Κρήτης, 1900-1950* [Ibbur: The Jews of Crete, 1900-1950], Athens 2018, p. 70; Eftichia Nahmias Nahman, *Yannina: A Journey to the Past*, New York 2004, p. 99; https://righteous.yadvashem.org/?search=Morfis&searchType=righteous_only&language=en&itemId=4022234&ind=0 (accessed on 28 June 2021).
10 Alexander Kitroeff, *War-Time Jews. The Case of Athens*, Athens 1995, p. 102, 117; Karatzoglou, *op. cit.*, p. 37; Karina Lampsa & Jacob Siby, *Η διάσωση. Η σιωπή του κόσμου, η αντίσταση στα γκέτο και τα στρατόπεδα, οι Έλληνες Εβραίοι στα χρόνια της Κατοχής* [The Rescue. The Silence of the People, the Resistance in the Ghettos and the Camps, the Greek Jews during the Occupation], Athens ²2021, p. 258; Carpi, *op. cit.*, p. 41; Leon Levy, *Θυμάμαι: Η ιστορία ενός διωγμού* [I Remember: The History of a Persecution], Halkida 2000, p. 51.
11 CZA S6/4657: CBJCG to Jewish Agency (29 January 1945); on the interned, see Iason Chandrinos, *Συναγωνιστές. Το ΕΑΜ και οι Εβραίοι της Ελλάδας* [Fellow Fighters. The National Liberation Front and the Jews of Greece], Salonika 2020, p. 259-260; ITS 8800880: Central Location Index to Joint (24 May 1945).
12 Molho & Nehama, *op. cit.*, 185-190; Lampsa & Siby, *op. cit.*, p. 274-283.

5. The Jewish Religious Community of Athens is appointed, with immediate effect, as the sole representative of the interests of all Jews in Greece. It should establish without delay a Council of Elders to undertake its business. Further orders will be given in due course.
6. Following registration, all male Jews over the age of 14 years must report daily to the above-mentioned authorities.
7. Jews are forbidden to frequent the streets and public squares between 1700 and 0700 hours.
8. The Greek police authorities are charged with the strict implementation of the above decree, and with arresting on the spot Jews who breach it or persons who help them to evade this decree.
9. Under this order, a Jew is deemed to be anyone who descends from at least three generations of Jews, irrespective to the religion to which he now belongs.

The order was primarily designed: a) To instil fear to "non-Jews" helpers; b) To actively involve the Greek authorities in the decree's implementation; and c) To lull into complacency at least some of their would-be victims by establishing an exclusively Jewish body as the "sole representative" of all Jews. The Germans were undoubtedly aware that even if they wanted to implement Blitzkrieg methods, these would not be effective – Athens was no Salonika. In late November, a further order was issued, whereby the movable and immovable properties of all native Jews who had so far failed to register were to be confiscated and handed over to the Greek [quisling] authorities, which henceforth would be responsible for their management. Thus, non-registered store and workshop owners and their mostly Jewish employees could neither continue to earn a living nor have valid ration books. Peddlers who sold their wares at stalls or traded in the streets could not renew their licenses. All should either become outlaws by going into hiding or discontinue flouting the order to register.[13]

That the first order was issued eleven days after Barzilai's last meeting with Wisliceny and was published in the Athenian Press only on 8 October deprived the Germans of the element of surprise. Arguably, this tardiness on their part provided the persecuted with a certain amount of time to organise their response in the wake of the Italian capitulation. Yet, in at least one recorded instance it came to nothing. Solomon Isaac Salario (b. Izmir 1898), a carpenter by trade, his wife Rachel (b. Athens 1903) and their four underage children left their house opposite the Jewish-owned textile factory Britannia in the suburb of Nea Ionia, where Solomon and his son Isaac (b. Athens 1927) worked, and sought refuge at the apartment of a Christian friend, Konstantinos Karamalis. The latter, a clerk at the registry office of the Athens municipality, provided them, free of charge, with false identity cards. On 29 September (i.e. before the publication of the German decree), Rachel and her daughter Matilda (b. Athens 1925) were arrested in a nearby street, having been denounced to the German authorities by unnamed neighbours. Not willing to compromise Karamalis, they seemingly revealed to their interrogators their "permanent residence". Isaac was arrested later in the day at Britannia. The three of them were incarcerated at the Haidari concentration camp. Solomon, who had escaped arrest, had no other choice but to register with the "Jewish Religious Community of Athens" (JRCA), while his two other children, Abraham and Moses, survived the Shoah by hiding at Karamalis' apartment. In the event, Solomon presented himself at the Beth Shalom Synagogue on 24 March 1944 and, together with Rachel, Matilda and Isaac, was deported on 2 April. Solomon and Isaac were murdered in October in the course of the abortive Sonderkommando uprising. Rachel and Matilda survived the death camps and returned to Athens. In 2006, the late Karamalis was recognised as Righteous Among the Nations.[14]

The trajectories of the Salario family in the context of the *Diogmos*, a term used by the historical subject itself to describe its persecution, are typical of many a Jew in German-occupied Athens. Foremost, they reveal agency on the part of the persecuted, debunking once more the convenient and outdated narrative of Jewish "complacency". Thousands of native Jews did not comply with the order to register with the JRCA. Like the hapless Salario family, that of Bohor Samuel Iossafat (b. Asia Minor 1885) chose to become "outlaws". A street retailer by trade, Bohor, his wife Eftichia (b. Larissa 1895) and their children – Fani (b. 1921), Samuel (b. 1922), David (b. 1926) and Mosses (b. 1927) – had moved to the capital from Alexandria in the early 1930s. In mid October 1943, having obtained false identity cards, they "granted" free of charge their one-storey house in the upcoming neighbourhood of Lofos Skouze to Christian friends, who formally appeared as the new owners. Then they moved – save Samuel who had joined the left-wing resistance movement of the National Liberation Front (EAM) and Fani who went to hide with a Jewish female friend in downtown Athens – to the empty cottage of another Christian friend on the slopes of Mount Hymettus. At their out-of-the-way hideout, young David became the family's bread winner. He used to cut wood from the nearby forest, transport it in a small cart to

---

13 Reproduced and translated in Richard Clogg (ed.), *Greece 1940-1949: Occupation, Resistance, Civil War*, New York 2002, p. 102; *Eletheron Vima* 7521 & 7560 (8 October 1943 & 24 November 1943).

14 *Eleftheron Vima* 7521 (8 October 1943); AA: Research file on the family of Solomon Isaac Salario; https://righteous.yadvashem.org/?search=Salarios&searchType=all&language=en&itemId=5730976&ind=1 (accessed on 28 June 2021).

Figure 2. (from left to right) *Matilda, Moses and Isaac Salario (circa 1937).* © Elias Tabakeas.

Pangrati (a distance of some 6 km) and sell it in exchange for black-market supplies and cigarettes for his father. And every fortnight, he walked to the bakery at Lofos Skouze (a distance of some 10 kms), had the family's old ration cards, which carried their Jewish names, stamped and got bread. "There was no way [the baker] would betray us", recalls David; "he was a trusted friend."[15]

The presence of "trusted" Christian friends, who, with or without "remuneration", helped the persecutees to implement their strategies of survival, emerges as a key feature of hiding. Indeed, of the 216 Greek families and individuals that are recognised as Righteous (as of January 2020), 133 (61.57%) carried out a variety of "rescue activities without remuneration" at the GAA. But there were also Christian "denouncers". In the case of the Salario family, one can only surmise what their motives were. In other recorded instances, derogatory stereotypes, revenge and foremost pecuniary interests are clearly discernible.[16]

Following the Italian capitulation, the merchant and former president of the Refugee Relief Committee Samuel Abraham Soussis (b. Arta 1895), his wife Esther (b. Salonika 1900) and their 13-year old daughter Rena hid at an apartment in central Athens, owned by a business associate of Samuel. The latter's wife, Esther's seamstress, apparently was after her rich collection of jewellery. Early in the evening of 29 January 1944, German soldiers, together with Greek collaborators, stormed the apartment and arrested the couple. As they were put in the truck to be transported for interrogation at the Gestapo headquarters on Merlin Street, the seamstress called Rena, who was playing at a nearby square, to approach; then, she said to the escorting fellow-Greeks: "Take this little bastard, she is also Jewish!" Some four months later, a similar-like contingent of Germans and Greeks arrested at their hideout at a suburb north of Athens Rafael Isaac Zakar (b. Arta 1889), his wife Anna (b. Preveza 1896) and five of their six children. They were tipped-off by a former girlfriend of the couple's eldest son, Isaac (b. Kerkyra 1912), who had left her for Samuel Soussis' eldest daughter, Edie (b. Athens 1924). The Sousis family was deported on 2 April, the Zakars on 20 June; save Emily Zakar, all were murdered upon arrival at Auschwitz. Isaac and Edie survived the Shoah and consummated their love in February 1945. Emily returned to Athens and married another survivor of the death camps.[17]

Helpers turned into denouncers underscore the hazards of hiding and escaping. This was true in the case of natives, newcomers and fugitives alike. The merchant Bension Solomon Alshech (b. Salonika 1906), his wife Clare (b. Salonika 1909) and their two children, Esther

---

15　Author's interview with David Bohor Iossafat (Athens, 6 April 2021 & 24 October 2021).

16　https://www.yadvashem.org/yv/pdf-drupal/greece.pdf (accessed on 29 June 2021).

17　Marios Soussis, *Καλή αντάμωση – Φιλιά εις τα παιδιά: Τα παιδιά που έχασαν το τρένο για το Άουσβιτς* [Until We Meet Again – Kisses to the Children: The Children Who Missed the Train to Auschwitz], Athens 2013, p. 136-137; General State Archives (Athens), Special Court Minutes (SCM) nos 1939, 1939a, 1946 & 1947 (7-8 November 1946).

(b. 1932) and Solomon (b. 1935), escaped from the ghetto and reached Athens in late spring 1943. Until the Italian capitulation, they lived together at an apartment at Koliatsou Square. Then, they split. Esther remembers:

> I hid at the house of [T] junior and his wife [R] in Iraklion. My nine year-old brother Solomon and my parents hid at the house of [T] senior, his wife and their daughter, 17 year-old [V], in downtown Athens. Mom, the only one who returned [from the death camps], told me the circumstances of their arrest. On 9 June 1944, father had given [T] senior a sum of money for safekeeping. The following day, a German officer, accompanied by a Greek gendarme, went to the house of [T] senior. Mom managed to hide Solomon at the courtyard. She didn't stay with him because she was afraid that they would torture father to tell them where I was hiding. The gendarme noted Solomon's shoes, but said nothing. Yet [V], who was the only member of the [T] family present at the scene, went out and came back with Solomon.

Semtov Haim Perahia (b. Salonika 1893), director of a tobacco factory in Drama, his wife Emily (b. Drama 1900) and their two children, Haim (b. Kavala 1919) and Rachel (b. Kavala 1922) moved to Athens in October 1940. In the wake of the Italian capitulation, they left the apartment they had bought in the capital, and hid at the house of a business acquaintance. "My father and my brother were getting tired", recalls Rachel. So they decided to flee to the Middle East. Their "helper" arranged that they get a taxi from Omonia Square, which would take them to the Attica coast. From there, they would board a rowboat to the west coast of Evia, then by foot and mule to the east coast, whence with a caique to Cesme.

> We decided that we we're going to get dressed as if we're going to a wedding, in case they stop us. And that's what happened. And [this] friend of ours gave us up. He [had lived] in Germany, and we thought he was working for the Greek government, trying to find out things from the Germans. And maybe he did, but he was on both sides. And maybe the Germans found out that he was hiding Jews [and for this reason] he gave us up. And all of sudden [the] Germans stop[ped] us, and since I knew German, I got out of the car, and I said: "I don't understand why you're taking us." He said: "Fraulein, we know everything about you. You don't have to tell us any[thing] more. You'll come with us."[18]

Others succeeded where the Perahia family failed. Between October 1943 and late August 1944, circa 880 persecutees (the majority refugees and escapees) in Athens reached the Turkish shore by crossing the Aegean. Such perilous journeys were organised by a network of Christians and Jews, Greeks and non-Greeks: Agents of the British secret services and the Greek government in exile, the EAM, which by late 1943 controlled much of the island of Evia, and the Jewish Agency in Palestine. Motivated principally by pecuniary concerns, sometimes the owners of caiques undertaking the journey would not hesitate to work for both sides. One such duplicitous skipper was convicted in 1947 for serving in the counter-intelligence office of the Special Security Service of the quisling Ministry of the Interior and for denouncing his would-be passengers, the family of Albert Moses Gatenio (b. Salonika 1899). Yet, he was acquitted for denouncing the Perahia and Gavriel (see below) families, while the native Errikos Caesar Fortis (Milano 1918) testified under oath thus: "We also wanted to leave, so we found [the said skipper], who hid us at his house until we were to leave, but I fell ill and we did not leave. [X] could have betrayed us. [Instead] he helped many of our own."[19]

Either way, fleeing was not an option open to all. It was a pricey affair, with the socio-economic status of the persecuted constituting a decisive factor. A qualitative analysis of the available data shows that most escapees belonged to well-to-do families, which could afford the payment, in gold sovereigns and jewellery, required by mediators, facilitators and executors. Early in the morning of 9 June 1944, the merchant Joseph Menahem Sion (b. Salonika 1888) and his three adult children (Matilda, Menahem and Jeanne) had been told to wait at a café of a sparsely populated village to the northeast of the capital.

> We found the café, drank something and paid the bill when all of a sudden a truck came, stopped in front of the café, the driver came to us, asked for the parcel, which immediately I gave it to him, he opened it and counted that there were twenty five gold sovereigns, told us to mount on top of the charcoal truck and started running.

They reached Evia by a rowboat, manned by two men, arriving at 6 a.m the following day. There, another two men, described by Matilda as "thieves", walked with them to the top of a mountain, which they reached at 6 p.m. They then began to descend the slope and after an hour or so they saw four other Jewish escapees and a wooden motorboat waiting for them at the seashore. "Someone

---

18   Author's interview with Esther Alshech-Florentin (Athens, 22 March 2019); USHMM, RG-50.030.0486: Interview with Rachelle Perahia Margosh (24 June 2004), https://collections.ushmm.org/search/catalog/irn515153 (accessed on 30 June 2021).

19   ITS 8800880: List of refugees of various countries who came from Greece overland (17 October 1944); Chandrinos, *op. cit.*, p. 125-140; SCM, no 1541 (3-4 February 1947).

asked us to hand over our [false] identity cards and to my sister her gold bracelet." Early in the morning of 12 June, they safely reached Cesme, "the dirt of which I have never seen in my lifetime."[20]

Among the successful escapees to the Middle East, the case of two unmarried Jews is revealing of another survival strategy that persecutees resorted to: Conversion, fake or genuine, to Greek Orthodoxy – with a total of 391 baptisms carried out between 1 January 1941 and 22 September 1944. As the secretary of the Archbishop of Athens and All Greece wrote in her diary on 20 April 1943,

> In absolute secrecy, we are baptizing Jews. At great personal risk, the Archbishop is making enormous efforts to save as many Jews as he can. He has come to an understanding with the Mayor's office in Athens. A special registry has been opened, and, after baptism, these people are given certificates which say that they are Greek Christians.

On 23 March 1944, Haim Abraham Koen (b. Larissa 1914) was paid a visit at his home by a fellow-Jew who was in the payroll of the SD (Sicherheitsdienst des Reichsführers – SS). A graduate of the Athens Medical School, Haim had been working at the capital's main hospital under a false name, having been baptised on 10 November 1943. Acting on his own, the traitor demanded of Haim ten gold sovereigns for not denouncing him, as well as his widowed mother and sister, whom the hapless doctor had placed at the Athens Old People's Home. Haim obliged, and subsequently fled to the Middle East, reaching Cesme on 14 April. On 10 May, his mother and sister were arrested at the Old People's Home, deported on 20 June and murdered. His two other sisters survived by hiding at the Athens Asylum for the Homeless. Before the Shoah, Ariel Raphael Strugo (b. Izmir 1918) worked as a junior reporter at the Athens News Agency, while studying Law at the National Kapodistrian University. He lived with his widowed mother and his sister Esther. On 14 October 1943, he and Esther were baptised. Seven months later, Ariel was registered with the British authorities in Izmir as a refugee "who came from Greece overland."[21]

Five days earlier, on 24 April 1944, Salvator Haim Gavriel (b. Preveza 1910), director of a textile company, his parents, his two brothers and his sister Leonie had been arrested while they were getting ready to get into a car, in this instance at Kaningos Square, that would take them to the Attica coast, the first part of the perilous journey to the Middle East. Evidently, their mediators had betrayed them. Save Leonie, who survived the death camps, all were murdered. In the case of Salvator, who was given the Christian name Sotirios (Saviour), his christening on 27 September 1943 did not save him from deportation. Admittedly, much further work needs to be done to determine to what extent conversion facilitated survival. And the same holds true in the case of those who were issued with – and/or paid for – false identity cards. As Nehama somewhat exaggeratedly put it: "Il n'existe pas un seul Juif, dans toute l'Attique, qui n'ait dans sa poche une fausse *taftotita*, de faux papiers". Either way, both strategies of survival highlight the existence of Greek Orthodox solidarity with the persecuted Jews.[22]

The perils of "hiding here, there and everywhere" are recounted in most accounts of the persecuted who survived in hiding. They might be lacking in detail, in some cases they are replete with factual errors but still they constitute forceful testimonies on the human will to confront and successfully overcome the ramifications of a world that had been turned upside down. These are eloquently summarised in the following extract from an article written by the telecommunications employer Raphael David Konstantinis (b. Athens 1888), who together with his wife and their five-year old child had hid at the suburb of Nea Smyrni.

> Human imagination cannot conceive the harshness of the living conditions of the Jews in hiding at the time. They were in constant fear of being arrested, day and night; they were obliged to consider at all times any reasons that might cause their identity to be revealed; they faced everyone with a suspicious and fearful cast of mind; they had to [always remember the narrative] they recited to neighbours and new acquaintances about where they came from and the reasons that led them to their new residence; they were forced to restrict their children's lives, fearful that, through carelessness, they might reveal the big secret concerning the crime they had committed and for which they were being persecuted. In most cases, they lived separated from their wives and children of whose fate they were unaware; they found out that whatever they possessed, the result of a lifetime's work, was confiscated; they learned of the arrest of a relative or friend, and compared their situation or

---

20   Written testimony of Menahem Joseph Sion (courtesy of Rina De-Goffer).
21   Holy Archdiocese of Athens: Registry of baptisms (courtesy of George Pilichos); Jeanne Tsatsos, *The Sword's Fierce Edge. A Journal of the Occupation of Greece, 1941-1944*, Nashville 1969, p. 56; AA: Research files on Haim Koen & Ariel Strugo.

22   VHA 28466: Leonie Yael (Buenos Aires, 25 February 1997); SCM, nos 1541, 1556 & 1557 (3-5 February 1947); Molho & Nehama, *op. cit.*, p. 196-197.

arrest to their own, to reach some conclusion, either comforting or despairing, as the case might be, about their own fate.[23]

A long-overdue duty

Errikos Leon Sevillias (b. Athens 1901), owner of a leather goods workshop, registered with the JRCA in early December 1943, as per the German order. Thereafter, every Friday he went to the Synagogue for the roll-call. His account of that "fateful Friday" reads thus:

> It was a sunny day and slowly many of us gathered in the little street before the synagogue. We talked in little groups about the fact that today we were late in getting started and, though it should have seemed strange, it didn't. Many of those who had either work or their shops nearby left and returned quickly. Someone who had forgotten his card left in order to get it and thus saved his life. All of a sudden someone shouted that we should all get into the synagogue because flour was going to be distributed for the Jewish Easter. Since the crowd was large some people remained outside, but a German told them that everyone had to get inside and that is how we got caught like mice in a trap. First of all there was no sign of flour and then, suddenly, the big door closed and two Germans who had been hidden stood in front of it, armed to the teeth. They stood facing the crowd with their machine guns. It all happened so quickly, so swiftly, that we were struck by fear and doubt at the same time. What did they want from us? Weren't we within the law? Weren't we on the roll?[24]

The testimony of a female deportee, who was arrested at the Beth Shalom Synagogue on 24 March and survived the death camps, highlights the role played by non-German agencies that fateful Friday: The Security Battalions of the quisling government of George Rallis, some members of which were dressed in the Evzone (*Tsolias*) uniform, and the notorious right-wing collaboration organisation of Yeoryios Grivas, which was particularly active in the neighbourhoods of Thissio and Petralona. Anna Nissim Koen (b. Chania 1923) moved to Athens in 1939 to marry the peddler Yesoula Ischaki (b. Ioannina 1914). Following the Italian capitulation, the couple heeded Rabbi Barzilai's advice to "disappear". They rented a basement at a suburb west of Athens. "We were hidden; our [new neighbours] did not even know that we were Jewish. I didn't have a fake identity card, I had nothing!" After some six months, they ran out of money and had to move back to their old residence at Thissio, which was owned by a member of Grivas' organisation. Having forfeited their status as hidden outlaws and under the watchful eye of their landlord, they of course registered with the JRCA. On that fateful Friday, Anna arrived at the synagogue around 9 a.m. "They had let it be known that they would give us matzo." Wishing to survey the scene, she did not enter directly the synagogue; but she was recognised by a German "Gestapite", who forced her in. After a couple of hours, numerous female arrestees were "escorted" by an armed *Tsolias* each to their residences to pick up "whatever they had." While Anna was collecting her stuff, her landlord signalled to the *Tsolias* that next door many Jews lived.

> He took me back to the synagogue and after a while they brought the others. The *Tsoliades* were disastrous for us Jews; they were traitors! They betrayed their own [Christian] brothers. Do you think they wouldn't betray the Jews?[25]

The centrality to the Shoah in Athens of that fateful Friday is undeniable. Out of a total of 622 Athenian Jews that I have identified to-date as having been arrested in the GAA between September 1943 and August 1944, and subsequently deported and murdered at the death camps, 496 (79.24%) were apprehended on Friday 24 March 1944 either at the round-up that took place at the Beth Shalom Synagogue on 5 Melidoni Street or at nearby streets or at their houses or at police stations. Another 36 Athenian Jews arrested on the day survived the death camps. Of these, only eight settled in Athens, the rest having moved to British Mandate Palestine, Israel, and to the USA by the 1950s. The same holds true for the 496 murdered victims' first- and second-degree relatives who survived the Shoah in hiding in Athens; most left Greece in search for new beginnings.

Unsurprisingly, the few Athenian survivors of both groups that stayed on at the capital did not come to constitute a community of memory. One that would seek to establish and promote "sameness and continuity across time", to memorialise their own and their ancestors' past in the face of the cataclysmic changes brought upon by the Shoah. The fact that by the mid-1950s the majority of the Jews in Athens comprised survivors of the *Diogmos* in hiding, natives, refugees and fugitives in equal measure, as well as newcomers, former members of by then destroyed communities, did not help either in cementing a sense of belonging over and above the common attribute of having survived. Additionally, at a time when thousands of their brethren from all over Greece had been murdered

---

23 VHA 48385: Eva Benmelech-Davis (20 July 1998); *Evraiki Estia* 5 (9 May 1947).
24 Errikos Sevillias, *Athens – Auschwitz*, Athens 1983, p. 6-7.
25 VHA 47849: Anna Varvara Koen (19 November 1998).

in the death camps, having survived the Shoah in hiding was very much something that few wished to talk about, even less so to publicly remember. It is hardly surprising that the few early post-Shoah testimonies by Greek-Jewish survivors focus on the paths to destruction within Greece, on deportation and the death camps. And it should not go amiss that even these early few and far between voices, as in other countries, were heard by a "relatively closed circle of survivors, their relatives and concerned individuals and groups." In any case, all this was very much in line with what followed: The repression of the memory of the Shoah in Europe and the USA from the late 1940s to the early 1960s, by victims and perpetrators alike. As Deborah Eisenberg has put it:

> Once a great public cataclysm has occurred, it is nearly impossible for people to recall what it is they felt and how they behaved during it or just prior to it. Misery is a potent aid in obliterating memory, and shame in distorting it.[26]

Before this "collective amnesia" took hold, on 19 October 1946 the draper and former board member of the JCS Saltiel Solomon Koen (b. Salonika 1876), who had hid in Athens during the *Diogmos*, had suggested to the CBJCG the construction of a monument in memory of those murdered at the crematoria, and expressed his willingness to contribute towards this end the sum of 200,000 drs. In its reply, the Board maintained that such a monument would be too costly and, crucially, that it would "remind the tragedy of our race" only to "our coreligionists in Athens" and not to those of other communities, which "suffered to a much greater extent." At a time when Athens had already become the centre of the Jews of Greece, the Board's quantitative reasoning seems somewhat hollow given that Koen's suggestion related to all victims of the Shoah in Greece and made no distinction on the basis of place of birth and/or of arrest and deportation. Instead, the Board proposed and carried through the placing of a commemorative plaque at the main surviving synagogue of each and every community. In Athens it was unveiled on 20 March 1947, in what was a solemn occasion attended

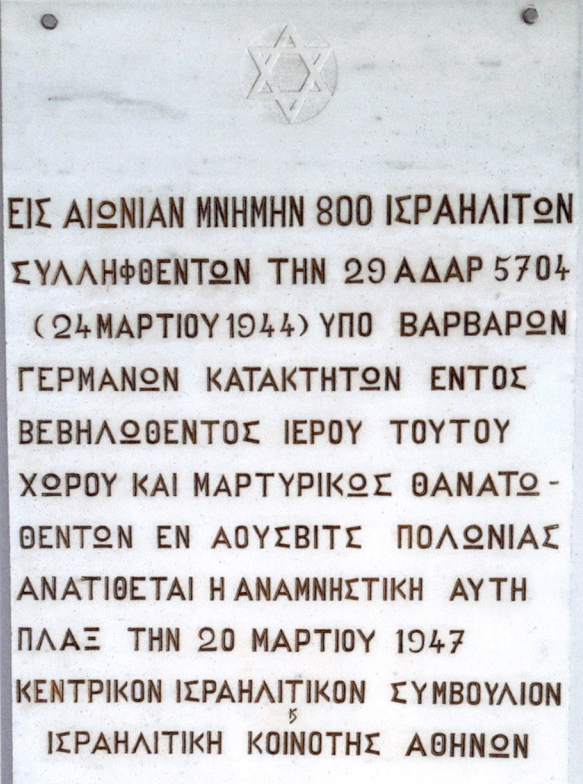

Figure 3. *"In eternal memory of the 800* [sic] *Israelites who were arrested on 29 Adar 5704 by the barbaric German occupiers inside this defiled sacred space and* [subsequently] *torturously killed in Auschwitz"*. © Soly Iochana.

almost exclusively by coreligionists. To-date, it remains the only such commemorative "monument" on the murdered Athenian Jews.[27]

Unlike the Holocaust Memorial that was unveiled in 2010, sixty-four years after Koen's suggestion, the commemorative plaque is tucked away from the public's gaze. Its existence is largely unknown; it is not mentioned on the webpage of the community; and one would search in vain for an image of it in cyberspace. As for its signifiers, these are cherished (and, in some instances, jealously guarded) by those who identify with them – the descendants of the identified murdered victims and the few survivors of the Shoah in Athens who are still among us. This introvert appropriation of the memory of the victims is in stark contrast with that exhibited by

---

26 W. James Booth, "Communities of memory: On identity, memory, and debt", *American Political Science Review* 93/2 (1999): 249; Saul Friedländer, "History and memory: Lessons from the Holocaust", https://books.openedition.org/iheid/2358 (accessed on 4 August 2021); Odette Varon-Vassard, "Η ανάδυση και η συγκρότηση της μνήμης της Shoah στην Ελλάδα (1990-2020)" [The emergence and constitution of the memory of the Shoah in Greece (1990-2020)], *Synchrona Themata* 150-152 (2021): 49-61; Dan Stone, "A victim-centred historiography of the Holocaust?", *Patterns of Prejudice* 51/2 (2017): 184; "Introduction" in Gregor von Rezzori, *Memoirs of an Anti-Semite. A Novel in Five Stories*, New York ²2008, p. ix.

27 Tony Judt, *Postwar. A History of Europe Since 1945*, New York 2005, p. 808; AA: Research file on Saltiel Solomon Koen; ACBJCG, file 300: Minutes of Board Meeting (22 October 1946); *Idem*, file 2: CBJCG to Koen (30 October 1946); Philip Carabott, "'Το νέον κέντρον του εβραϊσμού της Ελλάδος': Αθήνα, 1941-1947" [The new centre of the Jews of Greece: Athens, 1941-1947", paper delivered at the Netherlands Institute at Athens (16 March 2018); *Evraiki Estia* (28 March 1947).

other Jewish communities and its members in Greece as well as the communities of memory that have sprung up abroad. For example, Shoah victims hailing from Salonika and Ioannina are commemorated by name in monuments, memorial plaques and publications in Greece, Israel and the USA that are accessible to – and reachable by – the general public. Recent efforts to redress this in the case of the Shoah in Athens are undoubtedly commendable. But they fall short as they seemingly preach to the converted. "'Never again' means telling the story again and again," the UN Secretary-General recently noted. Not solely to a Jewish but to a worldwide audience, I would add.[28]

It is high time we begin to look at Athenian Jewish victims not merely as "numbers". Lest we forget, it was the Germans who turned those whom they deemed fit to pass the selection upon arrival at the death camps from human beings into a number, to anonymity. This infatuation with figures, though quite understandable in the face of the persistent rise of Holocaust denial and distortion, is hardly befitting to the memory of victims unless it goes hand-in-hand with their identification and their "recovery" as human beings. The mass industrial murder of six million Jews, its aftermath and its legacies have generated an abundance of documents and testimonies. In the case of the Athenian Jews, the reasons, the excuses and the deafening silence accompanying the failure of successive Boards of the JCA and the CBJCG to generate quantitative and qualitative lists of those who were murdered during the *Diogmos* cut no ice anymore. The 622 – and counting – murdered victims were *real people*, with *real lives*. It is our duty to reclaim their past to the best of our ability.[29]

---

[28] https://www.memorialmuseums.org/eng/denkmaeler/view/544/Holocaust-Monuments-in-Athens (accessed on 17 September 2021); Soussis, *op. cit.*, 441-470; Association of Descendants of Holocaust Victims, *Ημέρα μνήμης του Ολοκαυτώματος* [Holocaust Remembrance Day], Athens 2016; https://www.un.org/press/en/2020/sgsm19943.doc.htm (accessed on 17 September 2021).

[29] Indicatively ACBJCG, file 64/2: CBJCG to JCA (22 September 1947), and CBJCG, *Βιβλίο μνήμης* [Book of Memory], Athens 1979; Stone, *op. cit.*, p. 188.

The Silent Tree

Collaborationism, Political Power and Collective Guilt. A Dutch-Greek Case Study in Memory

Riki Van Boeschoten

Abstract

The chapter explores the micro-history of an appalling war crime that took place in the Thessalian village of Kato Lehonia in July 1944, the execution by hanging of three women. The victims of the crime were two wealthy Dutch women, Lucie Van Schelle-Topali, and her daughter Sophie, and Filitsa Kalavrou, the wife of a miller. The Topali family was widely respected in the village and considered as benefactors. After their death their property was looted by the perpetrators, Greek collaborators and German soldiers. The chapter examines how the villagers have tried to come to terms with feelings of collective guilt and fear by analysing symbolic story-telling against the background of local village culture. Written testimonies recorded shortly after the event and later oral history interviews illuminate the process of myth-making, the construction of meanings and the silences through which the legacy of the event lived on under the surface of public memory. This case-study may bring some fresh insights into our understanding of traumatic memory, by focusing on the grey zone between perpetrators and bystanders and on the notion of collective guilt.

Introduction

In the middle of the Thessalian village of Kato Lehonia a bronze tree stands as a reminder of an appalling war crime that took place on 7 July 1944: The execution of three women by the Germans and their local collaborators. They were hanged from the branches of a mulberry tree standing next to the railway station. Yet, as there is no inscription on the monument, only insiders may know its meaning. Most of them hastily move on and avoid talking about "the hanged women" (τις κρεμασμένες). This unobtrusive monument was inaugurated only in 1987, at the time of Andreas Papandreou's socialist government, on the initiative of mayor Dimitris Alexopoulos.[1]

For forty-two years absolutely nothing reminded the villagers of the crimes that had taken place during the last phase of the German occupation. Off the main road a street name, now full of graffiti, was once meant to pay tribute to one of the victims, but has since fallen into oblivion. Loukia Topali Street was named after Lucie Van Schelle, a Dutch

---

* I wish to thank Dutch historian John Loose for his work in the Dutch archives and our inspiring conversations about what he found there.

1 The monument was intended to honour as well the memory of other residents killed by the Germans during this period, in particular those hanged at the train station of Orman Magoula on 31 May 1944 (see below). This first and only commemoration in Lehonia was, however, boycotted by right-wing villagers; conversation with Dimitris Alexopoulos (3 August 2014).

Figure 1. *The Bronze Tree monument, Kato Lehonia.* © Riki Van Boeschoten.

patrician woman born in 1875 in Indonesia, who had married Panayiotis Topalis (1867-1939), a Greek wealthy landowner and wine-grower established in Romania. Both members of a cosmopolitan educated upper class, they had met during holidays in Switzerland and married at the Netherlands in 1896. Around 1907 the young Topali family had bought a vast landed property full of olive and fruit trees in Kato Lehonia.

Next to Lucie hang her daughter Sofia, or Sofika as she was lovingly called in the village. Born in Romania in 1900, she was a well-known botanist with a large network of connections among European and Greek academics, artists and writers. In 1927 the Topali family had funded the establishment of a top-notch modern primary school at the village, in memory of Sofia's brother Konstantinos, a well-known alpinist who had perished in an avalanche at the Swiss Alps. The third branch of the mulberry tree was used to hang Filitsa Kalavrou. She was the wife of the local miller Andonis Kalavros, who had joined the left-wing partisans of ELAS (Greek People's Liberation Army).[2]

During the war, Sofia had supported the left-wing EAM (National Liberation Front) resistance movement with money and food, as we know from a note left by Konstantinos Dondolinos, the director of the Commercial Bank in Volos and leading member of the EAM, who was in charge of the food kitchens set up by the organisation. In this note, written from his prison cell in March or April 1944, Dondolinos asked his wife to see to it that three million drachmas should be given back to Sofia.[3] On 21 April Dondolinos and his two sons were brutally murdered, together with sixteen other citizens, by the Greek collaborators of the EASAD (National Agrarian

---

[2] On 2 October 1961, the Court of First Instance at Volos granted her heirs compensation to the amount of 35,000 drachmas; General State Archives, Magnisia Branch, Volos (GSA-MB), Archive of Court of First Instance: "Nazi Decisions 1961". According to oral accounts, Filitsa herself had also supported the partisans.

[3] Archives of Contemporary Social History (ACSH), Athens, Archive of the Dondolinos family 1943-1947, 1963-1964: File 1.

League of Anticommunist Action).[4] These were the first victims of an unprecedented wave of killings, lootings and other forms of violence perpetrated by the EASAD, which terrorised the town from April to September 1944.

However, the involvement of two of the women, Sofia Topali and Filitsa Kalavrou, in the Greek resistance was not the reason why they were murdered. According to all accounts, the motive lying behind the execution was to loot the Topali property. Having carried out an investigation about this tragic event, using "the best possible sources," on 5 November 1945 the Dutch vice-consul in Volos, Henri Aslan, reported back to the Dutch embassy in Athens:

> These unfortunate ladies were betrayed and denounced to the German authorities of Volos by the faction of the EASADites, their gruesome instruments. The execution took place in the square of Kato Lehonia on 7/VII/44. The total amount of their rich fortune should be adjusted to about 100,000 pound sterling.[5]

The report also contains a full description of the property, which included a rich mansion with cellars full of produce, and on the upper floors luxurious furniture, jewellery and other valuables, about 4-5,000 olive trees, and 3-4,000 fruit trees, lots of cattle, a number of cottages to house employees and a large vineyard. In a follow-up report, Aslan added that all the movable property had been looted, at first by the Germans and then by the "rebels of EAM/ELAS."[6] Most local contemporary oral accounts agree with Aslan's version of events, with only one exception; the looting of the villa started immediately after the arrest, was carried out by the Germans, Greek collaborators and villagers and was completed even before the execution took place. The three women had been arrested in the first days of July 1944, transferred to the Gestapo prison of Volos and on the morning of 7 July they were brought back by train and hanged at the square.

This execution was one among thousands that took place in wartime Greece. Yet for a number of reasons it was an extraordinary event. Extraordinary, first of all, because of the identity of the victims; mother and daughter belonged to Europe's upper class, they were wealthy landowners, mistresses so to speak of the village, but because of their simple manners and their philanthropy they were well accepted by the villagers. And yet they were betrayed by members of the same village. Why did this occur?

It was an extraordinary event also because Lehonia was not an "ordinary" Greek village. It was a village with sharp social and political divisions – between rich and poor and between Left and Right. In 1944 Lehonia became the centre of activity of the EASAD collaborationist movement. Several young men of the village held a leading position in the League and committed numerous atrocities in the whole region. Why Lehonia?

The EASAD itself had links with the quisling government in Athens, with the German SD (Security Police), with Greek politicians and with some members of the Volos elite. In this way, both through the European connections of the Topali family and through the collaboration network, the events of July 1944 linked this Thessalian village with the wider world. One might say that, in spite of the insistent efforts of the villagers to "forget" the mulberry tree and all that it stood for, in 1944 the village had moved centre stage. The micro-history of this story may help us think about some of the larger questions at the core of the "troubled pasts" and the "unwanted stories" that form the subject matter of this volume. It raises questions about the grey zone between perpetrators and by-standers in wartime atrocities, and about the impact of feelings, in particular of fear and guilt, on the post-war structuring of memories on a community level. And ultimately, it raises the fundamental question of accountability in the post-war period. What happened to the perpetrators? Did they pay for their crimes or did they continue to exercise power in post-war society? If so, what are the consequences for local communities? And what are the consequences on memory? Are they transmitted to subsequent generations, and in what forms? Or are they silenced?

Here I address these questions by looking at the stories that the villagers of Lehonia have told each other for years on end. I intend to explore the role of story-telling as a collective coping mechanism in the aftermath of what must have been experienced by most as a hair-raising event. In order to understand the full meaning of these stories, however, we need to situate them in their socio-economic and political context.

The socio-economic context

Class divisions had marked the history of Lehonia since Ottoman times. Its fertile plain had belonged to wealthy Muslim landowners. After the annexation of Thessaly to the Greek nation-state in 1881, their lands had gradually been acquired by Greek large landowners. Most of them did not live in the area all year around. They formed a cosmopolitan, well-educated elite, whose members

---

[4] The information that the Topalis gave money to the left-wing resistance was confirmed by one of their employees in his account to a journalist; Giannis Mantidis, *Sofika Topali. Noose Around a Memory*, Athens 2016, p. 113.

[5] General State Archives of the Netherlands, Ministry of Foreign Affairs, Archive of the Dutch Embassy in Athens, 1940-1954 [ADEA] (original in French). In an earlier report, Aslan had estimated the property at about 60,000 pounds sterling.

[6] ADEA: Aslan to Dutch embassy (14 November 1945). The alleged looting by the partisans could not be confirmed by other sources. By the end of 1945, when Aslan collected his information, the tide had turned against the left-wing resistance, and the "best possible sources" which he claimed to have used, were obviously influenced by this political climate.

spent part of the year in Athens, Volos or abroad. Many were involved in commerce or early industrial activity. Class divisions were also expressed spatially; most of the wealthy landowners lived uphill in Ano Lehonia, where they had built sumptuous villas, the remnants of which are still visible today. By and large, their workers lived further down in Kato Lehonia, close to the railway tracks, overlooking the fertile plain with its lush vegetation spreading down to the seafront.

These class dimensions were still evident in the 1970s, when American anthropologist Diane Bennett (later O'Rourke) began to study village relations. She estimated that about 10% of households belonged to large landowners hiring labour, about 45% were middle class independent farmers and shopkeepers, and the remaining 45% were landless agricultural labourers.[7] Class distinctions were evident in architecture, clothing and social events. The wealthy would have their own place in church, would not invite their inferiors to Saint's Day celebrations or attend local weddings.[8] Daily life in the village was often fraught with class tension; landless labourers who depended for their income on the local landowners used to tell stories about inhumane treatment and talked of exploitation. The images of extreme poverty experienced by village labourers and of their tense relations with some of the landowners are also powerfully conveyed by local journalist Giannis Mantidis.[9]

At the same time, however, the ethnography also revealed how rich and poor had worked out a modus vivendi and a sense of symbolic community that helped them to avoid conflict and to integrate outsiders into their community. They did this, for example, by stressing equality in all death rituals and especially in the cemetery, by circulating stories about "good" landlords and "divine retribution" of moral trespassers, and by constructing a shared identity based on prosperity and progressiveness. More importantly, Diane Bennett singled out two strategies that allowed the villagers to live together in spite of past and present divisions: Ambiguity and strategic silences. Ambiguity creates a space for negotiating social relations and for multiple and flexible interpretations. Strategic silences meant that people were careful not to state explicitly things that everybody knew but might disrupt social harmony and cooperation.[10] Let us keep in mind these two principles; they might be useful in interpreting the stories about the execution that we will see later on.

This then was the community in which the Topalis settled in 1907. It seems plausible to suggest that many of the elements presented above were part and parcel of the community culture of Lehonia in the 1930s and 1940s. The Topali family belonged to the cosmopolitan proprietors described above, but in many respects they were different. They were the only ones that had settled in Kato Lehonia instead of Ano Lehonia and were, according to all accounts, regarded as benefactors of the community. While they socialised with people "of their own kind" in Ano Lehonia and in Volos, they had also established close personal contacts with the "commoners" and people appreciated their openness, generosity and simple manners. These views are confirmed by the notes of Daniel Baud-Bovy, a Swiss writer and close friend of the family, on his visit to the Topali family in 1937:

> The ways of this house, which could have been luxurious, especially in this village, were admirably simple. The only staff was a housekeeper, a joyful young girl who seemed part of the family and Stefani, the estate manager, who brought provisions on the back of a donkey! Rare visitors, and as clients all those who needed help, comforting or who were hungry.

And about Sofia Topali, he wrote: "She knew by instinct, without losing her native distinction, how to put herself at the same level with the people she spoke to."[11]

Reading these notes, against the background of the village culture described by Diane Bennett, it seems the betrayal of the Topali women by some of their co-villagers cannot be explained by class hatred, but should be rather sought in the general disruption of social relations brought about by the war. Bennett neither focused on the violence of the 1940s, nor does she mentions the Topali family or the execution. However, forty years after she had started her fieldwork, she acknowledged in a footnote that part of the village history probably played a more important role than she had realised earlier:

> It may be that the excesses of WWII and the civil war period and the fear these left behind were contributing factors to the stress on unity which I saw, for example, in the symbolism of the cemetery in the 1980s-1990s.[12]

It is to these factors I shall now turn my attention.

---

7   Dianne Bennett, "The poor have much more money: Changing socio-economic relations in a Greek village", *Journal of Modern Greek Studies* 6/2 (1988): 217-244; Dianne O'Rourke, "A failure of imagination: The decline of community in a Greek village", *The Journal of the Society for the Anthropology of Europe* 6/2 (2006): 3.
8   Dianne Bennett, "Bury me in second class: Contested symbols in a Greek cemetery", *Anthropological Quarterly* 67/3 (1994): 126-127.
9   Mantidis, *op. cit.*, p. 19-23.
10 Bennett, "Bury me in second class...", *op. cit.*, p. 129, 131; O'Rourke, *op. cit.*

11 Municipal Library of Geneva, Archive Baud-Bovy 134/1: Daniel Baud Bovy, "Une visite à M. Topali". I wish to thank Manuel Baud-Bovy, his grandson, for bringing this document to my attention.
12 O'Rourke, *op. cit.*, p. 11 (footnote 12).

The political context

Political divisions between Left and Right had begun many years before the war. In the 1930s a secret communist organisation used a haberdashery in Kato Lehonia as a meeting place,[13] but others in the village were horrified by the idea that communism might prevail one day. During the first war years the old social and political divisions partially broke down in a united cross-class movement of solidarity and support for the left-wing EAM. The climate began to deteriorate, however, at the end of 1943. After the capitulation of Italy in September, a German garrison was established in Lehonia, but the left-wing resistance movement gradually developed its own power structures and by mid-1944 had come to dominate both at a regional and a national level. Most notably, it had formed a provisional government and an elected assembly in the free mountains of Central Greece.[14] For those who feared a communist takeover after liberation, this sounded an alarm bell and eventually pushed part of the elite and its followers towards collaboration with the Germans. This included a section of the EDES (National Republican Greek League), which originally set out as a resistance organisation, the Security Battalions, and in Thessaly the EASAD.[15] In an extremely revealing document, initially published in 1977, Thrasyvoulos Papasakellariou, who served as mayor of Volos during the last months of the war, describes in detail how he took the initiative to set up the EASAD, his contacts with the quisling government in Athens, the Athens branch of the EDES, Greek politicians and leaders of anti-communist organisations. He mentions the difficulties in recruiting armed men and his reluctance to return to Volos for fear of being caught by the partisans and being executed. Finally, he writes about his dismay when he realised the organization he helped to create had turned into a bunch of ruthless murderers, killing over 200 people in one month.[16]

This was the setting which led to the eruption of violence in Lehonia and to the execution on 7 July 1944. According to testimonies collected by Mantidis, the Georgatzis brothers played a crucial role in both. Although Pindaros Georgatzis had initially supported the EAM, he changed sides when a representative of the EDES visited Lehonia. When the ELAS began to persecute EDES supporters, he fled to Athens. In February 1944 he took an active part in the negotiations mentioned by Papasakellariou with the aim to collaborate with the Germans against the EAM/ELAS.[17] On 1 May 1944, a few days after the killings of 19 citizens of Volos by the EASAD, a bunch of its local members, led by Spyros Kalabalikis, rounded up as many men as they could find. Twelve were executed one month later at Orman Magoula, while others were sent to concentration camps in Germany.[18] These events sealed the division of Kato Lehonia in two opposing camps, symbolised by the two coffee shops; the one, ran by the Georgatzis brothers, was frequented by the "national-minded" (εθνικόφρονες) and the other by supporters of the Left and the Centre. "This division", writes Mantidis, "was like a curse that went on for years."[19]

In June 1944, the ELAS arrested Pindaros and Andonis Georgatzis. Fearing that their execution might lead to further bloodshed, the local EAM organisation asked Sofia Topali to accompany Dimitris Kavouras, a respected landowner and leading member of the EAM, to intervene with the ELAS headquarters and set them free. This mission was accomplished successfully. One day after Sofia's return, she was arrested, together with her mother and Filitsa Kalavrou. Although nobody knows how, why and by whom the decision of their arrest was taken, the testimonies collected by Mantidis suggest that the Georgatzis brothers knew about it. The information that "something is going to happen tonight" reached Giorgos Alexopoulos through his girlfriend, Virginia Georgatzis. Alexopoulos used to spend the night at the Topali mansion, for safety reasons, together with three other young villagers. That night Alexopoulos neither went to the mansion, nor did anything to save his hosts. He warned only one of the three other friends, while the remaining two went to the house and witnessed the arrest.[20]

---

13 Archive of Audiovisual Testimonies, Department of History, Archaeology and Social Anthropology, University of Thessaly, Volos, S017/110: Kostas Frangou interview (1 February 2014).
14 Mark Mazower, *Inside Hitler's Greece. The Experience of Occupation 1941-1944*, New Haven 1993, p. 291-296.
15 On the EASAD, see *ibid*, p. 335-336; Vasiliki Lazou & Dimitris Skaltsis. "Εθνικός Αγροτικός Σύνδεσμος Αντικομμουνιστικής Δράσης (ΕΑΣΑΔ): Οι πρόθυμοι συνεργάτες των Γερμανών" [National Agrarian League of Anticommunist Action: The willing collaborators of the Germans], in S. Dordanas et al. (eds), *Κατοχική βία, 1939-1945: Η ελληνική και ευρωπαϊκή εμπειρία* [Violence During the Occupation: The Greek and the European Experience], Athens 2016, p. 91-147. On the EDES and its cooperation with the Germans, see Hagen Fleischer, "Νέα στοιχεία για τη σχέση Γερμανικών Αρχών Κατοχής και Ταγμάτων Ασφαλείας" [New evidence on the relationship between the German occupation authorities and the Security Battalions], *Mnimon* 8 (1982): 189-203, and *idem*, *Στέμμα και σβάστικα. Η Ελλάδα της Κατοχής και της Αντίστασης* [Crown and Swastika. Greece of the Occupation and the Resistance], Athens 1995, vol. 2, p. 251-257.

16 "Report to the Athens branch of the EDES (27 September 1944)", cited in S. Papayiannis, *Εθνικός Αγροτικός Σύνδεσμος Αντικομμουνιστικής Δράσης. Τα Τάγματα Ασφαλείας της Θεσσαλίας* [National Agrarian League of Anticommunist Action. The Security Battalions of Thessaly], Athens 2007, p. 347-356.
17 *Ibid*, p. 350-353.
18 Mantidis, *op. cit.*, 125-131.
19 *Ibid*, p. 78.
20 *Ibid*, p. 137-153.

Although some villagers, as well as the Metropolitan of Volos, claimed they had tried to save the two women, a muted sense of collective guilt has poisoned the lives and memories of many Lehonia inhabitants in the post-war era.[21] They preferred to keep silent, because after the war those who had collaborated with the Germans in the EASAD ranks continued to hold power. Even though they were at first convicted – most of them in absentia – by the Special Court for Collaborators in Volos, when civil war violence began to escalate they were soon back in the streets, committing new crimes against supporters of the Left (see below). In his reports on the situation in Volos in 1946, British vice-consul A.M. Rendel denounced the total impunity granted to Spyros Kalabalikis, spoke of Lehonia as his "Kingdom" and attributed to him racketeering practices.[22] Even long after the end of the Civil War, former collaborators or their relatives continued to maintain a powerful position in the community; for example, during the military dictatorship of 1967-1974, Tilemachos Georgatzis, the third of the Georgatzis brothers, was appointed mayor of Lehonia.

Local power relations, harrowing questions to which no answer could be found and mutual suspicion have nurtured feelings of fear and guilt, which are still perceptible today. Inevitably, these processes have left their traces in the collective memory of the 1940s.

Oral testimonies and the question of truth

> From that night on, after 7 July 1944, no one ever talked again about the hanging of the [three] ladies, no one from the village at least. In their heads the horrible film played over and over again, but they wouldn't dare discuss it, at least with someone who didn't feel any guilt of betrayal. The crime was covered by silence. It was like some kind of *omertà* that kept their mouths closed.[23]

What are the challenges facing the researcher who wants to uncover stories nobody wants to hear? Traces of memory can be found both in written and oral sources, but when these memories are dominated by feelings of fear and guilt the disentanglement of facts and myths poses some serious methodological questions. The crime of the mulberry tree has hardly left any written records. Most of the information found in archives was initially based on oral testimonies, such as those gathered by vice-consul Aslan in 1945 and the eyewitnesses accounts recorded in 1946. These oral/written testimonies should not be considered in any sense more reliable than the oral history interviews that were recorded decades after the event, because often those that provided the information had their own political agendas or were constrained by the same subjectivities as narrators whose stories remained oral. So we are left with stories, fragmented accounts, myths, and silence. But is this a problem? Following recent trends in oral history theory, I believe it is not. On the contrary, I consider that those stories and those silences can illuminate the deeper symbolic meanings of the narratives circulating in a particular community.

Silence, as Luisa Passerini reminds us, can be full of memory, is linked to forms of power, and may be considered a necessary step for local communities to be able to face the future. Painful and repressed memories may leave traces and in order to understand such "silent" memories, she argues, "we must look for relationships between traces, or between traces and their absences, and we must attempt interpretations which make possible the creation of new associations."[24] The exploration of such relationships between traces of painful memories means we are looking for the deeper structures of meaning in stories that people do tell each other. In other words, rather than looking for the factual truth of narratives, which of course is also important, we should try to understand the process of collective myth-making surrounding painful events. In this context, "myth" does not necessarily have the meaning of a "false" as opposed to a "true" tale. Much to the point, Alessandro Portelli, who grappled with such myths in memories about reprisal killings in Italy, defined myth as "a story that becomes significant as it amplifies the meaning of an individual event (factual or not) into a symbolic and narrative formalization of a culture's shared self-representations."[25] In his work on the massacre of 335 civilians by the Nazis in Rome, he was particularly interested in exploring how factually wrong stories can become "common sense":

---

21. GSA-MB, Archive of Notary Agoropoulos, doc. 24636, 24659: Sworn depositions by eyewitnesses Dimitris Koukousas (11 December 1945) and Dimitris Papadimitriou (2 January 1946); Mantidis, *op. cit.*, p. 164-167, 179, 223-224.
22. National Archives, Kew Gardens, Foreign Office (FO) 286/1173: Rendel to British embassy in Athens (9 June & 23 November 1946); "Report by A.M. Rendel on tour in Thessaly, 6-20 November 1946", p. 13.
23. Mantidis, *op. cit.*, p. 223.
24. "Memories between silence and oblivion", in Katharine Hodgkin & Susanna Radstone (eds), *Contested Pasts: The Politics of Memory*, London 2003, p. 240.
25. "The massacre at Civitella Val di Chiana (Tuscany, June 29, 1944): Myth and politics, mourning and common sense", in Alessandro Portelli, *The Battle of Valle Giulia. Oral History and the Art of Dialogue*, Wisconsin 1997, p. 153.

Oral history distinguishes between events and stories, between history and memory, because it considers that stories and memories are also historical facts. The fact that a wrong version of history becomes common sense, does not only invite us to reconstruct the facts, but also to ask ourselves how and why this common sense has been constructed, what this means and what is its purpose.[26]

In the following pages I will try to unravel aspects of this collective myth-making surrounding the Topali murders in Lehonia. I have selected four shared stories we encountered in oral memories that illustrate these processes particularly well because of the symbolic meanings we can read between the lines.[27] This "exercise" is based on the assumption that these shared stories, no matter whether they are factually true or not, convey meanings that are important for their narrators. By telling and retelling them, they contribute to creating the collective myths this community needs "to live by"[28] and to settle its accounts with a painful and shameful past.

A multi-vocal silence: Settling accounts with collective guilt

In fact the silence about the events of July 1944 was only partial; or rather, it was selective. In the post-war years, nobody dared to speak in public about the perpetrators and about the execution itself. As I have explained above, this silence was related to the continued influence of the perpetrators in post-war local power relations. Yet the multiple tales I have found in circulation suggest that in the private space of the home people continued to tell each other stories to make sense of what had happened. We could call it a "multi-vocal silence" or a silence full of memories, as Passerini has argued. These are stories with a mythical dimension, as meant by Portelli, which can be read as metaphors for the anxieties, fears and desires of those who tell them. Because of their shared nature, they have been transformed into "common sense". Often they are also based on a wider "cultural script", that is a "pre-existing cultural narrative or public representations according to which people make sense of their experiences and structure their memories."[29]

The trap: Partisans in disguise

This amazing story tells how two EASAD men and a German knocked at the door of the Topali mansion disguised as partisans, complaining to Sofia Topali that she had not sent any food lately. When Sofia protested and showed them the goods she had prepared for the partisans, the alleged "partisans" revealed their true identity and arrested mother and daughter.

Taking into account Sofia's close connections with local leaders of the Resistance, such as the Dondolinos family, and her important mission to the ELAS headquarters days before her arrest, it seems hard to believe she would have fallen into the trap prepared by the EASAD men. Yet it is a story repeated by most villagers, a shared story. In the version presented by Mantidis, entitled "the night of the traitors", the story gains in credibility, as it is supposedly based on an eye-witness account.[30] Apostolis Koukouselis and his brother Stathis, who were not warned by Alexopoulos about the imminent dangers of the night, witnessed the scene and recognised one of the "partisans" as a co-villager by the name of Mitsos. Moreover, Mantidis claims that minutes earlier the partisans in disguise had employed the same trick to arrest Filitsa Kalavrou and even came to his own house.[31] He had internalised this story to such an extent that when I paid him a visit in 2016 he took me by the hand and enacted the whole scene in situ, while the old fears re-emerged on his face. Had it not been for his elder sister, who saw through the trick, he told me, he might have hanged himself from the fourth branch of the mulberry tree.

Here, however, I am not concerned with the veracity of this narrative. The important point is that the people of Lehonia not only believe it to be true, but they also need to believe it. It is this need we must try to understand and explain. And to understand we have to place it within its own cultural context. There is, first of all, the immediate cultural context, the village culture. We can recognise here the two core social strategies identified by Diane Bennett: Ambiguity and "knowing but not saying." The identity of the false partisans remains ambiguous; we can suspect that many people knew who that Mitsos was, but it must

---

26 Alessandro Portelli, *L'ordine è già stato eseguito. Roma, le Fosse Ardeatine, la memoria*, Rome 2001, p. 18.
27 The oral history material presented here comes from life stories recorded for the City Museum of Volos (2013-2015), from unrecorded conversations described in my own ethnographic fieldnotes and from oral histories collected and published by Mantidis (*op. cit.*). As these stories were shared and repeated by virtually all narrators, I believe it is not necessary to mention individual narrators. The material has been deposited at the Oral History Archive of the Department of History, Archaeology and Social Anthropology of the University of Thessaly (Collection S017).
28 Raphael Samuel & Paul Richard Thompson, *The Myths We Live By*, New York 1990.
29 Loring Danforth & Riki Van Boeschoten, *Children of the Greek Civil War. Refugees and the Politics of Memory*, Chicago 2012, p. 224. A similar notion is the theory of the "cultural circuit"; see Lynn Abrams, *Oral History Theory*, London ²2016, pp. 68-69.
30 Mantidis, *op. cit.*, p. 149-153. Mantidis did not interview the only eyewitness who lived to tell the story (Apostolis Koukouselis), but his sisters. The other brother, Stathis, also present that night, was arrested and sent to a concentration camp in Germany, from where he never returned.
31 *Ibid*, p. 154-157.

not be stated. Secondly, there is the question of visibility/ invisibility. Just as in 1976 the villagers of Lehonia opposed a new regulation that made class divisions too visible in the cemetery, even though these divisions were recognised as part of daily life,[32] here the perpetrators must remain invisible, even though many knew who they were.

The broader cultural context is that of the cultural script, which in this case can be easily identified as the biblical fable of the "wolf in sheep's skin", a moral tale intended to convey that evil, even in disguise, will eventually reveal its true nature. The story of the trap focuses on the notion of betrayal and clearly marks off good (Sofia Topali, trust, the Resistance) from evil (collaboration, treachery). By telling this story, one might suggest, the narrator and his community can place themselves on the good side and clear any suspicion of betrayal. In other words, it is a way in which the community can come to terms with its collective responsibility and its guilt for the murder of the three women. The fear expressed by Mantidis in his re-enactment is also part of this collective narrative. Fear of the EASAD men, who remained alive after the war because of their impunity, explains why nobody dared to react to the crime.

Stolen dowries

This is one of many stories about the looting of the Topali mansion. According to the tale, the Topali family was considered "above any suspicion" because of their social status and their European connections. Therefore many families entrusted their valuables to this "safe house",[33] especially their daughters' dowries. After the mistresses' death, these goods were stolen together with other valuable objects belonging to the Topali family. The stories recount how truckloads emptied the house for days on end, speak of floors being broken open to search for gold, and about precious books being teared apart and thrown onto the streets. This story stresses the relation of trust and the closeness between the villagers and the Topali family. The cultural script one might think of here draws on a historical precedent in the Ottoman era; villagers donating part of their property to a monastery in order to save it from the Ottoman state. The story might also suggest that the villagers could not have participated in the looting of their own dowries. On the other hand, this explanation is contradicted by other versions, often recounted in a humorous tone, about villagers recognising their own stuff (curtains, tea sets) in somebody else's house. Here we find another kind of ambiguity, which facilitates the co-existence of multiple interpretations. The second reading allows the villagers to assume part of their collective guilt by recognising their participation in the looting, but by making it a shared responsibility, thus alleviating the burden.

The honest jewellers

This is another story about the looting and its aftermath. It tells how some collaborators who had obtained part of the Topali family jewellery tried to sell the objects to a goldsmith in Volos. At that time there were only three goldsmiths in the town and they had personal connections to the family. So when this unidentified man entered the shop and offered the precious stone, necklace or golden belt for sale, the jeweller immediately recognised the objects and sent the man angrily away. The story also says that the three goldsmiths then informed each other and agreed to refuse to buy the stolen jewellery. Again this story clearly marks off good from evil and dissociates morally part of the local population from the collaborators that tried to profit from their crime.

The pardon that came too late – Can there be any good Germans?

There are some stories about alleged attempts by influential German friends of the Topali family to release the women. But there is only one story, most probably fictitious, about an actual pardon that came too late, just after the three women had been murdered. It is mentioned by Mantidis, two interviewees of whom claimed to have seen the Germans that came to announce the pardon.[34] This story might be interpreted as wishful thinking, as an imagined happy end that tragically failed to materialise. It reminds us of the story of the elderly Germans who had participated in their youth in the massacre of civilians in Civitella, Italy, and came to ask for forgiveness decades after the war.[35] But underneath there is another symbolic story, a template so to speak, which is the "story of the good German". In Mantidis' book there are two other instances of this template.[36] The story of the "good German" is a European cultural script that often emerges to counterpoise accounts of Nazi mass killings. As is often the case with symbolic thinking, the myth of the good German can be interpreted in contrasting ways. According to Portelli, it may either "confirm our faith in the remnant of humanity that survives even in the cruellest torturers, or highlight through the humanity of one the inhumanity of all."[37] In the case discussed here the need to believe in the existence of "good Germans" may also be seen as an effort to stress the cruelty of local collaborators and to dissociate oneself from such individuals.

The consequences of failed retribution

All these stories may be seen as attempts to come to terms with a haunting past, with feelings of shame, rage, fear,

---

32 Bennett, "Bury me in second class...", *op. cit.*
33 Mantidis, *op. cit.*, p. 137-138.
34 *Ibid*, p. 172-173.
35 Portelli, "The massacre at Civitella...", *op. cit.*, p. 153.
36 Mantidis, *op. cit.*, p. 133-135, 198-200.
37 Portelli, "The massacre at Civitella...", *op. cit.*, p. 154.

powerlessness and guilt shared by many villagers of Lehonia. The only ones who did not show any sign of remorse or guilt were the two leadings members of the EASAD in Lehonia, Spyros Kalabalikis and Ioannis Velitsos, interviewed at the end of their lives by Mantidis. This unrepentant attitude can be ascribed directly to the impunity they enjoyed for their crimes in the wake of the unfolding civil war. The EΛSAD collaborators, among whom those of Lehonia held a leading position, were at first condemned to heavy penalties (death or life sentence), only to be acquitted later on. Most of them were condemned in absentia, but, as noted above, while their trials were going on, in 1945 and 1946, the same individuals were persecuting and killing former EAM members in their villages.

The way in which national states have dealt with former collaborators has had a profound impact on the ways in which the wartime period has been remembered, as well as on the political culture in post-war states. Accountability and justice are equally important structuring notions in post-communist states or post-conflict societies, such as Bosnia, Rwanda and South Africa. This has led to a growing body of literature on "transitional justice". While this notion focuses on an expendable temporal framework of "transition" from one (oppressive) regime to another, more democratic one, I find the concept of "retributive justice" more useful. According to anthropologist John Borneman, who employed it to analyse the post-communist transformation in East Germany, retributive justice includes both the "conviction of wrongdoers and the restoration of the dignity of the victims." He argues further that the relevance today of retributive justice "goes far beyond the fate of individual criminals and victims; its increasing importance is part of a global ritual purification of the centre of political regimes that seek democratic legitimacy."[38] One could doubt, of course, in the wake of the contemporary global political culture of "apologies", whether such repeated rituals of symbolic purification have today any effect on democratic legitimacy. It remains a fact that in the case of post-war Greece there has not been any "settling of accounts", in the sense intended by Borneman. The failed retribution of war-time collaborators in the wake of developments ushering to a full-blown civil war led to their re-legitimation in the name of the struggle against communism and to the de-legitimation of former participants in the EAM left-wing resistance movement.[39] As a consequence, there was neither political space for a ritual purification at the national level, nor for the "settling of accounts", including dealing with collective guilt, in local communities. The fragmented and muted memories we found in Lehonia about the hanging of the three women are the result of these global processes.

---

38 *Settling of Accounts: Violence, Justice, and Accountability in Post-Socialist Europe*, Princeton 1997, p. viii.
39 See Tasos Kostopoulos, *Η αυτολογοκριμένη μνήμη. Τα Τάγματα Ασφαλείας και η μεταπολεμική εθνικοφροσύνη* [Self-censored Memory. The Security Battalions and Post-War National-Mindedness], Athens ²2013; Dimitris Kousouris, *Δίκες των δοσιλόγων, 1944-1949. Δικαιοσύνη, συνέχεια του κράτους και εθνική μνήμη* [Trials of Collaborators, 1944-1949. Justice, Continuity of the State and National Memory], Athens 2014.

A Ticket of Re-Admission into Dutch Society

The Controversy on Amsterdam's Monument of Jewish Gratitude (1950)

Roel Hijink & Bart Wallet

Abstract

In 1950 the mayor of Amsterdam accepted from the hands of a Jewish committee a "Monument of Jewish Gratitude", intended to express the appreciation of Dutch Jews for the help of their fellow citizens during the Second World War. In our chapter, we analyse the initiative and realisation of the monument, arguing that it was from the outset a specimen of "conflictive heritage". The monument fitted the prevailing myth of collective Dutch resistance, but met with severe criticism from within the Jewish community. Through studying the prosopography of the committee members and analysing the various positions taken in the dispute, we argue that for some Jews who saw their future in the Netherlands the monument was their "ticket of re-admission into Dutch society", whereas others – mostly Zionists – objected to the monument as a symbol of traditional Jewish Diaspora attitudes of servility and assimilation, and juxtaposed it with the memorial "Joop Westerweel Forest" in Palestine/Israel – a living monument in the country of Jewish future. We also address the present endangered status of the monument and plead for its continued existence as a stumbling stone documenting postwar attitude towards Jews in Dutch society.

Introduction

On a cold winter day, 23 February 1950, a large crowd assembled for the unveiling of the Monument of Jewish Gratitude, located at Weesperplein, a square in the midst of the once vibrant Amsterdam Jewish quarter. The Jewish organising committee presented the monument as a token of gratitude of all Dutch Jews towards their fellow citizens for their help and support during the German occupation. Maurits (colloquially called Maupie) den Hartogh, chairman of the committee, addressed the crowd and specifically mentioned those who had hidden some 20,000 Jews, who thus had survived the Shoah. He considered the general strike of February 1941 as the main source of inspiration for all those who had helped Jews, "who more than others were persecuted and trampled,"[1] and did not fail to mention that some 100,000 Jews had not received the help they so much needed and, consequently, had been murdered. The monument consisted of a ten-meter-long and four-meter-high wall, with a two-steps-podium, five reliefs and on top a Star of David. It was designed by the Jewish sculptor Johannes Gustaaf (for his family

---

1   Amsterdam City Archives (SA), Topography Archive, no. 494: Speech by Dr M. Den Hartogh.

Figure 1. *The Unveiling of the Monument of Jewish Gratitude with Mayor Arnold Jan d'Ailly on 23 February 1950.* © City Archives Amsterdam.

and friends, Jobs) Wertheim (1898-1977). According to Wertheim, thousands of Jews had spontaneously contributed in order to bring to fruition the plan for the monument,[2] whereas in his speech De Hartogh stressed that even the poorest and weakest members of the Jewish community had given money.

Mayor Arnold Jan d'Ailly received the monument on behalf of Amsterdamians, but not without expressing some unease. What he felt was, next to pride, also shame:

> Have we always been our brother's keeper? Has everyone understood what gruesome injustice was done to their neighbours? Has everyone done enough to protect them against the heinous deeds? We all know that it was not like that. Our strength has been made perfect in weakness. But this monument honours a virtue that is an expression of the highest degree of civilisation. May it encourage us to always struggle against injustice and to stand up for our fellow human beings.[3]

D'Ailly promised that the city of Amsterdam would do everything to keep the monument as a solemn memory to the Jewish victims of the war. Then, a Jewish men's choir, directed by Hans Krieg, performed the Israeli national anthem Ha-Tikvah and Shir Ha-Ligyonot, the marching song of the Jewish soldiers who had served in the British army and fought in northern Africa during the Second World War. Attendees included members of parliament, aldermen and councillors of the Amsterdam municipality, officials of various governmental departments, representatives of the police and wartime resistance fighters, as well as professors and curators of universities.

---

2   *Nieuw Israëlietisch Weekblad* (14 April 1961).

3   "Monument drukt dank uit van Joden aan niet-Joden" [A monument expressing thanks from Jews to non-Jews], *Het Vrije Volk* (23 February 1950).

At the moment of its unveiling, the monument was one of the largest war monuments in Amsterdam and the only one commemorating the murder of Dutch Jewry, albeit indirectly by honouring Dutch resistance activities. In emphasising the heroic role of the resistance, the organising committee choose to interpret Jewish war time experiences through the lens of the dominant at the time discourse of remembrance. The idea was that the Dutch had been a nation of resistance during the years 1940-1945, with the resistance fighters acting as pars pro toto for the whole nation. Disregarding the relatively high number of collaborators, after 1945 the supposed unity of the nation continued as a unity discourse, aimed at combining forces for the rebuilding of society. The reliefs on the monument fitted neatly into the dominant frame, using classical and even Christian iconographic symbolism and ethical notions. The kneeling male nude expressed "Acquiescence in the will of God"; the standing nude with an arm protecting the head stood for "United with you in defence"; the standing woman in dress symbolised "Protected by your love"; the standing male nude with outstretched arm represented "Strengthened by your resistance"; while the kneeling female nude with her arms comforting around the naked child expressed "Grieving with you". The child was supposed to symbolise Dutch Jewry, the woman the Dutch population at large. All these reliefs and their titles aimed at connecting the Jews with the broader Dutch population, attempting to bridge the gap between the widely differing war experiences of both groups. "They were united with us," asserted De Hartogh in his address, emphasising how the Dutch had been complying with the biblical commandment to love your neighbour as yourself: "True heroism is not in the first instance contempt for death, but rather devotion to duty in obedience to the highest divine and human laws."[4] Already in 1945, in a speech to the Amsterdam municipal council, De Hartogh had praised the Dutch nation for their steadfastness in regarding Jews as Dutch citizens and expressing solidarity with their plight.[5] The February 1941 strike served De Hartogh and his fellow committee members well as a central element in the narrative of Dutch resistance and help for Jews.[6] Initially, the monument was planned to be unveiled on 25 February, the strike's Memorial Day, but because it fell on a Shabbat in 1950, the unveiling was moved to 23 February.[7]

While in 1950 hundreds of people assembled to witness the unveiling, at National Remembrance Day on 4 May 2017 only four persons commemorated the war victims at the Monument of Jewish Gratitude. It had been moved to a new location in a small park next to the Weesperstraat in 1968. Despite the fact that a nearby primary school adopted the monument, it now seems to have been fairly forgotten. At present, there are even far-fetched plans to replace it with a new Holocaust Names Memorial. These plans have thus far barely raised any debate or protests – and for a clear reason. The monument has increasingly become a specimen of troublesome heritage, reflecting the 1950s dominant memory discourse that is very much at odds with the naked fact that proportionally the number of Dutch Jews who were murdered in the Shoah was the highest amongst all Western European Jewries. This worrisome fact was partly caused by active and passive collaboration from Dutch citizens and institutions.

However, even before it was conceived, the Monument of Jewish Gratitude was highly disputed.[8] Our chapter will analyse the process that led to the construction of the monument and inquire what motivated the initiators to propose this particular monument. We will also examine the opposition to the monument and reconstruct what arguments had been brought forward in this very intense debate. Our aim is to demonstrate that the monument reflected a phase in postwar Dutch society in which Jews could only effectively "enter" the public sphere by adopting the predominant mode of war memory. For this reason, as much as it symbolises the war period itself, the monument also denotes the postwar memory culture that was created in order to mediate war experiences in the postwar period of reconstruction.[9]

---

4   SA, Topography Archive, no. 494.

5   *Gemeenteblad Amsterdam Tweede Afdeeling: Verslag van de vergaderingen van den Gemeenteraad, enz.* (21 November 1945): 20.

6   Annet Mooij, *De strijd om de Februaristaking* [The Battle for the February Strike], Amsterdam 2006, p. 5.

7   Initially the committee aimed for the unveiling to take place on 25 February 1949 but, due to financial reasons, it was unable to have the monument erected on time; Netherlands Institute for Art History, The Hague (RKD), Archive Jobs Wertheim, NL-HaRKD0129, Box VII. Because of the change of dates, the unveiling of the monument by Queen Wilhelmina did not materialise; E. Wouthuysen, "Johannes Gustaaf Wertheim, van bankier tot beeldhouwer" [Johannes Gustaaf Wertheim, from banker to sculptor], in C. Van Blommestein et al. (eds), *Joh. G. Wertheim*, Scheveningen 2017, p. 83-84.

8   Indicatively see Marja Vuijsje, *Ons kamp. Een min of meer joodse geschiedenis* [Our Camp. A More or Less Jewish History], Amsterdam 2012, p. 165-166.

9   Our chapter focuses on inner-Jewish debates and considerations concerning the monument. The "reconstruction" of the monument's history partly overlaps with an article on the broader societal context of its history; Roel Hijink & Gerrit Vermeer, "Het Monument van Joodse Erkentelijkheid, teken van trots en schaamte" [The Monument of Jewish Gratitude, a symbol of pride and shame], *Amstelodamum* 105/2 (2018): 51-67.

The committee

It is still difficult to say when exactly and at whose behest the idea for the monument was conceived. As early as November 1945, the committee's founding was announced in the Jewish community's weekly mouthpiece, including its objective to erect "a sober, worthy monument."[10] In an interview to art historian Jan Teeuwisse in 1986, Bob Nijkerk, one of the plan's initiators, came up with a remarkable story. He remembered that in June-July 1945, Queen Wilhelmina, via a palace official, had informed a few "prominent Jews" that in her view it was odd that the Jews had thus far shown such little gratitude towards the Dutch who had hidden them during the war.[11] This could have been the start of the initiative for the monument. Thus far, however, this is the only source we have – indeed, not a contemporaneous one – to document the beginnings of the project. It nevertheless substantiates a widely held recollection in Jewish circles that the monument was erected in response to the Dutch authorities' wish for such a type of memorial.

A clue to the rationale behind the initiative might be the composition of the committee that was formed to bring to fruition the project of erecting a monument to express the gratitude of Dutch Jewry. Eleven "prominent Jews" comprised the committee. Their prominence, however, did not stem so much from their position within the Jewish community, but rather their political, social and economic standing in society.[12] The chairman, Maurits De Hartogh (1876-1952), was a medical doctor and already before the war a well-known liberal politician, a member of the Amsterdam municipal council and of the Provincial States of North-Holland.[13] He was in numerous boards and the founder of the so-called Parkherstellingsoorden, sanatoriums for patients released from hospital but still in need of professional care. Queen Wilhelmina and her husband Prince Hendrik had visited these sanatoriums several times, where they came to know De Hartogh.[14] In contemporaneous Press accounts, he was portrayed as the main instigator behind the initiative to erect the monument.[15]

The vice-chairman, Marinus Benjamin Barend (Bob) Nijkerk (1894-1987), hailed from a business family and stood at the helm of a metal company, whereas the committee's secretary, Louis Weijl (1879-1972), was a medical doctor from Middelburg. Weijl was the only committee member who was active in the Nederlands-Israëlitisch Kerkgenootschap, the moderately Orthodox largest Jewish organisation encompassing the vast majority of the country's Ashkenazim. Treasurer Jacob Nathan (Jacques) Kattenburg (1877-1947) was founder and director of the raincoat factory Hollandia Fabrieken Kattenburg & Co. Following his death, his son Alfred took over. George van den Bergh (1890-1966) hailed from the prominent industrial family by the same name, which was active in the production of margarine within the Unilever multinational concern. Contrary to the liberal political leanings of most family members, he became a social democrat and was active as a municipal and provincial councillor. Professionally, he worked as a constitutional law professor at the University of Amsterdam, but also published on astrology and meteorology. Before the war, Van den Bergh had been very active in relief work on behalf of German-Jewish refugees.[16] The presence of Esther Teeboom-van West (1904-1986) in the committee is somewhat surprising. Both before and after the war, she had served as an Amsterdam local councillor for the communist party. During the war she lost her husband, but survived herself in hiding in the Gelderland province. De Hartogh and Teeboom-van West knew each other from the municipal council. Herman Leijdesdorff, a musician, had been first violinist of the Amsterdam Concertgebouw Orchestra and was head teacher at the Amsterdam Conservatory.[17]

A few other individuals were only temporarily involved with the committee. M. de Groot and M. Swaab are mentioned as members in 1945, but they were soon replaced by Dr A. Tannenbaum and Dr A.S. de Vries. Two other members are also mentioned, but their names both times are spelled differently, thus making it hard to identify who they might have been: M.H. or A.A.M. van Hertzfeld from Amsterdam and Is.S. or J. Zadoks from

---

10   *Nieuw Israëlietisch Weekblad* [*NIW*] (9 November 1945).
11   Personal archive of Roel Hijink: Transcript of interview.
12   The names of the committee's members can be found in a letter to possible donors; SA, Topography Archive, no. 494: Undated letter, stamped AA 695042 no. 4. For biographical data, see R.G. Fuks-Mansfeld (ed.), *Joden in Nederland in de twintigste eeuw. Een biografisch woordenboek* [Jews in the Netherlands in the Twentieth Century. A Biographical Dictionary], Utrecht 2007, and the database at www.jodeninnederland.nl.
13   N. Japikse (ed.), *Persoonlijkheden in het Koninkrijk der Nederlanden in woord en beeld* [Personalities in the Kingdom of the Netherlands in Words and Images], Amsterdam 1938, p. 612.
14   *Nieuwe Tilburgsche Courant* (15 May 1923); *De Telegraaf* (16 May 1925); *De Tijd* (9 September 1925); *De Indische Courant* (25 June 1930).

15   Indicatively, *De Volkskrant* (23 February 1950); *Alkmaarsche Courant* (21 February 1950); cf. Hinke Piersma & Jeroen Kemperman, *Openstaande rekeningen. De gemeente Amsterdam en de gevolgen van roof en rechtsherstel, 1940-1950* [Bills to Be Paid. The City of Amsterdam and the Consequences of Robbery and Restitution, 1940-1950], Amsterdam 2015, p. 12, 15.
16   Hans Blom et al. (eds), *Geschiedenis van de Joden in Nederland* [History of the Jews in the Netherlands] Amsterdam 2017, p. 344.
17   "Esther Teeboom-van West morgen 50 jaar", *De Waarheid* (29 April 1954); "Esther Teeboom: Een begrip in Amsterdam", *De Waarheid* (11 May 1956).

The Hague.[18] The last two represented Dutch Jews who did not reside in Amsterdam. It was important to reach out to the sparse remaining Jewish communities around the country in order to get their help as well. Weijl, for instance, had informed the chairman of the Middelburg Jewish community, Polak, of the committee's existence, and had requested the addresses of all Jews living in his area in order to ask for their financial help in establishing

> A modest monument in the capital to express the gratitude of the Jews towards their fellow-citizens in the Netherlands, for all they have done for us: Assistance to those in hiding, sympathy strikes, etc. Many paid for this with their own lives and many others had to suffer imprisonment and [deportation] to concentration camps.[19]

Most committee members shared at least two features. Almost all were part of the rather small elite of the Jewish community that was highly integrated into Dutch society. Most of them did not live a Jewish religious life, never or barely visiting synagogues, some of them intermarrying with non-Jews. However, as the community's elite they felt highly responsible, and they were often involved in enterprises on behalf of the poor or persecuted Jews, as well as sitting in the boards of Jewish institutions. Already from the first half of the nineteenth century, this mode of representation had characterised the small Dutch Jewish elite and the committee's members were no exception to this rule.[20] At the same time, many committee members had a shared war experience. Most were part of what has been called by a historian "the chosen people of Frederiks and Van Dam."[21] Karel Johannes Frederiks was secretary-general of the Home Office and during the occupation functioned as a de facto minister, although without contact with either the queen or parliament. Thanks to the rivalry between Generalkommissar zur besondere Verwendung Fritz Schmidt and Höhere SS-und Polizeiführer Hans Rauter, Frederiks managed to compile a list of prominent Jews who were considered to be of great value to Dutch society and culture. Professor Jan van Dam, a pro-German Germanic scholar, was secretary-general of the department of Education, Science and Culture and collaborated with Frederiks in this matter. The Jews on their lists were interned at a camp for privileged people, in Barneveld, before been sent to Durchgangslager Westerbork, while ending up in Konzentrationskamp Theresienstadt. Most committee members were so-called "Barnevelders".[22]

Therefore, all committee members with Barneveld and hiding experiences felt some sort of gratitude towards those who had been instrumental in saving their lives. De Hartogh, without doubt the driving force behind the whole enterprise, had already in the first post-war session of the Amsterdam Municipal Council on 21 November 1945 positioned himself as the spokesperson of all surviving Dutch Jews in expressing "gratitude". The formal minutes summarise his interposition thus:

> If it were not for the help of Dutchmen in hiding many Jews, if it were not for their sabotaging of the measures against the Jews, probably not even one would have survived this catastrophe. Next to grief, the speaker therefore feels pleased with the fact that during the occupation years once more it had become clear that the Dutch people did not position themselves against their Jewish fellow-citizens. It is his strong desire to testify in this [session] part of the deep gratitude that fills the hearts of the Jews in the Netherlands [because] during these five anxious years they were considered to be Dutchmen and [because] the people asserted their solidarity with them.[23]

There is an obvious continuity between this address by De Hartogh and his subsequent involvement in the founding of the monument. The "deep gratitude" expressed in words in 1945 was monumentalised in stone in 1950.

The Monument, Jews and Dutch Society

The initiative to erect a monument of Jewish gratitude for the Dutch people led to a painful controversy within the Jewish community. It was fought out partly in the public sphere, in newspapers and journals, and partly behind closed doors. The dispute uncovered various ideas on the position of Jews in Dutch society, on Jewish identities, on the commemoration of the Second World War and on the future of Jews.

There were at least two important divisions at play. The first was that, although all committee members were "prominent" Jews, they were so mostly in society, not within the Jewish community. Few of

---

18 *NIW* (9 November 1945).
19 Jewish Historical Museum [JHM] Amsterdam, Archive Nederlands-Israëlietische Gemeente Middelburg [NIG-M], file D12188: Weijl to Polak (8 December 1945), and Polak to Weijl (14 December 1945).
20 Bart Wallet, *Nieuwe Nederlanders. De integratie van de joden in Nederland 1814-1851* [New Dutchmen. The Integration of the Jews in the Netherlands 1814-1851] Amsterdam 2007, *passim*.
21 Jacques Presser, *Ondergang. De vervolging en verdelging van het Nederlandse Jodendom* [Demise. The Persecution and Extermination of Dutch Jewry], Soesterberg 2005, p. 426.
22 Abel Herzberg, *Kroniek der Jodenvervolging, 1940-1945* [Chronicle of the Persecution of the Jews, 1940-1945], Amsterdam 1985, p. 172-175; Boris de Munnick, *Uitverkoren in uitzondering? Het verhaal van de Joodse "Barneveld-groep" 1942-1945* [Exceptionally Chosen? The Story of the Jewish "Barneveld Group" 1942-1945], Barneveld 1991.
23 *Gemeenteblad Amsterdam Tweede Afdeeling: Verslag van de vergaderingen van den Gemeenteraad, enz.* (21 November 1945): 20.

them participated in organised Jewish community bodies; their prominence was societal- rather than Jewish-centred. They might have enjoyed a position of influence in Dutch society, but in the Jewish community they were without doubt considered to be peripheral. By reaching out to this specific group among Dutch Jews, De Hartogh estranged from the very beginning the established Dutch Jewish leadership from the initiative. The more De Hartogh positioned his committee as speaking on behalf of the Jewish community, the more the leadership distanced itself.[24] The question that lay behind this part of the controversy was one over representation.[25] Who was representing Dutch Jewry in society? Prominent, mostly secular Dutch Jews, or the nationwide Jewish bodies, the Ashkenazi Nederlands-Israëlitisch Kerkgenootschap (NIK) and the Sephardi Portugees-Israëlitisch Kerkgenootschap (PIK), both of which had shared a near monopoly in the pre-war period? After 1945 it was no longer self-evident that NIK and PIK would resume their representative roles, and from various angles new groups of people challenged the traditional Jewish organisational structures.[26] This also played out in the commemoration issue. Whereas the committee sought to erect a monument of gratitude, already on 14 October 1945 NIK had set up its own committee to erect a monument in memory of the victims of the Shoah.[27] This committee was ultimately much less successful in erecting a monument in a public space, and eventually had to resort with the Jewish cemetery in Muiderberg.[28]

The second divisive line was even more important, as it underscored the clash between Zionists and non-Zionists and their respective evaluation of the position of Jews in Dutch society. Before the war, Zionists comprised only a tiny, although vocal, minority within the Jewish community. Yet, in the wake of the Shoah, their popularity and influence rose to unprecedented levels. In many local and national Jewish organisations Zionists now dominated the boards, whereas the membership and moral authority of the Nederlandse Zionistenbond (Dutch Zionist Organisation) grew rapidly. Many Dutch Jews saw Zionism as a natural response to the horrors of the preceding war years.[29] Not all Jews, however, turned to Zionism; a few remained outspoken anti-Zionists, while many took a more neutral stance as non-Zionists. Yet, although De Hertogh's committee was composed of non-Zionists and their initiative fitted exactly their broader agenda, it was at odds with the Zionists' convictions.

The problem Zionists had with the proposed monument was threefold. First, they could not perceive the initiative as anything else other than demonstrating the traditional galut mentality of Diaspora Jewry. This meant that Jews had become accustomed to behave as a dependent minority, following a stance of servility towards the general non-Jewish society and specifically towards the authorities. The Zionists, instead, argued for a resolute attitude of Jewish pride, defending without shame the collective objectives of the Jewish community. The era of Jews assimilating in Dutch nationalism had come to a halt, they argued; now it was time that the Jews perceive themselves as constituting a nation. From this perspective, the monument and its Dutch nationalistic rhetoric, including the servile use of the concept of "gratitude", was in stark contrast to Zionist beliefs.[30]

At the same time, the Zionists did not believe there was any future left for Jews in the Netherlands. The Shoah had brought their history to an end; all that the surviving Jews had to do was to make sure the process of restitution was brought to a satisfactory end. Thereafter all conscious, principled Jews would leave for the Jewish State of Israel, whereas the remaining few would easily assimilate into Dutch society at large. After 1945, the focus of the reconstruction of large parts of the Jewish community in the Netherlands was not so much Dutch society, but Israel instead.[31] The monument, however, conveyed a different message: That the Jews self-identified as Dutchmen, that they were shielded by their fellow-citizens during the war

---

24 SA, Nederlands-Israëlitische Hoofdsynagoge Amsterdam [NIHS]: Minutes of Board meeting (14 February 1950).

25 *Ibid*: Minutes of Board meeting (28 January 1948), wherein it is explicitly argued that the committee cannot represent the Jewish community at large; also see the minutes of 17 August 1949 and 12 February 1950.

26 Bart Wallet, "Om 'een uitgeteekenden joodsche levensweg'. De reconstructie van het religieuze jodendom in Nederland, 1945-1960" [About "a drawn Jewish way of life". The reconstruction of religious Judaism in the Netherlands, 1945-1960], in Hetty Berg & Bart Wallet (eds), *Wie niet weg is, is gezien. Joods Nederland na 1945* [Anyone Who Has Not Left Has Been Seen. Jewish Netherlands After 1945], Amsterdam 2010, p. 96-113.

27 SA, NIHS: Minutes of Board meeting (14 October 1945). All active within the NIK, the committee's members were: Dr B. Stokvis, S.M. Sohlberg, J. Biet, J. Flörsheim, A. van Dam, M. van Embden, D. Eitje, Dr Lusa, Philip Polak, Rabbi A. Schuster, and the architect J. Baars.

28 *Ibid*; *Jaarverslag Nederlands-Israëlietische Hoofdsynagoge Amsterdam* (1948).

29 Evelien Gans, *De kleine verschillen die het leven uitmaken. Een historische studie naar joodse sociaal-democraten en socialistisch Nederland* [The Small Differences that Make Up Life. A Historical Study of Jewish Social Democrats and Socialist Netherlands] Amsterdam 1999, p. 561.

30 SA, NIHS: Minutes of Board meeting (14 February 1950).

31 Bart Wallet, "Een familie van gemeenschappen. De dynamiek van joods Nederland in de naoorlogse periode" [A family of communities. The dynamics of the Jewish Netherlands in the post-war period], in P. van Dam et al. (eds), *Achter de zuilen. Op zoek naar religie in naoorlogs Nederland* [Behind the Columns. In Search of Religion in Post-War Netherlands], Amsterdam 2014, p. 135-154.

years, and that they were expressing their will to continue living in the Netherlands next to – and together with all of – Dutch society. Clearly, the burgeoning myth of collective Dutch resistance against the Nazis was embraced as well by part of Dutch Jewry.[32] This was their strategy to secure a continued existence as Jews in the Netherlands.

Furthermore, the Zionists considered the monument superfluous. True to their convictions, they had already embarked on another initiative to honour the relatively few Dutchmen who helped Jews in myriad ways to escape Nazi anti-Jewish policies. In 1946 the Dutch branch of the Jewish National Fund, the main Zionist fundraising organisation for land acquisition in Palestine, had collected money in order to plant, a year later, the Remembrance Joop Westerweel Forest at the Ramat Menashe plain.[33] Westerweel (1899-1944) and his wife Wilhelmina ran a resistance group that saved between 300-400 Jews, by and large Zionist pioneers (halutzim) preparing for emigration to Palestine, before being caught and executed in August 1944. The forest bearing his name was to honour all those Dutch resistance groups and individuals that had assisted Dutch Jews. That Westerweel was chosen as pars pro toto was hardly coincidental. The fact that he had saved Zionist pioneers was most significant. The manner of memorialising was also telling: Not with a monument of stones in the country of the past, where these terrible things had happened, but with a living monument of trees in the country of the Jewish future. As the Jewish lawyer David Barmes put it at a radio address on 11 March 1946:

> We have sought to erect a monument in Palestine to commemorate the Dutch love of liberty and Dutch protest against the barbaric persecution of the Jews. A young country as Jewish Palestine has no appetite for lifeless monuments or commemorative plaques. Where everything is growing, where everything is developing, all expressions of life should be connected to this process of growth.[34]

For the Zionists, the only legitimate way of commemorating the victims of the Shoah was to invest in the remembering and reconstruction of the Jewish nation in the State of Israel.[35]

Last, but not least, Dutch Zionists strongly resisted the suggestion that the Jews should express their gratitude to the Dutch. The initiative caused unrest and quite substantive resistance from within the largest Jewish organisation, the Amsterdam Ashkenazi community, which withheld its support by arguing that it was the sole representative of the feelings of the majority of its members. Most outspoken was Mozes Heiman (Max) Gans, who at a board meeting maintained that he would be "very deeply troubled" should the official Dutch-Jewish institutions were represented at the unveiling of a monument offered to the Dutch people by Dutch Jews as a token of gratitude for their rescue, when his whole family was "eliminated" and no one had extended them any assistance. "Already the mere existence of the monument disturbs him."[36]

Jobs Wertheim and "anti-Goyism"

Much was at stake for all Dutch Jews involved in the fierce debate over the monument. Their stances were determined by each group's central or peripheral position within the community at large, by their Zionist or non-Zionist beliefs, by their espousal of a Dutch or a Jewish national language of commemoration, and by their resolve to stay in the Netherlands or leave for Israel. In the middle of all of this was Jobs Wertheim, the sculptor. He was a member of the Dutch Zionist Organisation, but nevertheless cooperated in bringing to fruition the monument. This made him the subject of heavy criticism. Defending his position as firmly as possible, he even went on the offensive by accusing his fellow-Zionist opponents of "anti-Goyism". Wertheim created this neologism in analogy to antisemitism, and defined it as Jewish hatred towards non-Jews. In his view, the opposition to a monument devoted to the Dutch people was nothing less but an expression of this very anti-Goyism. He even interpreted it as symptomatic of the crisis of Dutch Zionists, many of whom did not immigrate to Israel according to Zionist ideology, but stayed in the Netherlands and sought to compensate for their decision by attacking the Dutch people at large.[37]

---

32 I. De Haan, *Na de ondergang. De herinnering aan de Jodenvervolging in Nederland 1945-1995* [After the Downfall. The Memory of the Persecution of the Jews in the Netherlands 1945-1995], The Hague 1997, p. 80, 93.

33 Central Zionist Archives, Jerusalem, Keren Kayemet Leyisrael, Dutch files 1945-1947.

34 "Het K.K.L. richt zich tot de Joden van Nederland" [The Keren Kayemet Leyisrael addresses the Jews of the Netherlands], *De Joodse Wachter* 37/4 (22 March 1946): 12.

35 Cf. the dispute between the State of Israel and Dutch Zionists over the future of Hollandsche Schouwburg, the concentration and deportation centre of Amsterdam's Jewry; Bart Wallet, "Een levend gedenkteken. Israël, joods Nederland en de herinnering aan de Sjoa" [A living memorial. Israel, the Jewish Netherlands and the memory of the Shoah], in Frank van Vree et al. (eds.), *De Hollandsche Schouwburg. Theater – Deportatieplaats – Plek van herinnering* [Hollandsche Schouwburg. Theatre – Deportation Centre – Memorial Site], Amsterdam 2013, p. 190-199.

36 SA, NIHS: Minutes of Board meeting (14 February 1950).

37 Jobs Wertheim, "Nog eens anti-gojisme" [Again anti-Goyism], *De Joodse Wachter* 42/14 (1951): 12.

The term quickly came at the forefront of the inner-Jewish debate on the monument. The Zionist leader and teacher of German Hartog Beem rejected the entire concept outright, whereas others found it helpful but redefined its meaning. Elie Cohen, a concentration camp survivor, used it in order to explain this inner debate according to the Dutch Jews' varied Shoah experiences. He distinguished between Jews who had returned from the death camps, Jews who had survived in hiding, and Jews who had returned from abroad after having fled to Switzerland, Britain or elsewhere. The last two groups had survived mainly because they were helped by non-Jews in hiding and escaping the Nazis. For that reason, they either felt gratitude towards non-Jews or projected their feelings of shame and dependence on them by trying to distance themselves as rigorously as possible from Dutch society. From this perspective, anti-Goyism was a strategy employed by survivors in order to reclaim their independence and identity. The only ones who would be able to take an objective position vis-à-vis non-Jews were camp survivors.[38]

Once it became clear that the monument would be erected, the formal leadership of the Jewish community had to take a decision regarding its strategy. They resolved to continue with a twofold strategy. Neither the Jewish institutions nor any of the rabbis and lay leaders would support the initiative or even attend the unveiling of the monument. But in order to contain the damage as much as possible, they would try to influence the format and the design of the monument to the best of their abilities. This was relatively successful, in at least two respects.

Initially, the committee had chosen that the monument would comprise a bronze statue of the mourning prophet Jeremiah. This choice demonstrated once more its estrangement from Jewish artistic and commemorative traditions, as it clashed with the traditional interpretation of the Second Commandment.[39] After the rabbinate protested, the committee finally opted for Wertheim's limestone monument.[40] This was slightly better, although the reliefs still showed people – some even naked. The monument's commemorative language clearly was not Jewish, but rather classicistic or even Christian. It fitted quite neatly the dominant Dutch mode of remembering the Second World War in the late 1940s and early 1950s but was at odds with the two "languages of commemoration" that prevailed among Dutch Jews. These were, respectively, the Zionist language of honouring the dead through supporting Jewish life in Israel, and the Diaspora language, which employed traditional religious iconography and rituals for the dead and victims of the Shoah.[41]

Furthermore, the Jewish community leadership successfully intervened on the issue of the wording of the inscriptions. Initially, the committee had chosen the line: "The Jews of the Netherlands to their protectors during the years of occupation." The chairman of NIK, notary Eduard Spier, informed De Hartogh that this was completely unacceptable to "the official Jewish community" and threatened to inform the Amsterdam municipal authorities that it should not accept the monument at all. The wording was too generalised, Spier argued, since the majority of Dutch Jews did not have protectors at all. Moreover, the monument was not an initiative of "the Jews of the Netherlands", but just of a peripheral group of individual Jews. De Hartogh sought to compromise by suggesting as an alternative "to the protectors of the Dutch Jews during the years of occupation." Spier and his fellow leaders were still not enthusiastic, inter alia because now the wording excluded the rescue of German and East European Jews, but at least it no longer assumed they were involved in the initiative.[42]

In a clear show of rebuke, the official Jewish organisations chose not to attend the unveiling of the monument.[43] According to the NIK board, their presence would be erroneously interpreted as an expression of the "official gratitude of Dutch Jewry to the Dutch people for the help offered by a few." Max Gans, one of the board's members, informed accordingly the mayor of Amsterdam.[44] This formal opposition might well have led Mayor Van Hall to express a more nuanced view on Dutch resistance and its assistance to the Jews in his speech at the unveiling of the monument, instead of reiterating the dominating national myth of a whole nation in resistance. By taking this position, he came close to the stance taken by the influential Dutch Jewish weekly Nieuw Israëlietisch Weekblad. Its Zionist editors argued that there were compelling reasons why many Jews were quite reserved towards the monument; it could be appreciated only if its message was restricted exclusively to the few who had risked their lives to save Jews during the war, not to the Dutch people at large.[45]

---

38 Elie Cohen, "Splijting in eigen kring" [Cleavages in your own circle], *De Joodse Wachter* 42/14 (1951): 8-9.
39 Exodus 20: 4-6
40 "Monument op het Weesperplein te Amsterdam" [Monument on the Weesperplein in Amsterdam], *Algemeen Handelsblad* (11 January 1950).
41 Frank van Vree, "Iedere dag en elk uur. De jodenvervolging en de dynamiek van de herinnering in Nederland" [Every day and every hour. The persecution of the Jews and the dynamics of memory in the Netherlands], in Berg & Wallet, *op. cit.*, p. 57-72.
42 Jewish Cultural Centre [JCC], Amsterdam, Archive NIK: Minutes of board meeting (16 February 1950).
43 SA, NIHS: Minutes of board meeting (20 February 1950).
44 JCC, NIK: Minutes of board meeting (16 February 1950).
45 "Erkentelijkheid" [Acknowledgment], *NIW* 81/10 (1950).

Conclusion

In every single respect, the Monument of Jewish Gratitude is an exemplar of the prevailing mode of commemorating the Second World War in the late 1940s and early 1950s. To begin with, the rhetoric used to raise support and funds for its construction was tied to the myth of collective Dutch resistance against the Nazis. Although the wording on the inscriptions, and even the speeches during the unveiling, were somewhat more nuanced, the central message was clear: The Dutch nation had upheld its long and dear traditions of tolerance and shielded Dutch Jews against Nazi terror. The fact that the vast majority of Dutch Jews were not protected but murdered was left largely unstated. In reality, just five percent of the total Dutch population was involved in resistance and rescue activities.

Furthermore, for those Jews, who despite everything saw their future in the Netherlands, the monument was – with a twist to Heinrich Heine's oft-mentioned dictum – their "ticket of re-admission into Dutch society." Through it, they communicated to society at large that they adhered to the myth of resistance and that they were willing to present their own war-experiences through the prism of the new national narrative. This might have resulted from a mixture of socio-political considerations, external pressure and barely outspoken expectations, but also from a sincere feeling of gratitude towards the resistance and those individuals who had hidden them during the war years.

Finally, the debate on the monument unveiled deep tensions among Dutch Jewry: On the issue of who was representing the community; on the future of Jews in the Netherlands or in Israel; and on the various modes of commemorating the victims of the Shoah. Despite the intentions of the organising committee and the expectations of the authorities and society at large, from the very beginning the monument constituted a bone of contention. At the moment of its unveiling in 1950, it had already become one of "conflictive heritage". For some, it honoured Dutch pride. For others, it commemorated Jewish gratitude. And for many amongst Dutch Jewry, it generated strong feelings of shame.

Particularly since the 1960s, memory culture on the Second World War has shifted from focusing rather exclusively on the resistance and the unity of the Dutch nation to a growing awareness of the fate of the Jewish victims and the various stances taken by Dutchmen during the war. This led to the marginalisation of the Monument of Jewish Gratitude, as it affirmed the former rather than the latter memory culture. In the context of the larger reconstruction of the entire former Jewish quarter, in 1968 it was removed from its rather prominent site at Weesperplein to a small park-line location next to Weesperstraat, where most pedestrians pass it without even noticing it. It never assumed a prominent place in the calendar of commemorations, either of the municipality of Amsterdam or, indeed, of the city's Jewry. It has been fairly, and partly deliberately, forgotten.

It is only recently that the Monument of Jewish Gratitude has once more entered public debate as a result of the initiative to erect a Holocaust Names Memorial where it stands. This would erase it as an unwelcome memory of the immediate postwar period and the prevailing attitude towards Jewish survivors at the time, and subsequently replace it with a monument expressing today's memory culture: Focusing on the victims instead of the resistance, and on individuals – hence the names – instead of collective bodies. However, one might wonder if such a development would be enough to do away with this specimen of "conflictive heritage", as its removal would also make it harder to demonstrate and explain the delicate position of Jews in postwar Dutch society. Over time, the Monument of Jewish Gratitude was transformed from a monument of Dutch pride and Jewish gratitude into a large "stumbling stone". Its possible demolition would push aside a conflictive chapter in the history of the Dutch and Dutch Jews, which is still central to understanding the dynamics of the post-war community of Jewish survivors.

Persecution Through Demonisation, Condemnation Through Silence

Reflecting on Left-Wing Violence in 1940s Greece

Iason Chandrinos

Abstract

The Organisation for the Protection of the People's Struggle (OPLA) constitutes one of the taboos of modern Greek history and historiography. The OPLA was an urban guerrilla formation that operated in Nazi-occupied urban centres and liquidated real and imaginary traitors, informants, rank-and-file members of the collaborating security services, but also Trotskyites and KKE renegades; in other words, a broad spectrum of opponents denoting the culmination of the emerging civil war blocks. After the December Events of 1944, which marked a critical point in Greece's political history, the OPLA became a synonym for left-wing violence and fuelled a demonisation process matched by the total absence of any similar counternarrative from the Left. In my chapter, I highlight the basic features of the anticommunist narrative built around the OPLA and contextualise its use within right-wing propaganda. Apart from selective insights into literature, memoirs and Press accounts, I also rely on a collection of interviews conducted between 2007 and 2009 with former OPLA members as part of a research project about communist militancy in occupied Athens, in an attempt to discuss both the individual and collective framework of silences around one of the most unwanted stories of 1940s Greece.

Introduction

In the evening hours of 14 February 1944, the BBC Greek Service broadcasted a rather alarming statement by Emmanuel Tsouderos, prime minister of the Greek government in exile. It read thus:

> With surprise and sorrow the Greek government was informed that some *groups for the Protection of the People's Struggle*, which collaborate with or are steered by the enemy, are committing fratricidal acts in a manner unacceptable to Greek

tradition. It is our duty to notify all citizens and organisations that the perpetrators will be prosecuted as political criminals after the end of the war and will be accorded the same fate with the other enemies of the motherland. [1]

After almost three years of rivalry and conflicting interests, at the beginning of 1944 the Cairo-based Greek government in exile for the first time had become aware of two things: Its importance as a consolidating factor for the so-called national camp and the formation of an alliance of pre-war politicians, from liberals to staunch royalists, based on their desire to push out the left-wing National Liberation Front (EAM) from the postwar political spectrum; and the perception of the Left as a national and social threat. Until then, the leitmotiv of the anti-EAM propaganda, both within and outside the borders of occupied Greece, was that the communists were undermining the national liberation struggle by eliminating any actual or potential adversaries in a deliberate effort to monopolise the resistance.[2] Now it seemed as though the fear of a *coup d'état* was being superseded by the scale of the implemented violence itself. The changing perspectives concentrated on the most ambiguous offspring of the Communist Party of Greece (KKE), the Organisation for the Protection of the People's Struggle.

The OPLA was a shadow group officially formed by the Politburo of the KKE in December 1942 in order "to protect the lives of the fighters of the people," who were exposed to denunciations, arrest or execution.[3] In the autumn of 1943, after the escalation of resistance activities all over Greece and the eruption of armed conflict between the EAM and other resistance groups, the OPLA was re-established as a special, loosely structured armed group, operating mainly in urban centres and consisting of small hit-squads who engaged in a gang-like war of attrition against a wide spectrum of enemies, from small-time informants of the occupation authorities to high-ranking Police and Gendarmerie officers, and from sympathisers of rival resistance groups to blacklisted Trotskyites. No less than 400 people were assassinated in Athens alone during the last year of the Occupation (October 1943 to October 1944).[4] Not least because of the clandestine nature of its activities, credible data about numbers, structure and modus operandi are particularly scarce or completely absent, thus giving ample space to schematic, polarised interpretations, in an ongoing discussion that by no means constitutes a Greek peculiarity.[5]

By the end of 1943, clashes between the EAM and other resistance groups had not only alarmed but also indirectly unified the fragmented pre-war political spectrum, from the collaborationist government to the government in exile. The armed activism of the left-wing resistance in Athens and other cities sped up this convergence of interests, since the deployment of hit-squads, operating under a deliberately provoking acronym (in Greek, όπλα stands for weapons) seemed to legitimise the fears of a communist takeover in the wake of Liberation. But it was more than that. In Tsouderos' condemnation, the OPLA emerges as an instrument of pure terror, totally alien to the Greek tradition of doing politics, fundamentally different from the mainstream of partisan rivalries. Interestingly, the same interpretative schemes, revolving around sheer definitions of political morality, were also used by the non-communist resistance Press. Thus, following the assassination of a young member of the nationalist resistance organisation Sacred Brigade, who had been accused of passive collaboration with the quisling security forces, its mouthpiece condemned the act as profoundly unjust, claiming that political assassination was not the "Greek way."[6]

Dekemvriana: The moralistic approach to political violence

The arrival of the government of national unity, which the EAM had recently joined, in Athens in mid October 1944 marked the beginning of liberation, albeit one that was stillborn. Political tensions culminated around the demobilisation of all armed formations, a critical issue linked to the implementation of postwar justice and the treatment of collaborationist forces. After protracted negotiations, which ultimately failed, all six

---

1 Cited in the right-wing underground newspaper *Doxa* (20 February 1944), emphasis in the original.
2 Hagen Fleischer, "The National Liberation Front (EAM) 1941-1947: A reassessment", in John Iatrides & Linda Wrigley (eds), *Greece at the Crossroads. The Civil War and its Legacy*, Pennsylvania 1995, p. 48-89.
3 Giannis Ioannidis, *Αναμνήσεις* [Memoirs], Athens 1979, p. 149.
4 Iason Chandrinos, *Το τιμωρό χέρι του λαού. Η δράση του ΕΛΑΣ και της ΟΠΛΑ στην κατεχόμενη πρωτεύουσα 1942-1944* [The People's Punishing Arm. The Activities of the ELAS and the OPLA in Occupied Athens, 1942-1944], Athens 2012, 95-137, 225-280.

5 On the verge of Liberation, the "revolutionary justice" of the communists had already caused sharp divisions as to whether collaboration or acts of treason should be met by retaliatory-like measures. In post-war Holland and France, the debate in the Press on whether "communist assassins" should be persecuted alongside collaborators echoed the redefinitions of political morality after the Occupation. For Holland, see Werner Warmbrunn, *The Dutch Under German Occupation 1940-1945*, Stanford 1963, p. 206-208; for France, Herbert R. Lottman, *The People's Anger. Justice and Revenge in Post-Liberation France*, London 1986, p. 13-26.
6 *Ellinika Niata* 20 (May 1944). It is noteworthy that exactly the same line of argument is to be found in the censored Athenian Press following the execution of the quisling minister of Labour: "Political murder is a custom foreign to the Greek way of doing politics, that's why public opinion will always condemn it;" *Eleftheron Vima* (28 January 1944).

ministers of the Left resigned. A massive demonstration organised in protest by the EAM on 3 December was brutally crushed by the Greek police, leading to open clashes between ELAS units and Greek military and security forces (Police and Gendarmerie, joined by former collaborationist troops) in the whole metropolitan area. A heavy British military intervention led to the defeat of the ELAS, which was forced to evacuate Athens and finally disband, in the wake of the Varkiza Agreement of 12 February 1945. The Dekemvriana (December Events) was a turning point. Violence was implemented on an unprecedented scale, including British air raids causing many civilian deaths, as well as the summary execution of about 1,000-1,500 people, combatants and non-combatants, by the National Militia, the EAM security branch that had evolved out of the OPLA. Available testimonies and judicial reports about perpetrators and victims reveal a desire for retaliation against real or alleged collaborators, fuelled by class hatred that obviously motivated a large part of the rank-and-file. It was the closest Greece has ever come to a class revolution.[7]

The impact of the events became the new point of departure for the establishment of an anticommunist discourse. By February 1945, the "horrors" that the communists had perpetrated the previous month, marked the redefinition of political violence. Details of executions, followed by horrific press-photos of corpses, were published and disseminated as part of a general recounting of atrocities, which shaped the new moral geography of post-liberation Greece. This moral geography invested heavily in the OPLA, as the main identifiable agent of violence, and its perception as a murderous mechanism, whose brutality had reached immeasurable levels.[8]

Right-wing newspapers were filled with references to "gangsters", "bandits" and "EAM terrorists".[9] On a wider perspective, political assessments were supplemented – or even substituted – by a widespread, vague notion of "murderous instincts". A liberal mouthpiece argued that "it is a deplorable fact to realise that such violent passions could grow into the traditionally mild climate of the Greek soul."[10] During the first trials against OPLA members as early as March 1945, some newspapers emphasised the particularly young age of the perpetrators now being persecuted and attributed the crimes to the mental distortion and disorientation of the youth rather than to ideology.[11] Reflecting the impact as well as the intimacy of urban violence, the bloodiest civil war clashes of modern Greek history were narrowed down to a scheme of senseless massacres carried out by "crooks", "thugs", "burglars", "rogues" and "dim-witted nihilists". This belittling perception, which drew heavily upon the fact that among OPLA victims one finds industrial workers, clerks and housewives, introduced biblical names, like "Cain" and "Abel," to denote that the bloodshed had more in common with multiple fratricides than with any commitment to a revolutionary cause.[12]

This highly moralistic narrative remained dominant during the Civil War and its aftermath. The re-emergence of the Left as a parliamentary force in the late 1950s was met by a burgeoning flurry of publications and brochures that revived the earlier rhetoric of communist crimes, highlighting the attempt of the Right to counter the emergence of positive attitudes towards the idea of reconciliation. This was even more alarming than the prospect of left-wing violence itself.[13] The anticommunist narrative remained embedded in ethical schemes, while at the same time the perpetrators were elevated to the status of deliberate and well structured "Stalinist organs", staffed by "agents of international communism who committed crimes, treasons and cannibalisms, comparable only to [those of] the Soviet secret police."[14] The scheme of a continuous communist agitation shaped by the emerging Cold War mythologies is best summarised in a livre noire published in 1961, which through selected – mostly falsified – documents and graphic images essentialised the KKE both as a conspiratorial force capable of every treacherous endeavour and as a structurally murderous mechanism with no respect for human life. Almost one third of this almanac of communist aggression since 1918 is devoted to the institutionalised violence of the OPLA during the *Dekemvriana*.

> More haunting than the crimes that the communists committed against 65,000 Greeks [in December 1944] is the gruesomeness of their implementation. They

---

7   Polymeris Voglis, *Η αδύνατη επανάσταση. Η κοινωνική δυναμική του εμφυλίου πολέμου* [The Impossible Revolution. The Social Dynamics of Civil War], Athens 2014, p. 83.
8   Tasos Kostopoulos, *Κόκκινος Δεκέμβρης. Το ζήτημα της επαναστατικής βίας* [Red December. The Issue of Revolutionary Violence, Athens 2016, p. 21-24.
9   Indicatively, *Dimokratiki Simea* (26 December 1944); *Dimokratia* (3 January 1945); *Megali Ellas* (5 January 1945).
10 *Eleftheria* (3 February 1945).
11 This remained a basic interpretative framework of the governmental propaganda during the Civil War; indicatively, "Greek Red stirs riot. Guerilas near Athens found to be only youths", *The New York Times* (12 October 1947).
12 *That is KKE – EAM – ELAS in Greece*, Athens 1945, p. 35: "The fratricide crime[s were] committed by the Cains of Internationalistic Communist Totalitarianism against the Abels of lawful Greek Democracy"; cf. Kostopoulos, *op. cit., passim*.
13 Mark Mazower, "The Cold War and the appropriation of memory: Greece after Liberation", *East European Politics and Societies* 9 (1995): 276.
14 Evangelos Kalantzis, *Σαράντα χρόνια αναμνήσεις, 1920-1961. Μία ζωή αφιερωμένη στην πατρίδα* [Forty Years of Recollections, 1920-1961. A Life Dedicated to the Motherland], Athens 1968, p. 108.

[employed] special methods for the annihilation of the national-minded, democratic people, *as if in a People's Republic*.[15]

Such vastly exaggerated figures on alleged victims had become an inseparable part of the narrative. Victim enumeration was pervaded by what could certainly be described as the same

Economic logic [that] underlies our cultural understanding of the political act of terror – an economy of violence that speaks of, measures and compare acts of violence and damage in actuarial terms of loss, magnitude and compensation.[16]

The OPLA was profoundly instrumentalised by the propaganda of the anticommunist state, which sought a shorthand for communist aggression. In 1963, a major right-wing newspaper went on to attack the first amnesty picket march carried out by a few relatives, women and children, of the remaining political prisoners, by degrading it as a "painful replay of the Dekemvriana; we [have] witnessed the first EAM demonstration after many years, claiming mercy for the butchers."[17] Such a moralising narrative was supplemented by the condemnation of "street anarchy", which remained vivid and more frightening than the possibility of a resurrection of the partisan army. Despite being frequently associated with real or imaginary communist atrocities of ELAS partisans and during the Civil War of the communist-led Democratic Army of Greece (DSE) in the countryside, the OPLA always struck a chord as a self-contained agent of violence that operated in an urban battlefield, with all social and class connotations this placement may infer. Even at the peak of the Civil War, fought mainly outside urban centres, the term οπλατζής (member of the OPLA) stood as the extreme version of the communist militant, the remote end of an imaginary hostile territory to be located not in the partisan strongholds of northern Greece but in the diachronic hotbeds of radicalism, class cleavages and social unrest: the Athenian proletarian neighbourhoods.[18] When dealing with captured urban guerrillas, military and civil tribunals excluded their crimes from

The common criminal law in which every person falls. They belong to an exceptional Law, they are placed in a line of offenses distinguished by the complete absence of conscience, the absence of human features, the domination of brutal instincts, the rooted cultivation of evil.[19]

The unwanted legacy of the Left

To-date, this anticommunist narrative has never been actually met by a counter-narrative. What solidified the demonisation of the OPLA was the reluctance of the KKE to take responsibility for its actions. Unable to question the new establishment of public moralities in the aftermath of 1945, the defeated and disillusioned KKE attempted to shake off the charges of moral accountability, by merely seeking to disprove the accuracy of figures and attribute at least a portion of the assumed "red terror" victims to other causes of death.[20] The strategies employed to legitimise the party's choices during the *Dekemvriana* avoided confronting the essence of implemented violence. The explanations, if any, allotted the killings to the "outraged masses" that had opposed a British-backed attempt to restore the quisling political order against the will of the people.[21] Given that in the aftermath of the *Dekemvriana*, the policy of calling for reconciliation became a key element in the KKE's strategy, while the purge of former EAM rank-and-file intensified, the party saw no reason in thematising its own aggression and slid comfortably into victimhood; a process that presupposed the eradication – with almost no exceptions- of literal references to the OPLA from any kind of public debate.[22]

---

15 *Η Βίβλος της εθνοπροδοσίας* [The Black Book of National Treason], Athens 1961, p. 79 (emphasis in the original).

16 Allen Feldman, "Political terror and the technologies of memory: Excuse, sacrifice, commodification, and actuarial moralities", *Radical History Review* 85 (2003): 70.

17 *Vradyni* (20 December 1963).

18 For example, two days after the announcement of the Truman Doctrine, the Athens daily *Kathimerini* (14 March 1947) appealed to the KKE to join the vision of reconstruction, to sit among equals on the table of all political and social forces, where there would be place even for the "poor οπλατζής of Kesariani."

19 *Πρακτικά της δίκης της στενής αυτοάμυνας ή Ο.Π.Λ.Α. Θεσσαλονίκης* [Minutes of the Trial of the OPLA in Salonika], Salonika 1947, p. 252.

20 Indicatively, *Το ελληνικό Κατύν* [The Greek Katyn], Athens 1945; ΕΑΜ, *Λευκή Βίβλος: Μάης 1944 – Γενάρης 1945* [The White Book: May 1944 to January 1945], Athens 1945.

21 Myltiadis Porfyrogenis, "Οι όμηροι" [The hostages], *Kommounistiki Epitheorisi* 34 (1945): 12-14. The EAM preferred to directly cite the leftist British Press that condemned the interventionist policy of Churchill in Greece; ΕΑΜ, *Οι ξένοι για το Δεκέμβρη* [Foreigners on the December Events], Athens 1945. The only outspoken defence of the killings was assumed by two, probably commissioned, communist literary figures who emphasised the anti-imperialist nature of the struggle and pointed out the social turmoil in the country after "eight years [sic] of fascist rule"; Melpo Axioti, *Απάντηση σε 5 ερωτήματα* [Answers to Five Questions], Athens 1945, p. 34, 58-59, and Menelaos Lountemis, *Ο μεγάλος Δεκέμβρης* [The Great December], Athens 1945, *passim*.

22 In a notable exception, in March 1945 the mouthpiece of the EAM in Salonika, *Laiki Phoni*, engaged in a spirited public debate around the OPLA, by defending the "national duty" to track down and liquidate collaborators and traitors; Sofia Iliadou-Tachou, *Μέρες της ΟΠΛΑ στην Θεσσαλονίκη. Τα χρώματα της βίας* [The Days of the OPLA in Salonika. The Colours of Violence], Salonika 2013, p. 18-26.

Figure 1. *Monument for the fallen fighters of the KKE during the 1940s at the village of Ano Lousoi, near Kalavrita.* The graffiti on the right reads: *EAM – ELAS – EPON* [United Panhellenic Youth Organisation] *– OPLA – DSE. Glory and Honour to the KKE.* Source: https://www.kalavrytapress.gr/ekdilosi-sta-soydena-kyriaki-09-aygoystoy-2020/.

During the dark times of the Civil War and its aftermath, the Left retained its resilient silence on the matter and invested in victimhood as the proper commemoration of wartime experience. Tasoula Vervenioti has posited this memory trend not to the obedience of the rank-and-file towards imposed interpretations but to the self-consciousness of former resisters themselves, forged in the harsh postwar persecutions that enabled martyrdom to overlay and even supersede revolutionary morale. As a distinct memory community with its own mechanisms of selection, repression, displacement or denial, the Greek Left – or at least its mainstream versions – structured its own representations of the past into a conceptual binary construction of patriotism and victimisation, within which the resistance fighters of the Occupation and the victims of the Civil War persecutions were entwined in a mutual embrace. At the individual level, it was the need "to preserve a perfectly unified image of themselves, an increasingly idealized memory constructed largely inside prisons or in exile, which became the memory of their youth and bravery."[23]

The shadowy existence of the OPLA seems to have remained unaffected by all political and institutional changes later on, since the shift of perspectives in Greek public memory as a product of social configurations actually favoured the persistence of taboos. The transitional policies after the restoration of democracy in 1974 and especially after 1981 may have finally integrated the Left in the national memory but have also favoured oblivion rather than reconciliation. Such policies invested in silences rather than memory.[24] The EAM/ELAS became a new trend

---

23 Tasoula Vervenioti, "Left-wing women between politics and family", in Mark Mazower (ed.), *After the War Was Over. Reconstructing the Family, Nation and State in Greece, 1943-1960*, Princeton 2000, p. 106.

24 Philip Carabott & Thanasis Sfikas, "Fifty years on", in *Idem* (eds), *The Greek Civil War. Essays on a Conflict of Exceptionalism and Silences*, Aldershot 2004, p. 2.

in memory culture, as the socialist government of Andreas Papandreou, which came to power in 1981, made the Resistance the cornerstone of Greek historical memory, next to the 1821 War of Independence. The moment was probably too festive to generate more sophisticated views on the turbulent 1940s, whereas the new narrative of the "national liberation struggle" was built on the dismissal of the political dimension of the EAM/ELAS, avoiding engagement with subjects whose historical boundaries were either difficult to determine or too controversial to be publicly addressed. It was therefore hardly surprising at the time, less than it seems today, that the 1982 "Law on the Recognition of the Resistance of the Greek People against the Occupation Troops, 1941-1944" acknowledged as resistance organisations all EAM-linked formations, fourteen in total, save the OPLA. Instead of negotiating wartime violence, these correctional politics of memory replaced the anticommunist narrative with a nostalgic view of an EAM-dominated past, suggesting an imagined, alternative reiteration of postwar national history.[25]

Strategic silence or untellability: Interviewing former OPLA members

Silences around the OPLA, including distorted or schematic interpretations, go well beyond the borders of safeguarding a concealed partisan memory from the intervention of "outsiders". For Greek communists, the discourses of violence, as well as the notions of legitimacy, legality and authority for political actors remain in many ways filtered through a sense of guilt for the mass killings during the *Dekemvriana*.[26] In a rather non-Bolshevik manner, the party abstains from any line of argument that would make literal the trope of the class war it theoretically propagates, and recycles a never-ending debate on comparative cruelty.[27] This deniability reduces violence to a side effect rather than the core element of a political struggle, let alone the driving force of a national liberation movement with articulated revolutionary aims. Most memoirs, including those of high-ranking party members, are fixed to the realm of lost good causes and tend to reduce self-criticism around "poor" decisions, the infiltration of traitors or, at best, "reckless elements without class consciousness."

In this context, the OPLA could have never been part of any self-referential triumphalism. Far from it, it served and continues to serve – in a way much similar to that of the opposite side – as the ultimate scapegoat on which all excesses and mishaps are comfortably attached, in order to avoid a deeper confrontation with all revolutionary elements that would underline party failures, such as individual violence, complex social dynamics, and class-war undertones.[28]

Even if we perceive the topic as a territory that belongs only to the party, one that others are discouraged to talk about, its exclusion from any form of narration, even within the framework of a closed memorial community, remains baffling. Jo Stanley has pointed out that the recorded interviews carried out between former communist party members in Britain about their past experiences "can reveal the potential for the deep rapport and revelation that can come out of a number of discussions between people with a broadly similar political history and set of desires."[29] A similar collection of taped recordings from the 1980s, when KKE veterans were conducting extended interviews with co-resisters in the course of a country-wide project for the documentation of the history of the Resistance, revealed that even in the most secluded form of discussion – comrades taping comrades – there are specific taboos apparent in the interview process itself; even little hints about the OPLA were discouraged or suppressed by the interviewers, who felt compelled to repeat that "this" should be better excluded from the conversation agenda.[30]

In the case of the OPLA, on the one hand the haunting absence of a narrative and on the other the hopelessly one-sided sources have made the search for testimonies more and more intriguing.[31] The following section of the chapter is based on a collection of one video and ten audio interviews with former OPLA members (ten men

---

25 Hagen Fleischer, "Was wäre wenn… Die 'Bewältigung' der kommunistischen Niederlage im griechischen Bürgerkrieg nach Wiederherstellung der Demokratie (1974-2006)", in Ulf Brunnbauer & Stefan Troebst (eds), *Zwischen Amnesie und Nostalgie. Die Erinnerung an den Kommunismus in Südosteuropa*, Cologne 2007, p. 32-34.

26 Kostopoulos, *op. cit.*, p. 67-92.

27 For the instrumentalisation of violence by the Bolsheviks during the October Revolution and the rhetorical strategies implemented for its legitimisation, see James Ryan, "The sacralization of violence: Bolshevik justifications for violence and terror during the civil war", *Slavic Review* 74 (2015): 808-831.

28 Vasilis Bartziotas, *Εθνική Αντίσταση και Δεκέμβρης 1944* [National Resistance and December 1944], Athens 1979, p. 185: "In general, the operational forms as well as the ambiguous name of the organisation had brought us more losses than gains. Such organisations should be constantly supervised by party local operatives, otherwise they tend to excesses. In my opinion, the OPLA should have never been founded. Its creation was unnecessary."

29 "Including the feelings: Personal political testimony and self-disclosure', *Oral History* 24/1 (1996): 60-67.

30 Archive of the KKE, Athens, Audio collection of the Panhellenic Union of National Resistance Fighters (PEAEA) of Kokkinia, tapes no. 6, 10, 18.

31 Most sources about the OPLA are police reports published in the Press (in an interesting continuity with the trend that was initiated during the Occupation), and the very detailed minutes of post-war trials from early 1945 to 1948, accessible in the General State Archives (GAK). No documents of the organisation itself have been traced, whereas the existence of an archive whatsoever remains speculative.

and a woman),[32] which I conducted in 2008-2009 as part of my MA dissertation on the communist resistance in occupied Athens.[33] The main scope of the research was to understand the dynamics of violence, shaped through historical and spatial circumstances, social interactions, class divisions and daily realities in the short-term; in other words, factors important in our understanding of the functionality of a militant terror group bound to operate in an urban landscape. Seeking testimonies was a task of its own. Access to most of the informants had to be gained through the PEAEA, the Resistance veterans' association of the KKE, to which all but two still faithfully belonged.

My main hypothesis was that narrating resistance violence can be a subliminal form of rejection of imposed silences aligned to the "cleansed" official discourse of the national liberation struggle. During the interviews, I had in mind (and hope to be able to verify) that oral testimonies of former militants of the Resistance would dismantle the myth of a pacified, almost non-violent resistance, prevalent in all European countries. Researching through individual accounts the battle of Poggio Bustone in Italy in October 1944, the killing of a fascist group by the partisans that became a site of conflicted memories, Alessandro Portelli realised that those who had participated

> Tried to make space for violence in their narratives – to justify it as a necessity of the times, sometimes to redeem it as revolutionary value. They also try to rescue the memory of the Resistance as class war and civil war from under the suffocating whitewash of the exclusively patriotic war.[34]

The last point draws upon the perception of oral narratives as psychological structures of remembering that enable the historian "to explore points of conflict and rupture in people's lives that create confrontations with discourses of power."[35] Indeed, the level of consciousness with which old members of the Resistance or the communist party frame their story is always intriguing for an oral historian, as it sets individual memories against dominant narratives, in fact within the boundaries of a shared ideological framework. Moreover, interviews with former hit men of the Resistance, unable for decades to document their experiences or disseminate their recollections even within their own partisan collectivity, stimulate our interest to compare time and spatial contexts of different forms of narrative: Postwar trial hearings, memoirs, oral history interviews conducted by researchers. Searching the ways in which people deal with unwanted stories in which they have participated, especially through the informal setting of the interview, enables oral history to set a reminder that "history is made up of events that happened to persons and groups at some point in time: they are always personal to someone."[36]

My engagement with the subject was shaped in a specific intellectual environment. By the end of the 1990s, the "social turn" ushered into a new historiographical era that brought with it a post-revisionist approach of the period, which still looms large on academia and the public sphere. The work of Stathis Kalyvas on the region of Argolida in 1943-44 engaged critically the formulaic memory of the communist Resistance by provocatively emphasising its unrestrained exercise of violence against civilians.[37] It generated a new perspective according to which the civil strife in occupied Greece should be attributed primarily to the KKE, i.e. the communist resistance. In equal measure, it was hailed as "restorative" or discarded as either flawed or deliberately revisionist, in the sense that it diminished complex social realities to a vicious circle of retribution.[38] This new academic strand remained entangled in the civil war and post-civil war era schemes I described above, particularly by placing the instrumental violence of the KKE against the, allegedly, non-ideological motivation of the perpetrators on the micro level.[39] It became quite clear that Greece stood out among other European case studies, as it was the Civil War that "conditioned [the] debate on the Second World War rather than vice versa [and] affected interpretations of violence for which the occupying regimes [were] responsible."[40] Growing up as a historian in the midst of this debate, I have refrained from dealing with violence as a form of commensuration and have became more attuned to Allen Feldman's conclusion in his remarkable article on political terror and the technologies of memory in Northern Ireland:

---

32   References to the interviews appear in brackets [] in the main body of the chapter thus: First name of interviewee in full, surname (only initial), place of interview, type of interview (audio or video).
33   See Chandrinos, *op. cit.*
34   "The battle of Poggio Bustone", in Alessandro Portelli, *The Battle of Valle Giulia. Oral History and the Art of Dialogue*, Wisconsin 1997, p. 139
35   Anna Green, "Individual remembering and 'collective memory': Theoretical presuppositions and contemporary debates", *Oral History* 32/2 (2004): 42-43.
36   Sarah De Nardi, "'No one had asked me about that before': A focus on the body and 'other' Resistance experiences in Italian Second World War storytelling", *Oral History* 42/1 (2014): 76 (emphasis in the original).
37   "Red Terror: Leftist violence during the Occupation", in Mazower (ed.), *op. cit.*, p. 142-183.
38   Polymeris Voglis & Ioannis Nioutsikos, "The Greek historiography of the 1940s. A reassessment", *Südosteuropa* 65 (2017): 325.
39   Indicatively, Stathis Kalyvas & Nikos Marantzidis, Εμφύλια πάθη. 23 ερωτήσεις και απαντήσεις για τον Εμφύλιο [Civil War Passions. Twenty-three Questions and Answers about the Civil War], Athens 2015, p. 236-252.
40   Sabine Rutar, "The Second World War in Southeastern Europe. Historiographies and debates', *Südosteuropa* 65/2 (2017): 199-200.

We have to think violence both within and beyond actuarial closures of memory, as well as to think beyond restorative and retributive violence and its assumption of historical balance books.[41]

In the event, I gained more than I had bargained for. Every interview was a mixture of dry, awkward obfuscation of facts, on the one hand, and an eagerness to openly admit personal involvement, on the other. My questionnaires were loosely formulated and designed in order to penetrate defensive attitudes through name-dropping and discussion on specific incidents of which I knew beforehand. This was not always productive; sometimes it caused negations, small outbursts and bits of advice: "You may want to blunt some of your questions. Your approach is somewhat crude, forcing me to answer with a yes or a no. 'No' is still a perfectly valid answer" [Giorgos K., Piraeus, audio interview]. Despite the fact that the level of "honesty" and self-reflection varied greatly, there were surprisingly no downright refusals and, with one exception, no reluctance to sit in front of a tape-recorder.

The interview process revealed overlapping fields of self-censorship, some of which could be considered odd. Even for life-long party members, the mere use of the acronym "OPLA" itself remains alarming, making the most common silences – those that are mere responses to simple questions – seem odd or misplaced. Following up on one interviewee's admission about his "honourable enrolment in a special armed organisation with particular duties," I naturally filled in "so, an OPLA member," to which my interviewee, after a short pause, replied: "I won't certify that with an answer" [Giannis M., Ampelokipi, video interview]. This self-disclosure recalls the loyalties forged during the Occupation, according to which the organisation's established hierarchy was a powerful source of legitimacy that made personal judgement redundant. An OPLA squad leader from an industrial neighbourhood still believed that the liquidation of the local party secretary and hero of the resistance labour movement was justified, on the grounds that "he was a traitor. We received an anonymous tip from above, three words on a piece of paper. I still argue with his brother, also a partisan, we are neighbours. I still say right to his face: 'Your brother was a traitor, so don't push me!'" [Nikos S., Peristeri, audio testimony]. In general, the organisation was described as something abstract, detached from any notion of human initiative and, thus, stripped from any perceivable accountability:

Don't get me wrong, I would never speak openly about the OPLA. It was a mass organisation, dedicated to protect the people. No more, no less. Picture it as a giant bat that disappears in the darkness without leaving traces. Those who claim they were "members" remind me of the Russian word for blabbering: "boltovna". And don't forget that those who blab always become prey to the security forces [Vangelis P., Palia Penteli, audio interview].

In such instances, which are rare, one can even trace hints of personal pride, stemming from a sense of belonging to an elite group of frontliners, whose special mission even comrades fail to grasp, let alone outsiders, researchers or "experts". In his testimony, a 17-year old at the time youth, attached to an OPLA squad as an "apprentice", emphasises his non-involvement while, at the same, articulates a liberating, sentimental confession about adherence to a group, a realm that resisters always invest with affective ties of longing and belonging:

I told you before that I was the youngest in the squad, among some real "gunslingers". I am not saying that out of timidness, it is the truth: I was free to speak my mind, I wasn't afraid of the others just because they were older. What I never did though was to ask for details every time they came and told me "Come, we have work to do." I was going to find out along the way anyway. There was no need to know, there was no trust even among us, it was those times [Kostas G., Vyronas, audio interview].

Undoubtedly, the most delicate topic was describing the "action" itself. Naming the target, the place or even the members of the execution squad was easy. Ascribing the deed to a specific individual was not. As the discussion gradually broke the outer circle of silence, describing actions that fit into the scope of "revolutionary justice" was less harmful than labelling them or connecting them to specific persons. "Is it really necessary to mention the name of the executioner? Why is it so important? The whole squad went and did the job, period!" [Savvas K., Nea Elvetia, audio interview]. The use of "we" here evokes a sense of collective *omerta* against any attempt to disclose delicate information. Speaking in terms of "we" was also a safe ground that allowed the discussion to address the necessity of violence. When openly discussed, the implemented violence naturally dissolved into a firm concept of inescapable circumstances that rendered any sense of self-justification useless:

I want to stress that we tried to exhaust all methods of persuasion, before resorting to killings. We talked to classmates or neighbours who wanted to enlist in the

---

41   *Op. cit.*, p. 72.

Security Battalions, explaining that collaborating with the Germans was unacceptable, even forcing them to change their minds, to defect. Otherwise... [Theodoros X., Nikea, audio interview].

Particularly revealing was the realisation that the retaliatory acts of the Resistance were widespread; in fact, an inseparable part of a wider vicious circle of violence. The cases in which the use of violence was personally admitted open up a window in the individual and collective motivation of militant action. In one of those instances, a high ranking member of the Athenian ELAS (the tactical urban guerrilla formations of the EAM, operating as OPLA counterparts), described how he ambushed an informant of the collaborationist Special Security Police on his own initiative and without giving much thought to the fact that "disposing of traitors" did not normally fell under his jurisdiction: "Jurisdiction and bullshit. Back in those days, anybody who was found to have betrayed, denunciated or tortured resistance fighters had a ticket to hell!" [Stelios Z., Faliro, audio interview]. The second case was even more eloquent. In a rather unique admission, Vangelis P. revealed that in April 1944 he had voluntarily taken part in an OPLA-coordinated summary execution of alleged collaborators in retaliation for the denunciation – and execution – of five left-wing youth functionaries, all comrades and close friends of his. This rare case of admitting revenge as a personal motive was emphasised by an outburst that plausibly recalled the actual words he had uttered while pulling the trigger: "I needed neither indoctrination nor instructions. In the name of the Revolution, you die!" [Palia Penteli, audio interview].

Labelling the enemy underscores both the ideological undertone of the conflict and the extreme circumstances under which urban guerrillas usually operate. The emphatic use of informal, derogatory terms like karakolia (an old, naturalised Turkish word for the gendarmerie), baskines (a slang term for policemen that does not fit at all to the official narrative) or bourantades (a generic term that brings together different types of adversaries by linking them to the police networks) indicates a rejection of the silences imposed by the party and the politically correct narrative that these silences had generated. This rejection correlates with opinions regarding the culpability of the victims, wrapped in personal ideological convictions. "Yes, I remember the priest, he was an informant. Do you know anyone of them who isn't?" [Theodoros X., Piraeus, audio interview]. The emblematic word "informant" (in Greek, χαφιές) demarcates a wide area of retribution carved along the fluent boundaries between combatants and citizens and codifies the *modus operandi* of guerrilla formations throughout history. Given the fact that the majority of OPLA victims during the occupation and the *Dekemvriana* were non-uniformed citizens, we should be reminded that the killings carried out by the Resistance were, in principal, neither vendettas linked to interpersonal motives, nor even acts of vengeance. The pattern of brutal partisan retaliations in northern Italy in April 1945 confirms that, apart from targeting all renowned fascists and functionaries of the Salò regime, "the merest suspicion that an individual was a spy had been sufficient during the course of the war and remained so during the period of transition, to provoke revenge attacks."[42]

Conclusion

How do the actors of violence understand their motivations and actions? How can anybody objectively determine during an interview the level of consciousness of the former OPLA hit man, the political prisoner of the Civil War or the seasoned member of the party respectively? Perhaps it is irrelevant to document whether a Resistance member was personally committed to "revolutionary action" rather than patriotism or social justice. What is important is that this consciousness was strengthened by brutal persecution and forged by silences imposed by comrades. Entering the room of the interview, Theodoros X. greeted me and sat on a chair with his back against the wall. He explained: "There always has to be a wall behind me when I sit. An old habit from those times." For a certain group of veterans, the historical process seems to have frozen, not out of nostalgia but out of vigilance. No time distance would reconcile them with a diachronically hostile political system and its long-term institutional memory that perpetuated their persecution. In an interesting remark about an IRA member that he interviewed, Feldman noted:

> [He] could reform, but his reputation constituted a narrative closure in his biography which was both imposed on him and with which he could also be complicit. He was both victim and perpetrator.[43]

Not all versions of self-censorship evident during my interviews seem to validate the assertion of war memory studies that the delayed (or, in this case, the missing) onset of debate about the meaning of conflictual events has more to do with political interest than with the persistence of trauma or any "leakage" in the collective unconscious.[44]

---

42 Massimo Storchi, "Post-war violence in Italy: A struggle for memory', *Modern Italy* 12/2 (2007): 240.
43 Feldman, *op. cit.*, p. 60.
44 Claudio Fogu & Wulf Kansteiner, "The politics of memory and the poetics of history", in Richard Ned Lebow et al. (eds), *The Politics of Memory in Postwar Europe*, London 2006, p. 285-310.

In themselves, personal accounts of former OPLA members speak up against the collective narrative that superimposed victimhood on violent action. Even in cases where the intentions of the participants to remember do not emanate from shifting conceptual perspectives, there is a strong sense of injustice, which is shaped by the decade-long unwillingness of the KKE to openly acknowledge the resilience of its most trusted fighters and the disgraceful scheme – refashioned as an academic trend – of innocent youngsters turned irrational criminals that had prevailed in the judicial courts of the Civil War. Indeed, an injustice that seeks to be expressed:

> I remember the Asylum case [the trial for the executions in Kokkinia during the *Dekemvriana*], seventeen death sentences in total. Five of us were given a life sentence because the prosecutor appealed to the court to take into account "our young age, the irresponsibility of youth," etc. We became furious, we stood up and shouted that we were not irresponsible youths, we were fighters! [Theodoros X., Nikea, audio interview].

The "Morality Narrative" on Jewish Rescue in Greece
Commemorative Practices and Representations

Anna Maria Droumpouki

Abstract

In recent years, various actors in Europe and beyond have begun to focus on attempts by non-Jews to rescue Jews during the Holocaust. This has also been evident in popular culture. In Greece, the topic of Jewish rescue seems to have become the perfect moral conduit and a key reference point of national self-identification. Never assuming a truly self-critical profile, Greek and non-Greek agents strive to devise strategies of commemorating Jewish rescue for the purpose of collective self-praise. The resulting narrative includes stories of heroism in a general yearning for heartening memories of the Second World War, particularly in the wake of the 2009 economic crisis. I argue that the developing interest in Jewish rescue and the contemporaneous discourse on the topic that have become visible in official and public memory stem from a need to construct a rather beautified view of rescue with the explicit purpose of promoting a narrative of tolerance and peaceful coexistence among Jews and non-Jews.

Introduction

The "myth of the Good Christian" demonstrating solidarity to Jewish neighbours persists until the present day. It is important to deconstruct the layers of different post-Holocaust memories and strategies from the perspective of Jewish victims since the narratives of those rescued by Christian efforts overshadowed the silent majority of those who perished or who survived despite the lack of solidarity. The Christian and Jewish shared narrative served to allow postwar coexistence with returning Jews. Those who did not migrate and remained in Greece gradually identified with the Greek nation-state in order to rebuild communal and social life and avoid social conflict.[1]

Indeed, the topic of Jewish rescue seems to have become the perfect moral conduit and a key reference point of national self-identification in recent years. The main narrative axis is that of Christian assistance to Jews. Orthodox Greeks are depicted as

---

[1] Giorgos Antoniou & Dirk Moses, "Introduction: The Holocaust in Greece", in *Idem* (eds), *The Holocaust in Greece*, Cambridge 2018, p. 7.

providers of consistent, decisive and moral help to their Jewish neighbours.² It has served as a vehicle for the celebration of Greek Orthodox kindness and valour and for telling a story of great bravery that focuses on non-Jewish heroes. It reinforces the self-aggrandising image of peaceful co-existence with minorities by emphasising "diachronic" tolerance as a predominant element of Greekness and as a moral principle continually praised in national discourse. According to this narrative, among the general population stances towards Jews were invariably positive, there was a lack of anti-Jewish violence, and Jews were fully integrated into society. In such accounts, the Holocaust is instrumentalised as a mechanism for building a nationalistic myth about the noble nature of Orthodox Greeks.³ By contrast, some writers have argued that Greek society was indifferent to the suffering of Jews and that overall it provided limited help. With reference to the assistance provided by the left-wing resistance movement, they have argued that the help on offer was conditional upon financial reimbursement.⁴ Either way, I believe that both narratives are based on an oversimplified understanding of what is undoubtedly a complex issue.

In what follows, I briefly document the rise in interest on the Greek Righteous Among the Nations. I argue that it constitutes an official Greek, Greek-Jewish and Israeli policy, a tool employed by numerous actors, especially the Greek Ministry of Foreign Affairs (GMFA). These supranational "agents of memory" emphasise collective action and solidarity, often blurring the specifics of particular rescue actions. I then map out the main features of the commemoration of Jewish rescue in cultural representations. Overall, I look at rescue not as a common story, but as a common field of symbolic activity, a common field of individual constructions of the past and of one's Jewish identity. Thus, I identify rescue as a formative component of Greek Jewishness among the country's Jews in the post-war period.⁵

---

2 Indicatively see Greek Ministry of Foreign Affairs, *Οι Έλληνες Δίκαιοι των Εθνών* [The Greek Righteous of the Nations], Athens 2017, edited by Fotini Tomai, who at the time of publication was Special Envoy of the Greek Ministry of Foreign Affairs for Holocaust Issues; and the impressionistic accounts of Paul Isaac Hagouel, former Representative of the Greek Delegation to the International Holocaust Remembrance Alliance, https://berkeley.academia.edu/PaulIsaacHagouel.

3 Katherine E. Fleming, "Gray zones", in Antoniou & Moses (eds), *op. cit.*, p. 365.

4 Karina Lampsa & Jacob Siby, *Η διάσωση. Η σιωπή του κόσμου, η αντίσταση στα γκέτο και τα στρατόπεδα, οι Έλληνες Εβραίοι στα χρόνια της Κατοχής* [The Rescue. The Silence of the People, the Resistance in the Ghettos and the Camps, the Greek Jews during the Occupation], Athens 2012, p. 287-288.

5 See Andrew Buckser, "Modern identities and the creation of history: Stories of rescue among the Jews of Denmark", *Anthropological Quarterly* 72/1 (1999): 3.

A turning point in commemorative practices

In recent decades, a rapidly growing interest on the subject of the history of the Holocaust in Greece can be discerned. Positioned at the heart of an on-going conversation, there is promise for greater academic and public understanding, even though scholarly research and its attempt to provide an integrated history of Greek Jewry is still confronted with widespread ignorance, nationalistic interpretations, self-justifying views, and popular antisemitism.

From September 2003 to February 2005, the Jewish Museum of Greece (JMG) ran an exhibition entitled "Hidden Children in Occupied Greece", which was hailed by the museum's director as "the most significant program on the Holocaust that [it] has undertaken to date" because, inter alia, it served to "fulfil the duty to keep alive the memory and recognise the contribution of the altruistic saviours." The second edition of the homonymous bilingual (in Greek and English) catalogue was published in 2007. It contains "accounts" by nineteen Jewish children who survived the Holocaust in hiding, principally in Athens. As the editor of the catalogue puts it, "another feature of the accounts is the strong expressions of gratitude the, now adult, hidden children of the time feel towards their saviours."⁶ "Notwithstanding the complete negation of Jewish agency on the part of the children's parents, the double-edged sword of 'altruistic saviours'"⁷ was taken up by subsequent public commemorative events related to Jewish rescue.

Public interest in the topic of Jewish rescue began to gather momentum as of 2016 in the context of a series of events to commemorate International Holocaust Remembrance Day (IHRD) under the aegis of the Prefecture of Attica, the Central Board of Jewish Communities in Greece (CBJCG) and the Jewish Community of Athens (JCA). On 27 January, the President of the Hellenic Republic unveiled the Greek Righteous Among the Nations Monument at the courtyard of the Beth Shalom Synagogue in Athens. In the presence of a handful of Greek Righteous and Holocaust survivors and a much larger number of their descendants, the president of the JCA Minos Moissis and the president of the CBJCG Moissis Konstantinis paid tribute to "these Heroes". In his speech, Moissis juxtaposed fear and persecution with the contrasting qualities of solidarity and heroism that had been displayed by those "who selflessly saved many Jews by risking their life and the lives of their families" and stressed the "true Greekness" of Greek Jews by emphasising their age-old presence in the country. Konstantinis' speech propounded the same narrative: "Our saviours were our only hope,

---

6 Jewish Museum of Greece, *Hidden Children in Occupied Greece*, Athens 2007, p. 5, 9.

7 Philip Carabott, "Το 'Ολοκαύτωμα' στην Ελλάδα" [The "Holocaust" in Greece], unpublished paper.

Figure 1. *Greek Righteous Among the Nations Monument. "And yet, in a world of utter moral collapse, there were People who with unparalleled courage defended universal values. They stood up against the indifference and hostility that prevailed during World War II and saved their Jewish co-citizens. These are the Righteous Among the Nations (January 2016)".* © Soly Iohana.

the light amidst the darkness."[8] As with the exhibition on "Hidden Children", rescue here is conceptualised as the outcome of a collective response by individuals acting on the force of personal convictions or altruism. Nor should it go amiss that a parliamentary session devoted to the IHRD that same January commemorated those Greek citizens, "Righteous Among the Nations, who risked their lives" to save the Jews.[9]

Despite the natural passing away of "saviours" and "rescued", since 2000 68 Greek Orthodox have been honoured as Righteous.[10] The "discovery" of rescuers ought also to be seen in the context of the strategic readiness of both Athens and Tel Aviv to build strong relations with each other. The two countries have established a fully-fledged alliance in which they conduct joint military exercises and cooperate on security operations in the Eastern Mediterranean.[11] It is thus not accidental that the Embassy of Israel plays a key role in most of the ceremonies honouring and commemorating "saviours" and in joint initiatives promoting Greco-Jewish friendship. Likewise, Greco-Jewish actors have accepted, if only grudgingly, as bona-fide interlocutors Greek politicians who, in the not too distant past, had expressed blatant antisemitic views.

This commemorative boom has attracted the attention of the general public through popular representations, in both print and digital media, that promote an uncomplicated, linear narrative of bravery. Such treatment provides a relatively unproblematic access point to the Catastrophe of Greek Jews. In 2017, the GMFA, in collaboration with Yad Vashem, published a volume that looks at the positive role played by the Church, the National Resistance, local administration officials, the police and other Greek actors in saving Greek Jews.[12] In the official site of the GMFA, one reads that the volume's explicit aim is to "restore the historical truth" about the Greek-Jewish experience during the Holocaust, as there was a silence concerning the topic of Jewish rescue.[13] This publication is a first-class example of the official historical narrative on the peaceful coexistence between Gentiles and Jews, which is based on a kind of Greek exceptionalism. The argument that the Greek state was founded in the early 1830s on the constitutional principle of full emancipation and freedom of religion for all its citizens forms the founding myth for the narrative of the supposedly full integration of Jews in urban centres, which allegedly was the main reason for their rescue. It is, of course, a narrative that does not stand up to serious scrutiny. For how can one account for the deportation and murder in the death camps of circa 90% of the country's Jews who lived in cities and towns?[14]

Museological representations

From 2000 onwards, the JMG (est. 1977) has been cooperating closely with the Ministry of Education and Religious Affairs and the director of the Historical Service of the GMFA (later, Special Envoy for Holocaust Issues) in educational programmes on the Holocaust, commemorative events and in exhibitions.[15] In 2019, with the kind support of another actor, the Embassy of the Federal Republic of Germany, it ran a temporary exhibition entitled *The Good Shepherds: Metropolitans and Chief Rabbis in the Face of the Holocaust*. The aim of the exhibition was to show "the conditions under which senior members of the Christian clergy and eminent rabbis decided and acted in various ways to assist persecuted Jews during the years of the Nazi Occupation." It showcased the activities of senior prelates, who either carried out public anti-German protests, such as the Archbishop of Athens and All Greece Damaskinos, or offered gestures of sympathy and support to the persecuted. The exhibition also sought to highlight the importance of individual choice within an oppressive, often contradictory and extremely complex context. In several instances, assistance rendered to Jews was recognised as only one element of an individual's positive character, rather than a defining characteristic. Overall, clergymen are portrayed as patriotic, altruistic and highly motivated individuals. Yet, the Church's stance was ambivalent. As the exhibition's title suggests, there were also "bad shepherds" and prelates who stood by and did nothing to assist the persecuted. Given that "the core source of information" for the exhibition, and the lavishly illustrated bilingual homonymous catalogue that accompanied it, was "a survey conducted by the Church of Greece in 1966," "good shepherds" are upheld as diachronic role models and beacons of inspiration for "us today."[16]

---

8   https://kis.gr/en/index.php?option=com_content&view=article&id=620:unveiling-of-greek-qrighteous-among-the-nationsq-monument-at-the-athens-synagogue&catid=49:2009-05-11-09-28-23; https://en.gariwo.net/photo-galleries/events/unveiling-of-greek-righteous-among-the-nations-monument-14535.html (accessed on 5 December 2020).

9   https://www.hellenicparliament.gr/Enimerosi/Grafeio-Typou/Deltia-Typou/?press=c6a89141-c107-453f-b559-a59a00fe95cc (accessed on 19 November 2021).

10 https://www.yadvashem.org/yv/pdf-drupal/greece.pdf (accessed on 10 December 2020).

11 Indicatively see Aristotle Tziampiris, *The Emergence of Israeli-Greek Cooperation*, New York 2015.

12 Greek Ministry of Foreign Affairs, *op. cit.*

13 https://www.mfa.gr/en/current-affairs/news-announcements/new-foreign-ministry-publication-the-greek-righteous-among-the-nations.html (accessed on 5 December 2020).

14 Carabott, *op. cit.*

15 For this "close cooperation", see the video on the occasion of the 40th anniversary of the JMG's establishment, especially from 16:09 min., https://www.jewishmuseum.gr/evraiko-moyseio-tis-ellados-i-istoria-40-chronon/ (accessed on 2 October 2021).

16 Jewish Museum of Greece, *The Good Shepherds. Metropolitans and Chief Rabbis in the Face of the Holocaust*, Athens 2019.

This representation of the Church is central to Holocaust memory in Greece. Today more than 90% of the country's citizens define their national identity based on their shared Orthodox faith. As is the case within the European Union, where attitudes towards Jews often serve as public barometers of morality,[17] the JMG's exhibition framed the Church as a fundamental opponent of Jewish persecution and reaffirmed its embedded morality during the Axis Occupation in general, despite the fact that there is evidence at hand to the contrary.[18]

Media and print representations
The self-aggrandising Greek image of peaceful co-existence with minorities, which rests on "diachronic" tolerance as a predominant element of Greekness and as a moral principle, is brought into high relief in a number of media and print representations of Jewish rescue. Unsurprisingly, given the "singularity" of the issue in question, most focus on the wholesale survival of the Jews of the island of Zakynthos. *Life Will Smile* is an award winning 2017 documentary produced by Steven Priovolos – a Los Angeles-based Greek producer and cinematographer working on commercials, feature films and TV shows. As the documentary's director Drey Kleanthous puts it, "the story itself is arresting – and unique in the chronicles of World War II. Coupled with the sheer courage and strength of the central characters it makes it so wonderfully important, not just historically but also in the current climate of the world."[19] Narrated by the late Haim Konstantinis, a nine-year old Zakynthian Jew at the time, it tells the story of the rescue of circa 275 Jews who evaded arrest and deportation in 1943-1944 because of the courageous Samaritan-like activities of Metropolitan Chrysostomos and Mayor Loukas Karrer. According to Yad Vashem, which recognised them as Righteous Among the Nations in 1978, both men headed off repeated demands by the island's "military commander" to provide him with "the list of the Jews of the island, including addresses and other details, such as professions and economic status," until "finally Chrysostomos gave the German a letter stating that the Jewish community had only two members – Karrer and himself."[20] In the interim, all Jews were safely hidden in mountainous villages. And although the whole island knew what was happening, not a single Greek revealed their whereabouts.[21]

That this "letter" is not extant does not necessarily mean that the incident in question did not take place. But does its existence denote that the Zakythian Jews were spared from deportation solely because of the Samaritan-like stance of the metropolitan and the mayor? Historian Hermann Frank Meyer has argued that "courage and solidarity was shown from the German commander of the island, Alfred Lüth, who expressed his concerns about the deportation of the Jews because they had very close ties to the local population and were culturally and socially assimilated. There was a danger that if they were deported, there would be reaction from the local population."[22] For the producer of *Life Will Smile* such arguments cut no ice. "Seeing life through the eyes" of Mayor Karrer, a 33-year old man with an eight-month pregnant wife who made a "life-changing decision in order to basically protect 275 Jews," constitutes an incredible story for Priovolos.

> A whole majority worked together to protect a minority and I think that's a huge message for the world to know today because out of the 35,000 Zakynthians not one of them during that period of eight months that the Jews were hiding up in the mountains, not one person was tempted by the Germans in order to give the Jews away. What I say to people is, I don't have the expectation to make a film as good as *Schindler's List*, but the story itself, if you ask me, it has better elements. For me, this is the Greek *Schindler's List* because of a bravery and [a] list that comes into the equation.[23]

The uniqueness of "the miracle of Zakynthos" is also emphasised in the homonymous book of an American-Greek media producer, Deno Seder.[24] Zakynthos, he argues, is "a modern parable for Christianity. During World War II, there was a saying among the Greeks: 'If you are a good Christian, save a Jew.'" Former Governor of Massachusetts and candidate for president Michael Dukakis claimed that "any student of World War II and the Holocaust -in fact, any student of history – should read this book because it is a testament to the human spirit and to the courage of two men who were willing to risk their own lives to save the Jewish community of the Greek island of Zakynthos. And they succeeded!" And Seder has recently expressed his desire to write a screenplay for a feature

---

17 John J. Michalczyk, "Introduction", in *idem* (ed.), *Resisters, Rescuers and Refugees. Historical and Ethical Issues*, Kansas 1997, p. xii.
18 See Panteleymon Anastasakis, *The Church of Greece Under Axis Occupation*, New York 2014.
19 https://filmfreeway.com/LifeWillSmile (accessed on 24 November 2021).
20 https://righteous.yadvashem.org/?search=Bishop%20Chrysostomos&searchType=righteous_only&language=en&itemId=4043029&ind=0 (accessed on 24 November 2021).
21 https://www.ushmm.org/m/pdfs/20130305-holocaust-in-greece.pdf, p. 17 (accessed on 24 November 2021).
22 *Blutiges Edelweiß: die 1. Gebirgs-Division im Zweiten Weltkrieg*, Berlin 2008, p. 609.
23 Priovolos interviewed by Anastasia Tsirtsakis in July 2017, https://neoskosmos.com/en/42875/the-greek-schindlers-list/ (accessed on 6.12.2020).
24 *The Miracle of Zakynthos. The Only Greek Jewish Community Saved in Its Entirety from Annihilation*, Washington 2014.

film based on his book, where he would love to have Tom Hanks and Rita Wilson in leading roles.[25]

In all these accounts on – and representations of – the Samaritan-like stance of two "dynamic humanists,"[26] what is strikingly absent is any mention to Jewish agency. The role the persecutees themselves played in their rescue is not acknowledged even by the narrator of *Life Will Smile*. As Philip Carabott has argued, this intentional absence could be seen as the mirror image of the outdated narrative of Jewish complacency. Specifically in the case of Zakynthos, an April 1946 Greek-Jewish report reads thus:

> As is well known, the German occupation of Zakynthos began a few weeks earlier than in the rest of southern Greece. On 15 August 1943, the German commander informed the president of the Jewish Community that henceforth restrictions on the movement of the Jews will be imposed. The president, foreseeing what would ensue, gave the signal to everyone to leave the town and make sure to hide. Indeed, all abandoned all and took refuge in the villages.

Intriguingly, there is no mention of the "letter".[27]

In contrast, anthropologist Karen Batshaw presents a more nuanced account on rescue, one in which Jewish agency is not downgraded, although once more the "brave attempts" of Christians to "protect" the Jews take centre stage. *Hidden in Plain Sight* (California 2016), a historical fiction book, narrates the story of Anna, a vibrant young Sephardic Jew from Salonika, who is sent by her father to close friends, a Greek Orthodox family in Athens, in an endeavour to keep her from harm. As the book's title suggests, she is hidden by posing as a nurse, pretending to be Greek Orthodox, attending services, wearing a crucifix and generally giving all outward appearances of being of the Christian faith. While living with this family, Anna falls in love with a member of the household, Alexander. *Hidden in Plain Sight* shines a light on the plight of Greece's Jews and the "brave attempts of the Archbishop of Athens to protect them." As regards her inspiration in writing the novel, in the course of her talk at the National Hellenic Museum in Chicago she said: "I went online and learned that almost all the Jews were killed in World War II. This man then told me the story about the town he came from and how Christians saved most of the Jews. So I started to do research on it. When I realized how many Christians stood up to the Nazis, I realized this was a story that people should know."[28]

These cultural products of the last few years have created a narrative pattern about the topic of Jewish rescue. As Andrew Buckser has shown with reference to the rescue of Danish Jews, studies on rescue have tended to depict it in epic terms, as a battle of tolerance and democratic values against prejudice and inhumanity. This fits well with a general tendency in Social Sciences to cast Holocaust rescue in universal terms, and to depict its heroes as exemplars of universal values.[29] It is an approach that enables a richer understanding of the narrative pattern in the context of the moral debate surrounding the Holocaust in Greece, which underscores the impeccable pro-Jewish attitudes of Christian compatriots.

Concluding remarks

On 12 October 1944, just as German troops were withdrawing from Athens, a group of "storm-tossed castaway" Jews gathered at the Beth Shalom Synagogue, elected a temporary committee for the administration of their urgent needs and issued a resolution of "gratitude to the Greek people for their fraternal support and assistance" in their rescue.

> We, the Israelites located around the city of Athens, survivors by Divine Grace of the savage persecution of the German hordes, feel as our next primary task to declare publicly and before all free mankind our feelings of profound gratitude that we and our descendants will carry toward the Greek people in their entirety, who by all kinds of moral and material support and assistance made our rescue possible. This truly brotherly stance of the Greek people at times so critical for us increased our love and devotion to our Greek homeland, where we have lived over so many generations in undisturbed harmony, and makes us eager to make every sacrifice for its well-being and its magnificence.[30]

Some forty-five years later, the idea of "undisturbed harmony" was still very much in play.[31] At the same time, among Salonikan Holocaust survivors interviewed by

---

25 https://www.einpresswire.com/article/359978675/miracle-at-zakynthos-the-only-greek-jewish-community-saved-in-its-entirety-from-annihilation (accessed on 4 December 2020).
26 Dionysis Vitsos, *Οι Ζακυνθινοί Εβραίοι* [The Jews of Zakynthos], Athens 2019.
27 Carabott, *op. cit.*

28 https://www.nationalhellenicmuseum.org/nhm/wp-content/uploads/2015/07/Karen-Batshaw-Book-Talk-PR.pdf accessed on 6 December 2020).
29 "Rescue and cultural context during the Holocaust: Grundtvigian nationalism and the rescue of the Danish Jews", *Shofar: An Interdisciplinary Journal of Jewish Studies* 19/2 (2001): 2.
30 Cited in Carabott, *op. cit.*
31 Indicatively, see Erika Kounio Amariglio, *From Thessaloniki to Auschwitz and Back. Memories of a Survivor from Thessaloniki*, London 2000 (first published in Greek in 1998), chapter 1: "A happy childhood in Thessaloniki".

British anthropologist Bea Lewkowicz in the early 1990s, none sought to apportion blame to the Greek people for the fate that had befallen their families. This was the upshot of the need to highlight the brotherly and sisterly relationships between Salonikan Jews and non-Jews.[32] Feelings of insecurity among Greek Jews, which in turn have diachronically led to public "declarations of allegiance",[33] stem from their perceived exclusion from the Greek Ethnos (Nation).[34] Greek Jews have lived, and continue to live, in an ethnically, religiously and linguistically homogenous society. Religion in particular has played a crucial role in the formation of modern Greek national identity. To be considered Greek, one has to be born in Greece or be of Greek ancestry, speak Greek, and profess the Orthodox faith.[35] This observation highlights the difficulties inherent in being Jewish in a nation state. Thus for Greek Jews the issue of rescue assumes a major significance as their social and cultural assimilation has always been contested. The perception that they are different from the rest of the population is not confined to the average citizen. It is a normative constituent part of a society that identifies Jews as strangers, who do not belong to the national family or to the religious patterns of the majority group.[36] Hence, rescue stories serve the need for self-assurance and reflect the uneasy feeling among the Jews living in a country that bears all the hallmarks of a state religion.

Greek-Jewish narratives reflect a defining myth produced mostly by national agents of memory, Greek and Israeli alike. In this respect, official commemorative practices and representations on rescue are inherently lop-sided. For they tend to lay emphasis on specific aspects of the past at the expense of contentious ones, revamping them in the process to underline the narrative of Greek solidarity, with the end result constituting a representative example of *selective remembrance*.[37] The broad public outcome seeks to reaffirm the rescuers' deeds as an honourable and heroic aspect of Greek wartime history. Informed by Joanna Beata Michlic's argument about the Polish case,[38] the subject of rescuers is usually brought up not because of its intrinsic intellectual and moral merits, but predominantly to defend the good name of Orthodox Greeks.

The story of Jewish rescue in Greece is a topic that has not yet been granted a separate treatment in the pertinent Holocaust literature, one that remains outside the scope of interest of researchers, despite the fact that it is an important and common experience of the Holocaust. The overall discourse finds expression in the tendency to depict the people of Greece as providers of consistent and decisive moral help to their Jewish neighbours. This *morality narrative* reinforces the self-aggrandising image of peaceful co-existence with minorities by emphasising "diachronic" tolerance as a predominant element of Greekness and as a moral principle repeatedly praised in national narratives. The past often plays an important role in the self-definition of Jewish communities, offering a symbolic language through which to express ideas of common origin. In this way, narratives of rescue become allegories for the relationship between Gentiles and Jews within a country.[39] The conventional narrative of the past produced by Greek, Greek-Jewish and Israeli actors should not be considered a simple counterpart of the individual memories concerning rescue. Jewish rescue is a striking part of the Holocaust story in Greece, at both the personal and the institutional level.

---

32 Bea Lewkowicz, *The Jewish Community of Salonika: History, Memory, Identity*, Hertfordshire 2006, p. 192.

33 Philip Carabott, "Έλληνες Εβραίοι πολίτες στα τέλη του 19ου – αρχές 20ού αιώνα" [Greek Jewish citizens, late 19th – early 20th century], *Archeiotaxio* 19 (2017): 43-62; Idem, "Έλληνες εβραίοι πολίτες της Παλαιάς Ελλάδας" Greek-Jewish citizens of Old Greece], *Chronika* 255 (2021): 14-20.

34 Kateřina Králová, "Being a Holocaust survivor in Greece: Narratives of the postwar period, 1944-1953", in Antoniou & Moses (eds), *op. cit.*, p.312.

35 Philip Carabott, "State, society and the religious 'other' in nineteenth-century Greece", *Κάμπος: Cambridge Papers in Modern Greek*, 18 (2011): 1-27.

36 Harris Mylonas, *The Politics of Nation-Building. Making Co-Nationals, Refugees, and Minorities*, Cambridge 2012, p. 121.

37 Indicatively see Terry Aladjem, "Memory, culture and critical reflection: Cultural mnemonics in a new era of selective remembrance", unpublished PhD thesis, University of Massachusetts 1986, https://scholarworks.umass.edu/cgi/viewcontent.cgi?article=2733&context=dissertations_1 (accessed on 26 November 2021).

38 "Memories of Jews and the Holocaust in post-communist Eastern Europe", in David M. Seymour & Mercedes Camino (eds), *The Holocaust in the Twenty-First Century. Contesting/Contested Memories*, New York 2017, p. 140.

39 Andrew Buckser, *After the Rescue*, New York 2003, p. 210.

"Narratives Don't Burn"

Understanding Oral Testimonies and Conceptions of Loyalty Among Exiled Greek Minorities in Central Asia After the Stalinist Repressions

Eftihia Voutira

Abstract

1949 was a critical year. September 1949 marked the end of the military phase of the Greek Civil War, while June 1949 the beginning of Stalin's deportations of Greek minorities from the Black Sea regions (e.g. Sokhumi, Batumi). The chapter considers the oral testimonies of survivors from the Stalinist repressions in Central Asia. It focuses on the encounter between Greek communist exiles from the Greek Civil War and the deportees (exiles) from the Black Sea regions of the former USSR in Tashkent. It addresses their competing conceptions of party loyalty and their notions of inherent "patriotism". It adopts an anthropological perspective in pursuing the logic of the encounter between the different Greek groups that found themselves in Central Asia under some form of exile.

Introduction

The title of this chapter is evidently borrowed from Mikhail Bulgakov's famous statement "Manuscripts Don't Burn." He, majestically, refers to the actual burning of his treasured manuscript in an effort to cleanse his mind from the troubles the work had brought him. Woland, the imaginary character in the novel, later gives the manuscript back to him saying: "Didn't you know that manuscripts don't burn?" There is a deeply autobiographical element reflected in this passage which has since become a motto for dissident writers working in totalitarian states the world over. Bulgakov burned an early copy of *The Master and Margarita* for much the same reasons, as he expresses in the novel itself. This, he famously rewrote from memory after putting the original on fire. In alluding to the Bulgakov case, I am making a pitch for the relevance of the oral narratives/oral histories[1] collected during my own anthropological fieldwork in the former USSR (1991-1999). The project of collecting evidence and documentation of the Soviet and post Soviet era has been a major

---

1 Ray Pahl and Paul Thomson, "Meanings, myths and mystifications: The social construction of life histories in Russia", in C.M. Hann (ed.), *When History Accelerates: Essays on Rapid Social Change, Complexity and Creativity*. London 1994, p. 130-158. The authors identify four caveats as regards methodological problems in conducting oral history research in post-perestroika: a) The practical inability to create a base for random sampling; b) The lack of trust between the researcher and the informant; c) The all-encompassing perception of people as victims of circumstances; and d) The lack of historical memory. Of these, it is the latter three that are particularly relevant in my own longitudinal research; Eftihia Voutira, "Post-Soviet Diaspora politics: The case of the Soviet Greeks", *Journal of Modern Greek Studies* 24/2 (2006): 379-414.

interdisciplinary and international effort culminating in the recent publication Series of Soviet Archives.²

The focus of the chapter is on a key anthropological concern: The survival, maintenance and reproduction of communities in exile. One of the least studied phenomena of the Greek Civil War concerns the issue of inter-marriage among communist and non-communist Greeks during their exile years. Getting married and being married is one of the most important priorities of adult life. It has been argued that marriage in advanced capitalist societies is the result of love rather than arrangement.³ My aim is to address some of the more complex issues relating to marriage choices and the types of arguments used by Greeks in Central Asia to legitimise, support or explain their choice of spouse during the "exile years" (υπερορία).⁴ The context within which marriage choices were to take place is a primary factor in determining the type of rationale and particular cultural idiom used as a response. I focus on the degree to which the ethnic minority norms are in agreement or in tension with the norms of the host society, as well as on the strategies people use to accommodate one, each or both.

In the Soviet context, inter-marriage among different ethnic groups was seen as part of the ideology of Слияние (*Sliianiye*, the coming together of the different nations) and served the promotion and continuous reference to the "Soviet People". As one of my key informants in Uzbekistan told me:

> The promotion of intermarriage among different ethnic groups and particularly with Russians was seen as part of the state ideology. Every marriage between members of different nationalities was seen as a step towards the realisation of the Soviet people, and a victory of communism!⁵

Yet, my case study is different. Under the protection of the Communist Party of the Soviet Union (CPSU) and in light of the dictates of democratic centralism, the Communist Party of Greece (KKE) had full control of the fates of individual party members. Indeed, the precept to be applied at all levels of social life was obedience to the order *το όπλο παρά πόδα* (on guard!).⁶

The theoretical framework of understanding and labelling forced migrations

Forced displacement and transplantation of populations is a familiar imperial policy used for centuries in different settings. Under the particular form of the Stalinist regime in the 1930s, exile, forced uprooting and mass displacement became a norm. After 1939, different ethnic

---

2   The issue of the opening up of the Soviet Archives (KGB, Regional, Army, and NKVD) and other relevant centres of totalitarian control is of course vast. For the Greeks in particular, the collecting of archival evidence from Soviet archives began in the early-1990s; see Andréas Notaras, "Les grecs pontiques de la région de Krasnodar, Fédération de Russie: Transformations historiques de l'organisation sociale et de l'Identité ethnique au XX siècle", unpublished PhD thesis, École des Hautes Études en Sciences Sociales, 2005; Kostas Photiades, "Οι διώξεις μέσα από τα σοβιετικά αρχεία" [The persecutions through the Soviet archives], in Vlassis Agtzidis (ed.) *Οι άγνωστοι Έλληνες του Πόντου* [The Unknown Greeks of the Pontus], Athens 1995, p. 125-135; *Idem*, "Παρευξείνιος Διασπορά. Οι ελληνικές εγκαταστάσεις στις βορειοανατολικές περιοχές του Εύξεινου Πόντου" [Black Sea Diaspora: Greek Settlements in the North-Eastern Regions of the Black Sea], Salonika 1997; N. Bugai, *Iosif Stalin – Lavrenti Beria: "Ikh nado deportirovat". Dokumenty, fakty, kommentarii* [Joseph Stalin – Lavrenti Beria: "They Must Be Deported". Documents, Facts, Commentaries], Moscow 1992. Here I only mention some of the major sources that have become available in English while the international trade and appropriation of the archives remains a wide field of engaged research; http://www.thehindu.com/news/international/world/a-kgb-archives-opens-in-cambridge/article6186650.ece# (accessed on 27 November 2021). On pertinent novel and heated debates in history and anthropology, see Ann Laura Stoler, "Colonial archives and the arts of governance", *Archives and Museum Informatics* 2/1-2 (2002): 87-109. Inspired mainly by Michel Foucault's "A critical approach to Historical Epistemology", most writers within the post-colonial paradigm reconceptualised the debates on memory, counter-memory and subjectivity in history, thus anthropologising history by using the archive as an ethnographic field with its internal codes and power relations. Indicatively, Donald Bouchard (ed.), *Language, Counter-Memory, Practice: Selected Essays and Interviews by Michel Foucault*, New York 1977. For more recent revisionist accounts of the role of "great men in History", see the publications of Stephen Kotkin: *Armageddon Averted: The Soviet Collapse, 1970-2000*, Oxford 2001; (with András Sajó, eds) *Political Corruption in Transition: A Sceptic's Handbook*, Budapest 2002; (with Mark Beissinger, eds) *Historical Legacies of Communism in Russia and Eastern Europe*, Cambridge 2014; *Stalin. Paradoxes of Power, 1878-1928*, New York 2014. Kotkin's revisionist account of Stalin is an illuminating example of what I would call an ethnography of archives in the former USSR.

3   Indicatively, see Alan MacFarlane, *The Culture of Capitalism*, Oxford 1987, p. 123-143.

4   The term (lit. beyond borders) is one with special meaning for members of the Democratic Army of Greece (DSE). It is employed to refer to the exile years in communist bloc countries that provided hospitality and assistance to DSE members who fled Greece after the formal defeat of the communist forces in Greece in August 1949. For a comprehensive comparative account, see Katerina Tsekou, *Έλληνες πολιτικοί πρόσφυγες στην ανατολική Ευρώπη, 1945-1989* [Greek Political Refugees in Eastern Europe, 1945-1989], Athens 2013.

5   Interview with Maria (June 1992).

6   Eftihia Voutira et al. (eds), *Το όπλο παρά πόδα. Οι πολιτικοί πρόσφυγες του ελληνικού Εμφυλίου Πολέμου στην ανατολική Ευρώπη* [On Guard! The Political Refugees of the Greek Civil War in Eastern Europe], Salonika 2015.

groups, the so-called "punished people",⁷ from various provinces of western USSR were rounded up and deported in separate groups to different locations in Central Asia or Siberia. Poles, Germans, Hungarians, Chechens and Jews, who were considered "enemies of the state", were forcibly moved ostensibly to protect the borders or develop poor regions. Ethnic Greeks were exiled in four distinct phases from 1941 to 1952, always following the displacement of the other ethnic groups.⁸

For the Greeks in particular a number of criteria were used. These included who was considered "Greek", where they happened to live and at what point in time. Exile created among the Greeks a treasury of "kinship capital", a concept I construct from three components: Cultural familiarity, interpersonal trust and inward-looking group loyalty. In this sense, "kinship capital" is a value system that the Soviet Greeks, who formed the focus of my research, are born into, buy into and employ to survive and thrive even today.

The nomenclature and conceptualisation of the different types of forced migrations in the former Soviet Union is a major issue that could only be addressed after the demise of the country.⁹ Accordingly, one can identify the following phases in the history of these displacements:

Repressions ("enemies of the People")

In Soviet nomenclature, *репрессии* (repressions) denote the 1936-1939 exiling of all "enemies of the People" in the aftermath of the Great Purge with its show trials and executions of members of the government who posed a threat to Stalin. Individual party members, typically male, were imprisoned or sent to labour camps in the Urals and Siberia. Ethnic affiliation was irrelevant. The figure is in the millions.¹⁰ A joke was going around Moscow at the time: "Who is worse? The Bukharinists to the Right or the Trotskyites to the Left? Both are worse, is the Stalinist answer!" In the case of the Greeks, who were accused of being both, the reason for their purge was the *Греческий роман* (Greek Affair), wherein Greek communists ostensibly tried to overthrow the central government. Greeks were called "socially dangerous elements" – a label conferring liability on all kin – and their repression fell under the jurisdiction of the Extraordinary Commission for the Struggle Against Counter-Revolution and Sabotage (Cheka).¹¹ The remaining few returned to their previous areas of residence only to become victims of the next waves of deportations.¹² The following account summarises the experiences of these exiles.

> In 1938 they gathered all the Greeks from Kuban. First they took the priests, then the teachers. We had many Greek communists, even judges. They got everyone over 18. No one thought that they would be sent to Siberia. We thought they were to be sent to Greece since they were only Greeks. A policeman came and told them: "Leave, they will kill you." No one believed him. I remember the day they took them, the guards on horses and the men on foot. They were taken 34 km on foot assembling people from all areas. From those who were exiled, one in a thousand came back.¹³

Evacuations

These displacements were carried out from 1941 until 1942 and had primarily a strategic- and defence-orientated *raison d'être*. They do not constitute a separate phase of mass displacement, but one that is recorded from below. Typical evacuees were foreign passport holders, exiled as families or households. The following dramatically captures the experience as a lived event.

> In 1942, as the Germans were moving in, Stalin ordered us to leave. He sent us 6,000 km away, on the border with Siberia. It was so cold, we thought we would die. We lived there in exile for six years and after the war we were allowed to move to south Kazakhstan.¹⁴

---

7 Aleksandr Nekrich, *The Punished Peoples: The Deportation and Fate of Soviet Minorities at the End of the Second World War*, Boulder 1978.

8 Eftihia Voutira, "Ethnic Greeks from the former Soviet Union as 'privileged return migrants'", *Espace Populations Sociétés* 3 (2014): 533-544.

9 See J. Otto Pohl, *The Stalinist Penal System: A Statistical History of Soviet Repression and Terror, 1930-1953*, North Carolina 1997; Idem, *Ethnic Cleansing in the USSR, 1937-1949*, Westport CT 1999; Pavel Pollian, *Against Their Will: The History and Geography of Forced Migrations in the USSR*, Budapest 2003.

10 Pollian, op. cit., p. 313.

11 This practice points to the disparity between explicit aim and unintended consequences. Despite the continuous usage of socially determined repressions after 1938, the focus shifts towards ethnic categorisation and "essentially nationalistic goals and methods;" Pollian, op. cit., p. 43. Such a shift towards ethnicity may have begun as wartime strategy concerning groups viewed as unreliable.

12 Recent research shows that the majority of the "lists" delivered to the Cheka were composed by local councils that included other Greek communists. The "directive" set as priority those who had kept their Greek passports and were deemed to be "socially dangerous" because of their professional affiliation (e.g., bankers, teachers, doctors); cf. John Archibald Getty, *The Origins of the Great Purges: The Soviet Communist Party Reconsidered*, Cambridge 1985. Eight thousand Greeks from Mariupol, 4,500 from Krasnodar and 3,000 from the Donetsk region were executed; I. Dzhuha, *Греческий роман* [The Greek Affair], St Petersburg 2006.

13 Interview with Yannis P. (b. 1933) from Kuban (8 June 1992).

14 Interview with Dimitris K. (b. 1938) from Kabardinka (22 June 1992).

A variant evacuation involved a lesser known wartime strategy. It entailed the deployment of dispensable populations as human shields in defending the frontlines.[15]

We were used as human shields against the enemy with no consideration about our survival. Most of the young men of our village were killed by the Germans.[16]

Deportations

Soviet deportations remained a well-kept secret for more than ten years.[17] Had it not been that I arrived in Central Asia six years after Perestroika, I believe that the Soviet Greeks would not have felt able to speak of their displacements and lives in exile to me forty-five years on from the "event". The concept of the "event" is central to both Anthropology and History, describing how the self is narrated as "being" in history. The interrelation between them is aptly identified by anthropologist Allen Feldman, who construes the "event" not "as something that happened but as 'that which can be narrated.'"[18]

The case of the Crimean Greeks, who were deported in 1944 (together with Crimean Tatars, Bulgarians, Jews, Germans and Kurds), is fascinating because it involves people being exiled in 1944 and, upon return, sent to exile again.

In 1944, when we had come back from Kirghizia, we were ordered to leave again. We still had our suitcases in our hands from the previous exile. In June 1944 they exiled us again; and again on the road, on the train for one month. This time we were sent to Siberia. It was late August when we arrived and it was snowing. Again they took us on trucks, on freight trains, together with the animals. On the wagons there were different letters written (A, B, C), so we knew that, depending on our names, from then on we would be separated. We were not a community anymore; we were divided according to the letters of the alphabet.[19]

Forcible displacement, for whatever reasons, is always introduced as a sudden, unexpected event. Deportations from the Caucasus took place after the war and people were apprehensive and, in some ways, *prepared*. This is captured in Marina's dramatic account of the "event".

In 1950, having heard about the 1949 deportations from Batumi, we were waiting in Borjomi [eastern Georgia] and we were preparing for our deportation. The winter passed and we thought we had escaped the exile. But on 2 February, there was a knock on the door at three in the morning. Mother said: "They've come!" First they knocked next door and we heard them dragging the people out. In our case they showed my father a piece of paper that declared him to be Iranian. They put us together in a truck and told us we were being sent to central Asia. Many years later we found out what had happened. A neighbour, who was Armenian and who was making passports, wrote my father down as Iranian because his cousin needed a house. On the way, the train stopped and picked up other people. They picked up Armenians and Azeris and the train was [moving] for 18 days. We had to make a hole in the floor in order to use it as a toilet. During the day, the train stopped. It only moved at night.[20]

Marina's account is significant, because it also identifies the actual experience and the realisation of what had really happened after the "event".

Finding the Greek communists in exile: "Political Refugees' of the Greek Civil War

Tashkent constitutes a focal point of the Soviet Greek deportation experience, bringing together segmented groups: Pontic Greeks, who had left for Greece in the 1920s and had become "Greeks", and those who had stayed behind in the Soviet Union.[21] Ташкент, Хлебный город (Tashkent, bread city!) was the popular Soviet name for the capital of Uzbekistan, a city whose identity has been tied with socialist development on a grand scale.

For modern Greeks, Tashkent is often referred to as Μικρή Μόσχα (Little Moscow). It has special significance because it was the place where the DSE leadership set base in September 1949 after the defeat of the communists in

---

15   Robert Conquest, *The Soviet Deportation of Nationalities*, London 1960. During fieldwork, I was taken to the exact spot where the "human shields" were placed. There is a memorial plaque with the names of the wartime heroes engraved on it. All of them Greek! Local people use this memorial as a meeting point and younger generations as an amusement place. I was told that the place is "haunted", since old believers had their sacred places in that forest.
16   Interview with Kostas S. (b. 1934) from Vladikavkaz (26 June 1992).
17   Conquest, op. cit., p. 82.
18   *Formations of Violence: The Narrative of the Body and Political Terror in Northern Ireland*, Chicago 1991, p. 14.
19   Interview with Aphrodite (June 1992).
20   Interview with Marina (June 1992). This family had been moved involuntarily several times with different experiences in each case. The father was exiled in 1936 as part of the repressions, the mother was deported in 1941 from the Caucasus as part of the deportations, and the rest of the family was deported with an aunt from Borzhom in May 1950.
21   Voutira, "Post-Soviet...", op. cit.; cf. Elaina Maria Lampropulos, "Belonging to Greece and the Soviet Union: Greeks of Tashkent, 1949-1974", unpublished MA dissertation, York University 2014.

Greece.²² In 1991, there were cafes and tourist pavilions in the park, where three blocks of KGB buildings still dominated the central city opposite the CPSU offices and Lenin's statue, emblems of Soviet power structures. Around noon, huge kettles of boiling pilaf produced an enticing smell mixed with that of corn cobs grilled on street corners. Traditionally dressed women, youth in jeans, and old men wearing *tiboukeitas* (Muslim caps) would buy their lunch and eat standing up or on the stools along the strip of paved road in the middle of the park. Meanwhile, in Moscow one could hardly find a loaf of bread at the local bakery, let alone buy anything in the street other than shrivelled tomatoes or sprouted potatoes sold outside grocery markets.

For the Soviets a critical issue concerning the city of Tashkent relates to the composition of its Greek and Pontic Greek element. Both groups arrived at the same time, the Pontic Greeks in June 1949 from the Black Sea, and the Greeks from the Greek mainland in late summer 1949. Each was seen as having mutually exclusive ideologies, and their identity was defined by their place of "origin" and what this denoted. From the standpoint of the CPSU, the Greeks from Greece were the elite leadership of the DSE which had been "evacuated" in the immediate aftermath of the civil war. The Black Sea Pontic Greeks were "enemies of the people," "collaborators" with the enemy, and "punished people." For a long time, the two groups remained isolated from each other. Within Tashkent, the dominant Greek identity was that of the политические мигранты (political migrants). Comprising a total of 11,110 souls, including 6,022 men and 1,142 women, their civic status remained that of люди без гражданства (stateless people) for at least ten years.²³

The term "evacuated" was coined by an informant who explained the deportation to Central Asia under party orders as a challenge that had to be met under conditions of war time flight. This rescue mission was coordinated through Albania, where boats were waiting to load women and men to be taken through the Black Sea and then from Batumi by trains to Tashkent. "Tashkent, a word written with a strange letter that looks like a reversed Poseidon's trident," writes Alki Zei in her autobiographical novel, connoting the alien and exotic impression the new setting made on the members of the "Patriotic Front" upon arrival.²⁴

Housing was the first challenge, as described in the memoirs of a number of these communist Greeks; they lived as "mobilised soldiers" in elongated wooden army barracks built for German and Japanese prisoners of war. This situation lasted until 1956, when they began building their own homes.

> Our people who were arriving in Tashkent were put in camps set up next to big industrial plants or construction complexes. These original barrack compounds, our μαχαλάδες [neighbourhoods], were later called πολιτείες [small towns]. Men lived in male wards and women in female wards. The majority of the women who were there with their husbands could not live as couples. Everyone was given work immediately. They would all line up in the morning and march to work and they would all line up in the evening to march to bed. We followed the same military discipline that we had in the mountains. It was forbidden for anyone to leave their barracks. It was also forbidden to form relations with Soviet citizens, especially for men to have relations with Soviet women.²⁵

The political migrants were not allowed to marry Russians, Uzbeks, Kazakhs or others but had to find a way to marry "within". This regulation was related to the long-term plan of the communist leadership to facilitate the select Tashkent group's return to Greece, whenever the fight to "establish communism" would be resumed. It was a precept that also guided the educational system of civil war evacuees.²⁶ Marrying a Russian meant putting down roots and this was not an option allowed by the KKE, although it was tolerated more often than not. For the younger Greeks who had not married while they were in Greece, the question of finding a wife was a preoccupation.

Vangelis' story is typical. Pontic Greek by origin, his father fled to Greece as a refugee in 1918 and settled with his family in the Katerini region. Born in 1928, Vangelis was recruited into the communist resistance in 1944.

---

22   There is a renewed interest in Tashkent as a locus of social identity formation, involving survivors of the Greek Civil War, their descendants and the "stolen children" of the civil war; Eftihia Voutira & Aigli Brouskou, "'Borrowed children' in the Greek Civil War", in Catherine Panter-Brick & Malcolm T. Smith (eds), *Abandoned Children*, Cambridge 2000, p. 92-110; Stelios Yatroudakis, *Τασκένδη: 30 χρόνια προσφυγιά* [Tashkent: Thirty Years in Flight], Athens 2000; Loring Danforth & Riki Van Boeschoten, *Children of the Greek Civil War: Refugees and the Politics of Memory*, Chicago 2012; Kostis Karpozilos, "The defeated of the Greek Civil War: From fighters to political refugees in the Cold War", *Journal of Cold War Studies* 16/3 (2014): 62-87.

23   Gavrilos Lampatos, *Έλληνες πολιτικοί πρόσφυγες στην Τασκένδη, 1949-1957* [Greek Political Refugees in Tashkent, 1949-1957], Athens 2001.

24   *Achilles' fiancée*, Athens 2002.

25   Thomas Dritsios, *Από τον Γράμμο στην πολιτική προσφυγιά* [From Grammos to Political Refugeeness], Athens 1983, p. 15ff.

26   See Voutira & Brouskou, *op. cit.*, and Maria Bondila, *"Πολύχρονος να ζεις, μεγάλε Στάλιν": Η εκπαίδευση των παιδιών των Ελλήνων πολιτικών προσφύγων στα ανατολικά κράτη (1950-1964)* ["Long Live, Great Stalin": The Education of the Children of Greek Political Refugees in Eastern Countries (1950-1964)], Athens 2004.

When he arrived in Tashkent in 1949, he was *της παντρειάς* (at the age to marry). He was retrained as a mechanic, but as he insisted:

> My problem was not finding work. It was finding a wife. The Party order was not to marry anyone non-Greek. In 1954, I heard that in the region there were members of our family, from both sides. They were in Kentau. I took the map and tried to find the town. I saw the train tracks and knew there was a station approximately 20 km distance from the town. I had to travel in a dusty road to reach the village. It seemed like being in the desert. I asked around and most people spoke *ρωμαίικα* [Greek]. I found the family. Then I decided to marry Aliki who was of marriage age, even though they were "Greek royalists." We got married in Tashkent.

For a DSE member like Vangelis, seeing a "Greek royalist" was like seeing red. The royalists were the enemy in the Greek Civil War. Yet, why would someone who was deported within the Soviet Union identify with the royalists in Greece? The answer relates to the preconceptions and perceptions of each about the other. Deported Greeks had a passport with the indication "Kingdom of Greece", sufficient in the Cold War climate to identify them with the opposition. In Greece, marriage between the opposing sides would have been impossible, yet, in exile the sub-national Pontic Greek affinal relation imposed its own rules of endogamy, which in exile was the priority.[27]

Aliki first thought about going to Greece when she was eighteen years old and her mother began mentioning marriage. Who would she marry? A Greek, of course. Why? This was the first time the rationale was explained to her. Because she can then go to Greece some day.

> We were not raised to think of Greece as a haven. Our parents did. I remember them talking about it as a dream. But then after we were deported there was very little that we could do. We were all trying to survive from one day to the next. No time to think or contemplate about a better or different life. Then, when marriage age came and we were thinking about who will marry whom the issue of Greece was always coming up. My brother was in love with a Russian girl; she was beautiful and kind but my mother did not want her because she was Russian. So she quickly arranged a marriage for him with a Pontic Greek to make sure that he doesn't "get a Russian." There were many people like my mother, they were all afraid of having a Russian in the family. If you marry, you can't leave; my mother said that if you marry, it is like sowing roots. How can you uproot yourself again then?

Another case of a political migrant marrying within the ethnic group against the interests of the party is Lefteris. His story is different in that he had managed to get permission from the KKE to go to his relatives at Tsalka in the Caucasus. (I met him in Greece, in Prohoma, where he had returned in 1987.)

> In 1965 my aunt wrote to invite me to Tsalka, where they lived at the village of Santa. I had grown up with the image of that place because my father always told me stories about Santa, where his brother and sister had stayed after he went to Greece in 1928. The party gave me permission to go. I went there and I found my aunt Areti and she was living in the family house. Imagine, I got to sleep in my father's house, in fact in his room! He had died in the war so I could not tell him that I got to realise his dream, live in his house and sleep in his room! I wrote to my relatives and told them that I was sleeping in my father's room in Russia. There I met Anna, who was my second cousin and we lived there [in Santa] for another 15 years before returning to Greece.

The story of his marriage is more than merely finding a wife. It involved retracing a whole part of his genealogy. Ironically, Lefteris did not merely find his wife by retracing his genealogy; he had to get married *in church* in order to repatriate to Greece with his wife, given that at the time (1979) civil marriage was not recognised in Greece. "We had to get married in church. Can you imagine me, a communist, trying to find a priest?"

After de-Stalinisation most marriages were between partisans and Black Sea women who had been deported. It is interesting how easily the ideological differences between the Stalinist *Греческие партизаны* (Greek partisans) and the anti-Stalinist deportees were waived in the interests of "endogamy". For the partisans, one can argue that this was not especially hard since KKE orders were to marry within the ethnic group. For the deportees, however, the social obligation to marry "within", not merely as a sanction but also as an advantage to "repatriation", was more significant, particularly since a number of these partisans were of Pontic Greek origin. When I arrived in Tashkent in the spring of 1991, most of the community had "repatriated", but the older people at the party offices, which had become an active cultural association during perestroika, would nostalgically remember the Pontic feasts they had in the community for these weddings. The association's archives I was allowed to see for the period 1957-1970, which were far

---

27 Voutira et al., *op. cit.*

from complete, showed 85 marriages between Greeks and 132 marriages with other Soviet nationalities, mainly Russian. The wives of these political migrants who returned to Greece with their husbands after the formal recognition of the KKE in 1974 and the "national reconciliation" of the early 1980s formed a cultural association in Athens with some 200 members in the mid-1980s.

Concluding remarks

The incident of meeting and marrying under conditions of exile is one of the ironies of the experience of the survivors of the Greek Civil War and the Stalinist deportations. The paradox to be resolved by each loyal member of the party depended on their competing loyalties and divided authority in the context of their kinship capital, which entailed marrying within while living without. At the same time, it involved interpreting the dictates of the party and their own sense of loyalty. After 1968 and the break-up of the KKE, loyalties were further segmented. Both in exile, for those who stayed, and in Greece, for those who had repatriated.

Possibly the most important longer-term unintended consequence of deportations, exiles and repressions was to bring all the dispersed groups of Greeks together in central Asia. Their collective identity and self-perception as "punished", "repressed" and exiled people created a strong sense of collective cultural capital, much stronger than any intentional educational or cultural activity programme could provide. In their own words, the most important experience they all shared was their forcible displacement to Central Asia. They met and recognised each other, while in exile. And for this, they all shouted: *"Thank you Stalin!"*

Narratives Competing for the Public Space in Post-Soviet Russia

A Case Study in Challenges to Transitional Justice

Nanci Adler

Abstract

Unlike in post-Nazi Germany, in post-Soviet Russia there are no *Stolpersteine* with the names, birthdates, and arrest, deportation, and/or execution dates of victims of the Stalinist terror at the sidewalks in front of the homes where they once lived. Quite the contrary, in post-Soviet Russia there is a persistent trend to manage national and public memory by repressing the memory of repression. This trend is characterised by the ongoing struggle to determine which truths are admitted to the public space. The efforts of victim organisations to assert their narrative of the Stalinist past have met resistance, which in one case led to the closing of the only Gulag museum on a former labour camp site. This museum was but one of the many recent battlegrounds for the clash of narratives, as old repressions become recycled into new ones. The chapter explores remembrance and civil society's efforts to publicise the history of repression amidst the state's parallel efforts to co-opt it. It looks *at* – as well as *through* – Russia to identify impediments to transitional justice that are similar to those found in a number of post- and still-repressive societies that have been unable, unwilling or resistant to embrace transitional justice measures.

Introduction

A casual glance at the sidewalks of Berlin and Moscow reveals the contrasting ways in which Germany and Russia approach their repressive history. Among Germany's many commemorative symbols, Berlin's sidewalks solemnly display over 5,000 *Stolpersteine* marking the homes where the victims of Nazism once lived. Inscribed on these blocks are their names, birthdates, deportation points, and dates of death. Over 50,000 such memorial stones have been placed in other European cities.[1] In post-Soviet Russia, such reminders of the Stalinist terror in the public space are scarce in number and spare in influence because they refer to an officially redacted or irrelevant past.

Post-Nazi Germany's full, if involuntary, acknowledgement of its repressive history, impelled by the defeat of Nazism, permitted it to progress toward a democratic political

---

*   Parts of the chapter appear in Nanci Adler, "Challenges to transitional justice in Russia", in Cynthia M. Horne & Lavinia Stan (eds), *Transitional Justice and the Former Soviet Union: Reviewing the Past, Looking Toward the Future*, Cambridge 2018, p. 45-65.

1   www.stolpersteine.eu/en/technical-aspects/ (accessed on 25 November 2020).

system. By contrast, the repression of individual rights continues in an undefeated authoritarian post-Soviet Russia. In consequence, over thirty years after the collapse of the Soviet Union, the achievements of the Stalinist system, and Stalin himself, are still – or again – being valorised. The present regime is no more than tolerant of the counter-currents that have been stirred by the anti-Stalinist organisation Memorial as well as other NGOs, which have challenged official attempts to ignore, subvert or co-opt the history of repression.

Nevertheless, small but significant steps on the part of these organisations may be noted. In 2014, Memorial orchestrated a campaign, entitled "Last Address", offering individuals the chance to place a name plaque on the buildings from which their relatives were removed, often never to return. These plaques display eight lines, for example: "HERE LIVED VLADIMIR ABRAMOVICH NIKOLAEV; PAEDIATRICIAN, BORN 1902, ARRESTED 1936, EXECUTED ON 19/12/1938; REHABILITATED IN 1961." To the left of the text, a starkly empty square has been cut in the metal, representing the void the repression created in the families of millions of Soviet citizens, arrested without warning and executed or incarcerated. It also represents the void created by the official avoidance of what actually happened.

As of 2015, nearly eighty years after the Terror, there were no more than 30 plaques in Moscow, each also representing a renewed struggle with the authorities – this time for permission to hang them.[2] As I hope to elucidate in this chapter, in post-Soviet Russia there is a persistent trend to manage national and public memory by repressing, controlling, or even co-opting the memory of repression to accommodate a select national narrative. This phenomenon is not unique to Russia. It characterises numerous post- and still-repressive societies that have been unable, unwilling or resistant to embrace "transitional justice" measures. So, this case study in fact illuminates some of the more pressing challenges facing transitional justice today.

Despite the long, politically expedient trend of imposing a national amnesia of the Gulag, efforts have been made to investigate and publicise a counter-history to the state-sponsored narratives. The chapter addresses these efforts and explains why they have had difficulty finding resonance. This is relevant because the success of transitional justice in post-Soviet Russia may depend on its ability to forge a dialogue between official and personal narratives and create an inclusive history of the Soviet state's repression of its own people based on credible evidence and validated by a credible audience. The chapter also looks at post-Soviet remembrance practices, national memory and the national narrative, truth and the national narrative, textbooks, and the recurrent practice of re-writing and reconstructing the past. Finally, it reflects on how to move beyond current impasses.

Which past to remember?

Among the difficulties of constructing the history of Soviet repression is grasping the intricacy of a process that moved so casually from non-existent evidence to lethal consequences.

> Nikiforov, Georgii Konstantinovich, age 54, writer, member of the Writers' Union, executed on 2 April 1938.
>
> Nikiforov, Mikhail Pavlovich, age 37, deputy chief engineer of the USSR Central Administration of Communications, executed on 9 December 1937.
>
> Nikolaev, Aksim Maksimovich, age 50, chairman of the All-Union Society for Foreign Cultural Relations, executed on 15 March 1938.
>
> Nikolaev Aleksei Petrovich, age 42, chauffer of the Zhilstroi Trust, former second lieutenant of the Tsarist Army, executed on 21 November 1937.

Contrary to what it might have been, this list was not offered in evidence for criminal proceedings against the Soviet regime. Trials or truth commissions are exceedingly complex undertakings in the aftermath of a 70-year dictatorship. Even such acts as acknowledgement, apologies, and commemoration can be difficult to accommodate. The Nikiforovs and the Nikolaevs were just a few of the individuals whose names began with the letter "N", and whose fates were publicly remembered on the Day of Political Prisoners.[3] These were the names on the piece of paper given to me to read aloud in 2011. They were found on *Rasstrel'nye Spiski* (execution lists) of the NKVD, along with tens of thousands of others, apolitical undesirables who were shot in the back of the neck on the day of sentencing and dumped in a mass grave on the outskirts of Moscow.

The commemoration ceremony is an annual event organised by the non-governmental organisation Memorial, with official permission to recite names from 10 am until 10 pm, barely enough time to recite two-thousand, let alone millions of names. It is generally not attended by government officials.[4] The gathering takes

---

2   Interview with Arsenii Roginskii (Moscow, 9 April 2015).

3   Memorial distributed such a list to each of the hundreds of participants who attended the Day at Lubyanka Square, Moscow, on 29 October 2011.

4   Interview with Arsenii Roginskii (Moscow, 31 October 2016).

place at the monument to the "victims of totalitarianism", a stone from the Solovetsky Islands (the first labour camp under Lenin), erected by Memorial in 1990, right across from the notorious Lubyanka.[5] Until 2015, there was not even one *state*-sponsored commemorative plaque in Moscow to victims of Stalinism. Now a well-funded Moscow city-sponsored Gulag museum opened in October 2015.[6] The museum depicts the Gulag relatively accurately, but its critical appraisal neither extends to the Soviet system nor presents human rights violations. Significantly, in October 2017, President Putin unveiled the state and crowd-funded "Wall of Sorrow", a monument to the victims of Stalinism. In his remarks at the ceremony, he asserted that we should mourn the victims, but not bring the country to renewed confrontation by "settling scores."[7] Victims are a politically-safe focus, but the state draws a thick line when it comes to the discussion of perpetrators.

Such a division has been enabled by a revision of the past, which has been the short-term remedy to circumvent the obligation to undertake "transitional justice" measures in post-Soviet Russia. This fashioning of a good future out of a "bad past" has been facilitated by the construction of a "usable past" for the national narrative.[8] This is also accompanied by a present patriotism that calls for Western franchises like McDonald's to be replaced by *Edim Doma* (Eating at Home),[9] and museum exhibitions that showcase Soviet interpretations of history.[10] It has also come to include publications like *Words that Changed the World*, a 2015 volume of Putin's collective wisdom edited by a youth group.[11]

A Soviet-era adage proclaimed that "Lenin is always with us." It alluded to the omnipresence of the leader of the Bolshevik Revolution in public and private spaces. Lenin, though still physically with us as he lays embalmed in a mausoleum on Red Square, has now been relegated to the communist past. Yet, twenty-four years after the collapse of the Soviet Union, the history of the crimes of Stalin and Stalinism had been so successfully glossed over that nationwide polls showed his popularity edging back toward pre-de-Stalinisation levels – and gaining momentum.[12] In 2015, a poll found that 38% agreed that the Soviet people's sacrifices during the Stalin era were justified by the high goals and results that were achieved in such a short period.[13] Apparently, the accomplishments of industrialisation and the Soviet dictator's wartime victory were more relevant to those polled than the millions of victimisations of that same era that had resulted from those same events. In 2016, 40% of those surveyed believed that Stalin should not be considered a state criminal, and appraised the Stalin era as being more "good" than "bad".[14] And, finally, in 2017, 46% of those polled viewed Stalin with respect, and even enthusiasm.[15] Stalin's burgeoning popularity reflects the longing to restore the country's former prestige and the security of a more strictly, if forcibly, ordered society – a trend led and followed by the present regime. In a hopeful sign, while 43% of those surveyed in July 2017 found that the repression was necessary for Stalin to bring about order, 49% asserted that repression could never be justified, and that it was a crime against humanity.[16]

Thus, despite official measures that purport to criminalise pro-Stalin propaganda,[17] the parallel process of the rehabilitation of Stalin continues – on busses, in monuments, in stores, in textbooks and in the public space. In 2016, the Communist Party of the Russian Federation (CPRF) seized the opportunity to, as it were, capitalise on this trend and the longing for order by declaring it to be the year of Stalin and the "Stalin Spring".[18] This marked the 80th anniversary of the 1936 "Stalin Constitution", proclaiming the primacy of the CPRF, while several local parties have developed initiatives to better educate the populace on Stalin. Such select remembrance led one liberal politician to cynically comment: "When they talk about the Stalin era, they imagine the holster at the side, but not the barrel to the back of their neck."[19]

---

5   See Nanci Adler, *Victims of Soviet Terror: The Story of the Memorial Movement*, Westport 1993.
6   The city-sponsored museum (in its previous incarnation, tucked away in an alley at the centre of Moscow) existed on a shoe-string budget in a very modest unpublicised form since the early 2000s.
7   http://en.kremlin.ru/events/president/news/55948 (accessed on 26 November 2020)
8   *Inter alia*, see Berber Bevernage, "Writing the past out of the present: History and the politics of time in transitional justice," *History Workshop Journal* 69 (2010): 111-131.
9   "Mikhalkov creates rival to McDonald's", *The Moscow Times* (10 April 2015).
10 Indicatively, "Krym: Na Puti k pobede" [Crimea: On the way to victory], visit to Muzei Revolutsii (Moscow, 12 April 2015).
11 Neil Macfarquhar, "A book for discerning Russians: The words of Putin," *International New York Times* (1-2 January 2016).
12 http://www.rbc.ru/politics/15/02/2017 (accessed on 21 March 2017); www.levada.ru/2016/01/13/rol-stalina-v-istorii-rossii (accessed on 13 January 2016); http://www.levada.ru/2016/03/01/praviteli-v-otechestvennoj-istorii/ (accessed on 9 March 2016).
13 www.levada.ru (accessed on 31 March 2015).
14 www.levada.ru/2016/01/13/rol-stalina-v-istorii-rossii (accessed on 13 January 2016); http://www.levada.ru/2016/03/01/praviteli-v-otechestvennoj-istorii/ (accessed on 9 March 2016).
15 http://www.levada.ru/2017/02/15/15388/ (accessed on 30 June 2017).
16 https://wciom.ru/index.php?id=236&uid=116301;https://www.novaya gazeta.ru/news/2017/07/05/133162-bolee-40-rossiyan-nazvali-stalin skie-repressii-vynuzhdennoy-meroy (both accessed on 5 July 2017).
17 Anna Dolgov, "Russian Senator introduces bill criminalizing pro-Stalin propaganda", *Moscow Times* (22 September 2015).
18 https://tvrain.ru/articles/lider_kprf_objavil_o_nastuplenii_stalinskoj_vesny-400547 (accessed on 21 December 2016).
19 Alec Luhn, "What Stalin owes Putin", *International New York Times* (12-13 March 2016).

So, the casual acceptance of repression has been successfully coupled with the valorisation of Stalin. His rise in popularity was accompanied by a sequence of measures, including the 2009 restoration of an ode to him engraved in a prominent Moscow metro station and the creation of a state commission to guard against the "falsification of history to the detriment of Russia's interests." These measures prompted human rights organisations to presciently argue in 2009 that "de-Stalinization is Russia's acutest problem at the moment."[20]

The identification of a human rights issue as Russia's "problem" is true, but the state asserts a competing truth and prioritises a different problem. As a human rights issue, the politically expedient imposition of a national amnesia regarding the Gulag undermines the integrity of the collective memory, further marginalises and victimises the dwindling generation of Gulag survivors, and is an impediment to transitional justice. By contrast, the issue prioritised by Russia's past and present rulers was not fully confronting this history of multiple regime abuses, but rather strengthening the stability and legitimacy of the regime. They were concerned about a de-Stalinisation that might emerge uncontrollably from below, a fear that is constant and probably correct.

The revelations regarding state-sponsored repression may not have been a major determinant in facilitating the collapse of the Soviet Union,[21] but their significance might be assessed from the importance placed on censoring them. Accordingly, rather than following the European example of recognising the victims and crimes of Nazism through commemoration, *Stolpersteine*, transforming campsites into memorial museums and substantive compensation, the only museum on a former Gulag site was co-opted by the authorities to misrepresent the Gulag as a bulwark against fifth column subversives seeking to undermine the Soviet people.

Nuremberg was not a voluntary exercise and it has been much criticised as victors' justice, but it set an institutional precedent for acknowledging grave violations of human rights committed by individuals and by a state system. And, despite its shortcomings, in the wake of a defeated apartheid regime, the South African Truth and Reconciliation Commission sought and forged a dialogue between official and personal narratives, and formulated an inclusive history. By contrast, decades after the collapse of Communism, we have no such history of the Soviet state's repression of its own people. And so, Russia's current official approach to the memory of Stalinism can most accurately be characterised by subverting George Santayana's oft-quoted admonition: Those who do not want to be condemned by the past should remember their history to provide a *positive* spin. The dominance of the state-sponsored or co-opted narrative reflects the persistence of a post-communist repression and totalitarian culture long after its formal demise.

Remembrance

The subject of who, what, and how to remember are particularly complicated questions in post-repressive states that believe their survival depends on the careful monitoring of selected omissions.[22] The history of the state's mass murder and terrorisation of its own citizens runs counter to the mythologised Soviet victory over the barbaric Nazi regime, a cornerstone of the state-generated narrative. Indeed, the Director of the State Archive of the Russian Federation, Sergey Mironov, was demoted in 2016 for publishing an archival document deflating the myth of the heroic defence of Moscow.[23] Moreover, an acknowledgement of culpability in Stalinist crimes undermines much that was foundational to some citizens today, such as industrialisation, the eradication of illiteracy and other achievements of the Stalinist era.[24]

For years, victims' organisations lobbied the government to acknowledge the crimes of Stalinism, present apologies, and launch a federal programme dedicated to remembering the repression.[25] Their recommendations included a call for the state to admit its culpability and acknowledge that the whole country was "one big Katyn,"[26] but they emphasised restorative justice and commemoration. Promises were offered to create a programme to eliminate the vestiges of Stalinism, but genuine official support for such an enormous mandate has been inconsistent and long in coming. For example, Medvedev was in favour of the idea of creating a data base on victims, but stopped short of supporting the request for

---

20 "Russia marks day of victims of political repressions," *Itar-TASS* (30 October 2009).
21 See Stephen Cohen, *Soviet Fates and Lost Alternatives*, New York 2009, chapter 5.
22 www.memo.ru (accessed on 12 March 2012).
23 https://snob.ru/selected/entry/94992 (accessed on 2 December 2021).
24 See Memorial's international appeal: "National Images of the Past: The twentieth century and the 'war of memories'", an appeal from the International Memorial Society" (March 2008); also see Irina Flige, "Predmetnaia i material'naia pamiat' o Bol'shom Terror" [Objective and material memory of the Painful Terror], unpublished paper (2007).
25 www.hro.org (accessed on 7 February 2011); Sergey Karaganov, "On the perpetuation of the memory of the victims of the totalitarian regime and on national reconciliation", *Rossiskaia Gazeta* (8 April 2011).
26 http://www.kremlin.ru/transcripts/10194 (accessed on 2 December 2021); see also Arsenii Roginskii, "Pamiat' o Stalinizme" [The memory of Stalinism], in E. Kandrashina et al. (eds), *Istoriia stalinizma: itogi i problem izucheniia* [History of Stalinism: Research Outcomes and Issues], Moscow 2011; Alexander J. Motyl, "Why is the 'KGB Bar' possible? Binary morality and its consequences", *Nationalities Papers* 38/5 (2010): 671-687.

a "political-legal judgment of the crimes of the Communist regime." He questioned what authority could condemn the former regime, and rejected the very idea that the state could admit culpability on behalf of the state by arguing that "legal judgments are passed by judges, not even the president or parliament."[27]

Notwithstanding all of its ambiguity, if not ambivalence regarding the Stalinist past, in 2015 the Russian government endorsed a bill on the remembrance of victims of political repression.[28] It addressed memorialisation, books of remembrance, data bases, archival access, and victim recognition and compensation. It allowed the monument to the victims of Stalin's terror to be placed in central Moscow, even if most survivors did not live to see it erected, and the city of Moscow allocated a building and funds for the construction of the Gulag Museum (see above).[29] Along with these measures, the state supported a parallel "practical patriotism", though it did not define precisely what that was. State support for a de-Stalinisation programme runs counter to the "militant patriotism"[30] it also endorses, so civil society is chronically tasked to monitor the Russian government's words and deeds.[31] Today the work of historians and civil society actors who challenge the official narrative of present or past events has become more marginalised and in some cases even dangerous.[32]

Memorial has been regularly accused of political activities and targeted for official harassment for not having declared themselves "foreign agents", in keeping with a 2012 law. They share this politically precarious status with a number of other NGOs. It appears that such state-sponsored measures could severely limit the functioning of this human rights watchdog, which emerged during Gorbachev's perestroika. In the last few years, the organisation has been increasingly threatened with liquidation (see here, Postscript).[33] In an interview I did with Memorial's founding chairman Arsenii Roginskii in Moscow on 8 April 2015, whose 2017 passing left a tremendous void in the human rights world, he reflected on the predicament of the organisation. He no longer characterised the state's obstacles to its work as "battles", rather he termed them a "chronic condition". Our interview took place outside of his office, actually literally outside.

The destruction of the museum at labour camp Perm

In 2002, I wrote: "Postwar Europe made the concentration camps an important theme in its efforts to expose the ideology and practices of fascism. Post-Soviet Russia has the potential to do the same. The beginnings are evident."[34] My discussion went on to identify and describe the efforts to transform the labour camp Perm, which Gorbachev had closed in 1987, into a museum. It was dedicated in 1995 and in subsequent years was substantially developed. Observers and participants in those years did not foresee that the government would view it as a threat that had to be eliminated.

In 2014, as electric power and water supply were shut off by the authorities, and the camp's watchtower bulldozed, it was evident that Perm's physical survival was in peril. The survival of its factual history was also imperilled by a state-run television report featuring interviews with former guards who claimed that only traitors were incarcerated in Perm. While there was no accompanying description of how citizens became labelled as "traitors" or "enemies of the people", there was accompanying praise for the "self-sacrifice and benevolence" of the camp guards. In response to this development, Irina Flige, chairman of St. Petersburg Memorial, concluded with dismay that "the executioner is masterfully ascending the hero's scaffolding."[35] Perm had become the latest battleground for contesting the history of the repression.

Katyn as a symbol of repressed history

The official efforts at acknowledging Soviet culpability for the 1940 Katyn massacre offer informative insight into the causes and effects of consistent ambivalence. In 1990 Gorbachev admitted that the Soviet Union was responsible for the murder of thousands of Polish officers in a forest near Smolensk. He handed over lists of Polish POWs to the Polish government, and instigated investigations. Yeltsin continued the de-Stalinisation trend, and in 1993 the Russian president laid a wreath as he asked forgiveness at the Warsaw monument to the victims of Katyn. In 2000, a Russian-Polish Katyn memorial gravesite was officially opened. However, by 2004 archives relating to the killings became re-classified. Memorial spent the following years battling these restrictions in court and by

---

27 www.hro.org (accessed on 7 February 2011).
28 www.government.ru/docs/19296 (accessed on 2 December 2021).
29 Vladimir Ryzhkov, "Attitude to Stalin reveals Russia's considerable divide", *Moscow Times* (22 September 2015).
30 Ivan Nechepurenko, "New policy on commemorating victims of repression at odds with actions", *The Moscow Times, John's Russia List #9* (20 August 2015).
31 www.memo.ru/d/243949.html (accessed on 2 December 2021); Lyudmila Alexandrova, "Russia condemns political repression officially", *TASS* (19 August 2015).
32 On the legal battle of researchers arrested for working in the archives, see Catriona Bass, "Controlling History", *Transitions Online* (6 December 2011).
33 www.novayagazeta.ru/news/1697854.html (accessed on 2 December 2021).

34 *The Gulag Survivor: Beyond the Soviet System*, New Brunswick 2002, p. 261.
35 Irina Flige, "Prostranstvo Gulaga: opyt i pamiat" [Gulag space: Experience and memory], unpublished paper (May 2016).

the fall of 2010 there was some progress.[36] Moreover, in April 2010 (seventy years after the tragedy), Putin joined the Polish prime minister at a wreath-laying ceremony at the site of Katyn, and called the executions of the Polish POWs a "crime of totalitarianism."

To date, there are several unresolved questions with regard to the consequences of this recognition. Victims of Soviet terror are eligible for rehabilitation (the only state-sponsored transitional justice mechanism available), however paltry the attendant privileges may be. But the Rehabilitation Law still eludes the surviving families of these victims, and the General Procuracy still refuses to name names of the individual perpetrators. In 2012, the European Court of Human Rights in Strasbourg found that ten of its applicants (families of Katyn victims) suffered a "double trauma", first losing their relatives, and then being subjected to "prolonged denial of information, together with dismissive and contradictory replies by the Russian authorities."[37] Some judges voiced the criticism for turning a "long history of justice delayed into a permanent case of justice denied."[38]

Not surprisingly, in this environment of mixed messages and politicised history, a 2010 survey found that only 43% of those polled knew anything about Katyn, 19% considered the Soviets responsible, and 28% maintained that the Nazis committed the crime; 53% weren't sure who was responsible.[39] The fact that nearly one-third of those polled still viewed the Nazis as the perpetrators of this massacre demonstrates the official and public unwillingness to fully confront this part of the nation's past.

National memory and the national narrative: State-generated history

The memory of the Gulag has not yet found an accommodating place in the national memory. While the current Russian administration can not get the historical genie back into the political bottle, they have attempted to constrain its effects.[40] Many Soviet leaders were concerned about de-Stalinisation and imposed limitations accordingly. Apparently, an accurate account of the victimisations under seven decades of Soviet rule could not be included in a Soviet history that Russians would be proud of – unless this disclosure was coupled with pride in the government's pledge to deal with the damage wrought by Stalin. The expedient solution they arrived at was to construct a purposively incomplete history that marginalised the repression and the Gulag. This strategy permits the government to condemn the Soviet terror and control history at the same time by co-opting some of the tasks of civil society.

The reforms a government imposes on curricula are clear indicators of what it wants students to learn about – and from – the past.[41] It is also the case that, although educational materials are fashioned to reflect the views of the government, in practice teachers still feel free to disregard the content of the official textbooks. The approved account of the history taught in Russian high schools today is a sanitised version of the Stalinist past. Putin, who famously decried the collapse of the Soviet Union as "the greatest geopolitical catastrophe of the 20th century" in a nationally broadcast address in 2005,[42] was an influential advocate of this narrative. He later argued that Russia should not be made to feel guilty about the Great Purge of 1937, because "in other countries, even worse things happened."[43] Putin admitted that there were some "problematic pages" in his country's history, but asked in the same breath what state had not had these.[44] This stance is part consequence and part symptom of the fact that Russia made no substantial attempts to come to terms with the legacy of Soviet communism. On the one hand, it has been impelled to disapprove of repression by prominent Russians like Solzhenitsyn, Sakharov, Khrushchev, and Gorbachev, among others. On the other hand, its leaders and many of its citizenry have become dependent on repression to maintain stability.[45]

In 2008, in an effort to promote patriotism among younger people, a manual for teachers covering the period 1900-1945 was officially approved for use in schools.[46] Achieving such a goal through the use of History required a considerable manipulation of the facts as well as contriving creative interpretations. Witness this revealing illustration of the systemic bias built into the state-

---

36 Aleksandr Gur'ianov, ""Katynskaia problema' v sovremennoi Rossii" [The "Katyn problem" in modern Russia], *30 Oktiabria* 97 (2010).
37 www.concernedhistorians.org/le/259.pdf (accessed on 2 December 2021), p. 37 and article 165 on p. 42.
38 *Janowiec and Others v. Russia* [GC], nos. 55508/07 and 29520/09, 160 (21 October 2013).
39 Levada Centre, "Rossiisko-Pol'skie otnoshenie i Katynskii rasstrel" [Russian-Polish relations and the Katyn executions], 8 April 2010.
40 *Ukaz* 549 (15 May 2009), www.politru.dokumenty/presidentprosledit (accessed on 4 December 2021); A.V. Filippov et al. (eds), *Noveishaia istoriia Rossii, 1945-2006 gg.: Kniga dlia uchitelia,* [Contemporary History of Russia, 1945-2006: A Teacher's Text-Book], Moscow 2007; A.S. Barsenkov & A.I. Vdovin, *Istoriia Rossii, 1917-2009* [History of Russia, 1917-2009], Moscow 2010.
41 Elizabeth A. Cole, "Transitional justice and the reform of History Education", *The International Journal of Transitional Justice* 1 (2007): 115-137.
42 http://archive.kremlin.ru/text/appears/2005/04/87049.shtml (accessed on 4 December 2021).
43 Douglas Birch, "Vietnam worse than Stalin purges," *Associated Press* (21 June 2007).
44 Leon Aron, "The problematic pages", *The New Republic* (24 September 2008).
45 Adler, *The Gulag...*; Idem, *Keeping Faith with the Party: Communist Believers Return from the Gulag,* Bloomington 2012.
46 A.V. Filippov et al. (eds), *Istoriia Rossii, 1900-1945: kniga dlia uchitelia* [History of Russia, 1900-1945: A Teacher's Text-Book], Moscow 2008

sponsored narrative found in a later manual. It instructed teachers to address the period of Stalinist repressions by focusing on "what we built in the 1930s."[47] They were told to explain that "Stalin acted in a concrete historical situation, as a leader he acted entirely rationally – as the guardian of the system."[48] Since the scope of the repression does not readily fit into the concept of "rational governance", the manual suggests working the numbers a bit.[49] The fact that some youth organisations today proudly proclaim "we leapt forward, we created a country of tanks from a country of ploughs"[50] attests to the effectiveness of this history lesson.

In 2014 the Putin administration initiated the creation of a textbook whose narrative would present a "unitary vision", emphasising the role of Stalin as an "effective manager." The central message was to be: "We are citizens of a Great Country with a Great Past;" Putin recommended that there be no "dual interpretations."[51] On top of that, in 2014 a Soviet-era publisher gained dominance of the textbook market. So, despite the introduction of Solzhenitsyn's *Gulag Archipelago* into the high school curriculum (an initiative supported, if not driven, by Putin), a subtext of this history lesson is that the political ethos was perhaps not fully ready to change. In fact, that much-publicised gesture was "Potemkin-like",[52] because Solzhenitsyn's text was used for *Literature* – not *History* – classes. However, while a culture of repression persists, there have been important political changes, which include the fact that the *Gulag Archipelago* and similar works, which were prohibited from being published in the Soviet Union, and even illegal to possess, are readily available.

Truth and the national narrative

In 2009 the state undertook the management of the historical narrative with the establishment of a Commission to Counter Attempts to Falsify History to the Detriment of Russian Federation Interests.[53] The commission was made up of state and public officials and historians, who were charged with looking at past events for misrepresented or manipulated facts that cast Russia in a negative light. Civil society organisations expressed concern that the "struggle against the falsification of History" was becoming an "affair of the state," because, they cautioned, the state can not be the arbiter of the "truth".[54]

But the question of who should be the arbiter is beyond complex, as attested by the experience of international criminal tribunals that are challenged by the persistence of incompatible and coexisting "truths",[55] based on the different perceptions of different groups, as well as different interpretations of those perceptions.[56] Thus, contending parties often enter and leave the court with "their own truths" still intact.[57] The moral credo of the South African Truth and Reconciliation Commission was that "the truth will set us free." That discussion becomes complicated when we recognise the co-existence of different truths, some explicit, and some implicit. One of Medvedev's last measures as acting president in 2012 was to dissolve the dubious History Commission.[58] A History Commission with a mandate to identify and analyse areas of agreement and disagreement on past events would have made a better contender for public trust.

However, the influence of verified facts could still be challenged by the influence of comforting fictions. For example, disconfirming evidence did not refute the idealistic claims of communist loyalists who had endured the Gulag, because their claims rested on other "truths", namely faith-based beliefs. Those who had incorporated the Party's narrative into their own struggled to accommodate to the post-Soviet revelations

---

47 "Stanovlenie mobilizatsionnoi politicheskoi sistemy" [The formation of a system of political mobilisation], www.prosv.ru/ebooks/Danilov_Istoria_1900-1945/12.html (accessed on 14 March 2012).
48 *Ibid*; Filippov et al. (2008), *op. cit.*, p. 19 and 267.
49 "Uchitel'iam istorii veleno prepodnosit' stalinskii terror kak ratsional'nyi instrument razvitiia strany" [History teachers are ordered to present the Stalinist terror as a rational tool for the country's development] www.newsru.com (accessed on 25 August 2008).
50 "Ensuring Stalin's victims are not forgotten", http://www.bbc.com/news/world-35611709 (accessed on 2 March 2016).
51 Lyudmila Aleksandrova, "Work on standard Russian History manual proves really daunting task", *Itar-Tass* (26 September 2013).
52 Arsenii Roginskii, Comment at "International Symposium on the Legacy of the Gulag and the Remembrance of Stalinism", Amsterdam 8 November 2013.
53 *Ukaz* 549 (15 May 2009), www.politru.dokumenty/presidentprosledit (accessed on 4 December 2021).
54 Paul Goble, "Medvedev Historical Falsification Commission 'Harmful' or 'Useless', Memorial expert says", *Window on Eurasia* (20 May 2009). Also see Vladimir Ryzhkov, "History under lock and key", *The Moscow Times* (9 June 2009), and "Medvedev seen making History more 'Politicized' with creation of Commission", *Vedomosti* (19 May 2009).
55 See Erin Daly, "Truth scepticism: An inquiry into the value of truth in times of transition", *The International Journal of Transitional Justice* 2 (2008): 23-41.
56 This, despite the efforts of the International Criminal Tribunal for the Former Yugoslavia to set the record straight, overcome ambiguity, and "police a violent past"; Roland Kostic, *Ambivalent Peace: External Peacebuilding, Threatened Identity and Reconciliation in Bosnia and Herzegovina*, Uppsala 2007, p. 33.
57 Andreas Gross, "Draft resolution and report on the use of experience of 'Truth Commissions'", Report to the Council of Europe (4 December 2007), p. 8.
58 Iuliia Kantor, "Bez falsifikatsii: 'Istoricheskaia' komissia pri prezidente raspushchena" [No falsification: "Historical" presidential Commission disbanded], *Moskovskie Novosti*, http://mn.ru/society_history/20120319/313741427 (accessed on 5 September 2012).

of Soviet injustice. For example, Mariia Kuznetsova, one of my interviewees for a project studying the enduring loyalty to the Party among Gulag prisoners and returnees, reported that she had managed to maintain a limited view of the chronology and scope of the repression up until Gorbachev lifted the censorship on public discussions of the terror. Mariia found herself forced to revisit and re-assess the old interpretations of the repression that she had learned from her mother and her cohorts. Now she was exposed to the fact that Lenin had used physical coercion to promote the communist ideology. She was embarrassed to admit: "I was the last of everyone I knew to really understand that so much of the system of repression started with Lenin, we always wrote everything off to Stalin." Mariia would have preferred to remain oblivious to this because it undermined so much that was foundational to her understanding of her family and her country. She had to search anew for meaning. She explained: "It was very hard, you lose the ground beneath your feet because you don't understand what the truth is."[59] However, many were protected from disillusionment by the state's positive revision of History, along with their own self-imposed censorship, both of which outlasted the official demise of communism.

Remembering (or reconstructing) the past

Since Stalin's death, the view of the Stalinist past has been adjusted to fit the state's needs. Organisations, such as Memorial, view the efforts to hide the scope and consequences of the repression as an unhealthy lost opportunity to learn from mistakes of the past. Its efforts to bring the full history of Stalinism into the arena of public discourse are regularly discouraged, and occasionally co-opted.

Semën Samuilovich Vilenskii, whose death at the age of 88 in 2016 marked the end of an era, was incensed by the fact that there had never been a moral condemnation of the CPSU. He spoke with the authority as head of the victims' organisation *Vozvrashchenie* (The Return), a Kolyma survivor, memoir publisher, and the only member of the Rehabilitation Commission who had been a Stalin-era prisoner. He further asserted that Russia would benefit from a "Nuremberg Trial without blood."[60] He ventured that those found guilty of these crimes against humanity could receive the maximum penalty, and then be pardoned. Vilenskii was one of the last remaining survivors of the Stalinist era. Until the end of his life, he called for the state to "recognise and repent".[61] However,

Arsenii Roginskii, an ex-prisoner of the dissident era and fellow member of the Rehabilitation Commission, argued that identifying victims is only the first step in dealing with the repression; identifying their oppressors, still mostly unnamed, is the next step toward remediating the past and improving the future.[62]

Stalinism and its victims occupy a lacuna in the nation's image of itself. But the vanishing community of Gulag returnees remains determined to remember, to record, and to publicise the crimes committed in the name of Soviet communism. Their efforts have been met by strong official resistance, because Russia has invested heavily in the creation of its purposively incomplete official history. In the Soviet era, there was a fairly consistent recognition that a fuller history of the repression could undermine the legitimacy of the regime, and in the post-Soviet era the gilded version of the past has been promoted as an inspiring rallying point for patriotism and national pride. In consequence, more than twenty-five years after the end of the Soviet Union, Russia crafted an approach to its Stalinist history that would burnish its national image: Its citizens were encouraged to flip past the "problematic pages" and focus on the "bright past" of national achievements.

This question brings me to a personal reflection. Over thirty-five years ago, on my first trip to the Soviet Union in 1983, as an American student, my movements were restricted and monitored from when I first stepped on Soviet soil, so there was little conversation of any substance during the one-hour taxi ride from the airport. By contrast, in the late Soviet and post-Soviet years, surveillance had become so much less restrictive that the hour of passage from Sheremetyevo airport to the city became my grapevine to the man on the street and the kinds of issues that had entered the public space. On one of my recent visits to Moscow, I abandoned my standard entry ritual for the modernisation of a high-speed train, and there I happened on a revealing indicator of the self-image that Russia is promoting for domestic consumption. The train's television monitor was airing an advertisement trumpeting the achievements of the city of Moscow. Under the heading "Era of Construction", it showed buildings constructed between 1948 and 1953, and informed the viewer that many more such structures had been planned, but the construction work – it seemed to imply "regrettably" – had stopped. The reason, it stated, was that Stalin died in 1953. Indeed, a number of construction projects – most of them dependent on forced labour – ceased when the dictator died. In these concrete images, we are asked to behold Stalin's contribution to the "bright past".

---

59 See Adler, *Keeping Faith...*, *op. cit.*
60 Author's interview with Semën (Moscow, 18 November 2003).
61 Author's interview with Semën (Moscow, 30 October 2011).

62 Roginskii, "Pamiat' o stalinizma", *op. cit.*, p. 23.

What can be concluded from all of this? In actual history, the chronology of events moves from past to present, and historical scholarship thrives on the assumption that the past produces the present. But in Russia's politicised history – and, as noted above, Russia is not unique in this practice – it is the present that produces the past by choosing which parts of the past should be remembered and how they should be construed. In consequence what could have been a *useable* "lessons learned from the past" history of Russia has been subverted. It now takes the form of what the needs of the present require the history of Russia to be. While integrating the story of the terror into the mainstream history of Russia is a relatively straightforward task at the level of historical scholarship, it has been frustrated by political obstacles. Overcoming them would require a fundamental shift from a system of governance that devalues human rights, toward a democratic ethos that prioritises them, which would include undertaking transitional justice measures.

However, the Russian government's efforts to focus attention on the material and military benefits under Stalin and de-emphasise Stalin's crimes suggest that promoting this skewed version of history is the best mechanism available for sustaining repressive governance. In consequence, organisations pursuing an accurate history of the Stalinist past are at risk for being charged with engaging in undesired political activity, and even of attempting to overthrow the Russian government. For example, in its continued crackdown on so-called "foreign agents", in 2016 the Ministry of Justice raided Memorial in Moscow and seized documentation from the previous four years, nearly 32,000 pages.

The survival of civil society depends on both the survival of the state and the individuals it governs. The narrative accounts of each should intertwine. However, such intertwining is proscribed in a post-Soviet Russia since it is attempting to relegate Stalin's repression to the past without recognising its impact on the present. From the foregoing, one might reasonably speculate that while the current regime may recognise the national and international resistance to repression, they fear that the only alternative would be the chaos that followed the dissolution of the Soviet Union. This approach has narrowed the field to two major narratives of the repression that compete for dominance in the informal marketplace of public opinion: The stories of the victims and survivors, still seeking recognition by and compensation from the government, and the official redacted history, aiming to both sanitise Stalin's repression and persuade the public that the survival of the state required the suppression of individual rights – and still does. This latter message has gained the competitive edge. The cost of Russia's inability and unwillingness to fully acknowledge its history of repression is one that will be borne by all successor regimes. It can be controlled by constant vigilance, but it is expensive to sustain and has the potential to be destabilising.

Concluding reflections

Given that the "bright future" of Communism now belongs to the "bright past" of the Soviet empire, what changes can be made in the present to actually proceed toward a bright future? In a broader context, this question is relevant to any number of states struggling to come to terms with a repressive past. To be sure, since many look back with pride at the accomplishments under the former regime, or remember it differently than it was, or differently from one another, it is not clear whether and how a confrontation with the factually accurate history would change such perceptions. Nor is it clear how much ability or willingness there is in any given group/nation/individual to undergo the wrenching process of self-judgment.[63]

On the other hand, we might be able to bridge the gulf between the official histories of repressive regimes and the personal narratives of victims by delineating the areas of agreement, disagreement, and negotiability. This endeavour has been neatly framed as "doing History, doing Justice."[64] It refers to the conciliatory effects of collating and analysing historically entrenched disagreements into a "shared narrative."[65] Furthermore, a recognition and analysis of the dilemmas conveyed in the multitude of "small stories", which qualitative research could document, will inform the approach that transitional justice must take in grappling with broadly diffused notions of moral or legal culpability. An understanding of such experiences could be incorporated in new and constructive public narratives.

Accordingly, the opening of archives in Russia or elsewhere, the proper placement of those records that have been accessed for, and produced by international tribunals, the exhumation and forensic examination of mass graves, and the gathering and analysing of personal and legal testimonies could provide the public with the "shared custody"[66] of a "common past", necessary for social repair. The "brightness" of the actual past may be dimmed for some, but in this age of transitional justice,

---

63   See the discussion in Elazar Barkan, "Truth and reconciliation in History", *American Historical Review* 114/4 (2009): 899-913.
64   See the thought-provoking discussion in Charles S. Maier, "Doing History, doing Justice: The narrative of the historian and of the Truth Commission", in Robert I. Rotberg & Denis Thompson (eds), *Truth v. Justice: The Morality of Truth Commissions*, Princeton 2000, p. 261-278.
65   Barkan, *op. cit.*, p. 903.
66   Erik Ketelaar, "Truth, memories and histories in the archives of the ICTY," unpublished paper delivered at the conference to mark the 60th anniversary of the Genocide Convention, The Hague (8 December 2008), p. 13.

a national process of reckoning might achieve sufficient consensus to interrupt the perennial recycling of old repressions into newly "justified" repressions – that have included the repression of the victims' stories. There is support, however limited, for such an approach in Russia. Arsenii Roginskii, an ardent advocate for non-violent change, emphasised the importance of the story we tell to ourselves and to others: "Society and the state will need to work together; and historians bear a special responsibility in this process."[67]

It may be that an inclusive history that recognises the victims and their heirs, while it verifies, analyses, records, acknowledges, and seeks to understand the competing narratives on the past could facilitate a shift from duelling monologues to engaging dialogues. Such a common undertaking might move Russia beyond the post-communist impasse, and shorten the long shadow of repression.

Postscript February 2022

On 11 November 11 2021, the Supreme Court of the Russian Federation gave notice to the International Memorial Society that the General Prosecutor's Office filed to liquidate the organisation.[68] This legal action followed years of harassment of Memorial by the authorities – now under the guise of failing to conform to the notorious 2012 "foreign agent" law (alleging that organisations which receive foreign donations, support foreign interests). Its researchers have also been arrested on other spurious charges.

Memorial began in 1987 as an eleven-person signature campaign for a monument to victims of Soviet terror under the honorary chairmanship of Andrei Sakharov, and had since grown into the most authoritative research centre on Stalinism today. In its 35 years, Memorial gathered thousands of eyewitness testimonies from Gulag victims and produced outstanding scholarly reference works on the Stalinist state apparatus. As attested by numerous accounts above, more than a generation of researchers benefitted from the material (sometimes literally) unearthed by Memorial.

At the end of December 2021, thirty years since the dissolution of the Soviet Union, the Procuracy of the Russian Federation decreed the liquidation of the International Memorial Society, and, days later, the liquidation of its Human Rights branch. Memorial had been in a tug of war with the state for years on how the story of the Stalinist past should be told. In its decades of operation, Memorial was faced with many existential challenges, but it managed to endure, and even prevail. Arsenii Roginskii foresaw that Memorial could simply be liquidated with fines; it ended up being forced out of existence with legislation. Ironically, in its nascent days, the Soviet regime had tried to use legislation to bar Memorial from establishing itself and growing. It did not succeed. The fact that the current regime was able to succeed in its move against the organisation manifests an entrenched, systemic repression, complete with hostility to freedom of expression, and the erosion of intellectual and academic freedom in Russia today.

---

67 Roginskii, "Pamiat' o stalinizma", *op. cit.*, p. 27.
68 https://www.memo.ru/en-us/memorial/departments/intermemorial/news/625 (accessed on 2 February 2022).

The Narratives of the Survivors of Srebrenica

Selma Leydesdorff

Abstract
The chapter is based on my oral history book with the testimonies of women who survived the massacre of Srebrenica. *Surviving the Bosnian Genocide: The Women of Srebrenica Speak* (Indiana University Press, 2015) is not a book about the genocide itself but rather discusses how the events of 1995 interrupted their lives, lives that would never be the same again. These are life stories about mourning, about rage, directed particularly against the Dutch whose army did not deliver on its promise of protection, and about disappointment that the world has forsaken the inhabitants of a small flourishing town.

The memories of genocide survivors contrast sharply with the reports and analyses through which the political debate has been conducted. Documents rarely mention the survivors and are, for the most part, commissioned by national governments. It is vital for survivors that their full voices be heard in the public domain. They want their ordeal to be known and their suffering to be acknowledged. In my opinion, the history of the war must include their own personal stories and perceptions of betrayal, survival and isolation. It should reflect their recollections of the mass murder and their efforts to come to terms with it. The debates and lawsuits on compensation that ensued after the carnage in Bosnia and Kosovo also demonstrate the need for the international community to acknowledge its utter failure in response to the Balkan Wars of the 1990s and to take the perspectives of the survivors seriously.

While the West intervened in the Balkan Wars, albeit only after the deaths of countless Bosnians, not enough thought has gone into how to bring about peace in damaged communities and to assuage the unsettled feelings of the many traumatised people living either in Bosnia or in the Diaspora. It is the case that sorrow, poverty and isolation persist. We tend to forget that the victims' core desire is usually for recognition, which goes far beyond financial compensation. Whoever looks at the survivors' wishes or reads the many psychological reports will see that the absolute central desire is to return to a normal daily life and to escape the legal and administrative web. These people are extremely poor; many still live in refugee camps.

During interviews, accounts of catastrophes are not immediately comprehensible. Narratives of trauma are not straightforwardly referential; rather, they are expressions of "a crisis of witnessing." The eyewitness account is rooted in dislocations of history. Whoever has interviewed trauma cases knows that chronology fails, lapses occur, and confusion is normal. Talking about trauma often means reliving it in all of its pain, difficulty, fear, confusion, and shame. I have called the stories behind the interviews a second voice, but I should write it in plural, because we deal with polyphony. In my chapter, I present and discuss examples of this polyphony.

Background

When war erupted in Bosnia in 1992, the federative entity that used to be called Yugoslavia – the multiethnic communist state that had existed for decades – crumbled. At that time, new nations began to declare their independence; Bosnia did so in 1991.[1] In Eastern Bosnia, Muslims became the victims of a brutal and bloodthirsty purge by various Serbian forces and the Serbian Army, which consisted of murder, rape on a massive scale, plundering, and forced relocation.[2]

The situation was so out of control in 1993 that the United Nations designated "safe areas" or "safe enclaves" in the region and sent in troops to protect the Muslims. Srebrenica, a small town sequestered in a fertile valley in Eastern Bosnia, was one of them. After it was declared a UN safe area, thousands of Muslims from surrounding villages fled to the town in search of safety. Despite the UN's guarantee of protection, Srebrenica was under constant shelling from forces in the surrounding hills. Tragically, the peacekeepers were unable to prevent a humanitarian disaster. There were no medical supplies, water and electricity had been cut off, food convoys were denied access, and the population was starving. The troops sent by the UN had a limited mandate and were insufficiently armed to keep peace in an area where a violent war was raging. Srebrenica was first protected by the Canadian Army and, later, by soldiers of the Dutch Army under the command of the United Nations. Despite promises of safekeeping, the town fell into Serb hands on 11 July 1995. Before the massacre of Srebrenica began, UN soldiers herded women, children, and older men into the UN compound at Potočari, where they expected to find shelter. However, in the days after the fall of Srebrenica, 7,749 people were killed, mostly men. The large majority who entered the compound at Potočari perished in the massacre. Although many younger men opted to flee through the woods to territory controlled by the Bosnian Army rather than enter the compound, only a few made it to safety.[3]

Besides the massive slaughter, the outcome of the events was very unclear in the Netherlands. While some accused the Dutch Army of murder since it had stood by and allowed it to happen, others proclaimed they had done a very good job. Indeed, the largest genocide since the Second World War had taken place under the eyes of Dutch soldiers. I am one of those in the Netherlands who is convinced that examining the role of the inadequately armed and unprepared soldiers, as well as the failing leadership of the military and the Dutch government, should teach us, the Dutch, a critical lesson. Instead, from the beginning, there have been powerful attempts to cover up what happened, and over the years that has not changed. For example, soldiers were ordered not to speak, rolls of film vanished, and contact with the victims was discouraged.

In fact, during the first days after the fall, the Press was informed that the mission to protect the population had been successful. Several days later, however, news of the mass murder appeared, and the Dutch population came to know that their soldiers had passively watched the Serbs separate the men from the women. An official inquiry was then started to reach an "independent judgment" about the role of the Dutch Army. When the findings of this inquiry were presented, angry women-survivors from Bosnia walked out of the presentation. I was shocked by the vagueness of the conclusions of the inquiry and the firm and intense rejection of them by the women. This is how my research started. Elsewhere, I describe the attempts of the Dutch government to hinder me from performing my research based on contact with survivors.[4] But I managed to gather the necessary funds to travel and undertake much needed research since other people as well no longer believed what they were told.[5]

My criticism is not only concerned with a distorted representation of what occurred, but also with the way in which victimisation was claimed by the traumatised Dutch soldiers. Their standing by and watching events was virulently criticised by many. There is an argument that standing by is morally and legally abetting the genocide because no help is given to people clearly in need.[6] This argument was confirmed by testimonies and a complaint filed against the Dutch state and the United Nations. The outcome of the war has had powerful and widespread reverberations, with monumental suffering. However, to

---

* The chapter bears some similarity with my "Narratives of the survivors of Srebrenica: How do they reconnect to the world?", in Elissa Bemporad & Joyce W. Warren (eds), *Women and Genocide, Survivors, Victims, Perpetrators*, Indiana 2018, p. 250-268. But the argument is different, since here I focus on the distortion of juridical language and official reports.

1 Sabrina Ramet, *The Three Yugoslavias: State-Building and Legitimation, 1918-2005*, Indiana 2006.

2 Edina Bećirević, *Genocide on the Drina River*, New Haven 2014.

3 David Rohde, *Endgame: The Betrayal and Fall of Srebrenica. Europe's Worst Massacre since World War II*, New York 1997.

4 Selma Leydesdorff, *Surviving the Bosnian Genocide. The Women of Srebrenica Speak*, Indiana 2011.

5 *Idem*, "When communities fell apart and neighbors became enemies: Stories of bewilderment in Srebrenica", in Nanci Adler et al. (eds), *Memories of Mass Repression. Narrating Stories in the Aftermath of Atrocity*, New Brunswick 2009, p. 21-40.

6 Nsongurua Udombana, "When neutrality is a sin: The Darfur crisis and the crisis of humanitarian intervention in Sudan", *Human Rights Quarterly* 27/4 (2005): 1149-1199; Erviv Staub, "Preventing genocide: Activating bystanders, helping victims, and the creation of caring", *Peace and Conflict: Journal of Peace Psychology* 2/3 (1996): 189-200; Arne Johan Vetlesen, "Genocide: A case for the responsibility of the bystander", *Journal of Peace Research* 37/4 (2000): 519-532.

the extent that it has remained solely within the private sphere of the survivors, the pain has become nearly invisible to the rest of the world.

Although there are no reliable statistics, I am inclined to concur with those authors who connect the widespread occurrence of domestic violence with war trauma.[7] In Bosnia, most families have also become single-parent families, and the women are less able to provide adequate role models for the many young men who were children during the war. Consequently, crime and unemployment are rampant. In truth, an entire generation has grown up in mud and dirt, with a hostile attitude towards a world that has forsaken them, failed to recognise their justified need to be acknowledged, and has not helped them to locate their loved ones. When we hear Bosnian women speaking up in the public arena, it is almost always in a court of law that is prosecuting the perpetrators, which means that their words only concern the war and the genocide.[8] A few, albeit sporadically, lawsuits focus on current living conditions and on how social networks have been destroyed and upward social mobility impaired.

Within the framework of this chapter, there is no place to expand on the several relevant judicial procedures and lawsuits. The international debate over who was responsible has continued. While we live now decades later, I am happy to note that the mood is changing. But, it has been a slow process. Although some judicial verdicts have been in favour of survivors, there still is no general recognition that something went horribly wrong. There is also another rather unexpected outcome of what happened: Many soldiers who were deployed have been severely traumatised. In some way, this trauma, while becoming the dominating discourse in the public domain, has started to conceal the fate of the real victims in television shows, in the Press, and in representations of the Bosnian war. The people who survived seem to have disappeared from public awareness. The soldiers want recompensation. Moreover, no one seems to care about those who still live in dire conditions and were victims of trauma that was often worse than that of the soldiers. It is also the case that many people do not want to be reminded of the role of the Dutch Army. In 2011 an official memorial centre was opened in Potočari and a documentary was shown on Dutch television.[9] Two conflicting stories about Srebrenica were being presented. Several times, the women survivors threatened to dissociate themselves from the centre. As for the documentary, it is very Dutch, part of the national obsession with Dutchbat, the name of the battalion serving in Srebrenica and, also, of the organisation of traumatised soldiers.

The memories of the genocide survivors contrast sharply with the reports and analyses through which the political debate is conducted. Documents rarely mention the survivors and are, for the most part, commissioned by national governments.[10] It is vital to the survivors that their full voices be heard in the public domain. They want their ordeal to be known and their suffering to be acknowledged. In my opinion, the history of the war must include their own personal stories and perceptions of betrayal, survival and isolation. It should reflect their recollections of the mass murder and their efforts to come to terms with it. This suppression of their experience has led them to accuse the international community and the Dutch Army of "betraying" them. I witnessed how, over the years, sadness and tears have been transformed and made antiseptic by judicial language. The testimonies in the writ of summons against the state of the Netherlands and the United Nations on 4 June 2007 are clearly accusatory, although it appears that these were the outcome of open interviews.[11] I have always been amazed at how, in the long and open interviews that I held, there was so much more within them than I had anticipated. We oral historians interpret silences and search for hidden stories.[12] This is our unique and essential contribution to clarifying the past. The debates and lawsuits that ensued after the carnage in Bosnia and Kosovo also demonstrate the need for the international community to acknowledge its utter failure in response to the Balkan Wars of the 1990s and to take the perspectives of the survivors seriously.

Going to court was not an obvious solution for the organisations of survivors. I was in the process of

---

7   Esmina Avdibegović & Osman Sinanović, "Consequences of domestic violence on women's mental Health in Bosnia and Herzegovina", *Croatian Medical Journal* 47/ 5 (2006): 730-741.
8   Dubravka Zarkov & Marlies Glasius (eds), *Narratives of Justice In and Out of the Courtroom: Former Yugoslavia and Beyond*, New York 2014.
9   https://srebrenicamemorial.org/en/news/netherlands-compensations-commission-potocari-visited-the-srebrenica-memorial-center/73; "Srebrenica, 16 jaar later" [Srebrenica, 16 years on] https://www.npo.nl/de-reunie/24-04-2011/KRO_1440703 (both accessed on 11 December 2021).
10 Indicatively, Nederlands Instituut voor Oorlogsdocumentatie, *Srebrenica, een "veilig" gebied: Reconstructie, achtergronden, gevolgen en analyses van een "Safe Area"* [Srebrenica, a "Safe" Area: Reconstruction, Background, Consequences and Analyses of a "Safe Area"], Amsterdam 2002.
11 https://www.internationalcrimesdatabase.org/Case/769/Mothers-of-Srebrenica-v-the-Netherlands-and-the-UN/ (accessed on 11 December 2021).
12 Selma Leydesdorff, "How shall we remember Srebrenica? Will the language of Law structure our memory?" in Yifat Gutman et al. (eds), *Memory and the Future. Transnational Politics, Ethics and Society*, London, 2010, p. 121-137.

interviewing when some important spokeswomen protested that such a procedure would not bring back the missing, and that attention should be much more focused on building the collective cemetery and a commemoration site. They were also worried that, while focusing on legal procedures, women would neglect to build up their lives or improve the horrible living conditions in their dilapidated neighbourhoods and camps. Most of all, they dreaded the psychological effects of their rage being presented in a lawsuit. In the end, 6,000 female survivors supported the writ of summons.

While the 1995 Dayton Agreement stopped the bloodshed, it established a system that instituted territorial separation on the basis of ethnicity. Srebrenica is located within the Serb part of Bosnia Herzegovina, and those who have dared to return have had to deal with the administration of a hostile entity. Many feel threatened there, while other survivors are too traumatised to return. I am convinced that the language of the Law and judicial thinking have removed the possibility of reintegrating feelings of deep traumatisation, although it is unclear if this would ever have been possible anyway. While the West intervened in the Balkan Wars of the 1990s, albeit only after the deaths of countless Bosnians, not enough thought has gone into how to bring about peace in damaged communities and to assuage the unsettled feelings of the many traumatised people living either in Bosnia or in the Diaspora.[13] It is the case that sorrow, poverty and isolation persist.

Talking to the victims

From 2002 until 2008, I travelled between Amsterdam and Bosnia, interviewing the female survivors of Srebrenica. At that time, many lived in shelters, camps and apartments that had been abandoned because of the war. While interviewing, I started to realise that the destitute women I was speaking with originated in a small, economically flourishing, town, where there was a large civil society composed of a middle class and skilled labourers. Interviewing in the refugee camps means adapting to the culture of a devastated remote countryside. In the early years, reaching some places meant crossing a small path through mine fields. As a historian, I was not used to such conditions. In fact, I like text; I am not particularly keen on doing fieldwork. However, in this case, it was essential. The women that I interviewed were well aware that the Dutch soldiers were no match for the heavily-armed Serbian forces. They also knew that the Dutch Army was not experienced in real war, nor did they have orders to fight. Their mandate was simply to separate the parties. In fact, however, they looked on while men and women were separated, and women with small children were evacuated to safe territories.

Both legal discourse and historical discourse attempt to understand the history of an epoch and its causality, but their outcomes are different. For instance, as a historian, I researched the daily life of Srebrenica during the siege (1992-1995). Early on, most information came from official reports and from the International Criminal Tribunal for the Former Yugoslavia (ICTY). The first type of information tended to meet the demands of the subsequent official Dutch commissions, whereas the second type, the demands of the law. Both presented a specific image of the town under siege, an image that was filtered through the lens of knowing that the people there would be slaughtered. Their common task was to discover who was accountable and to assign responsibility. Nonetheless, the picture that emerges is one of a people who were doomed.[14] But the people living there were not aware that they were going to be killed. Another, equally and perhaps more, viable perspective shows a town that was vibrant and full of people who strongly believed that they would survive because they were protected by the United Nations. There were also sharp divisions between population groups, with an upper class of endogenous inhabitants and masses of newcomers. In the end, of course, they were all destined for death and misery. It is certainly not the writ of summons alone that has provoked a transformation in attitudes and language. Many women I interviewed had testified at the ICTY and at the various local courts that have been established in the region. The massive attention given to the testimonies there has transformed the story of pain into defence and accusation. Feelings of revenge arise so easily, but revenge is in direct opposition to the building up of a town and a countryside where people can live together again.[15] A commitment to revenge would be utterly destructive, as people have to live on the same street with men who have committed crimes against Bosniaks or on the next plot of land that is owned by a Serb.

Recognition

We tend to forget that the victims' core desire is usually for recognition,[16] which goes far beyond financial compensation. Drawing on Hegel, political philosopher Nancy Fraser has described recognition as

> An ideal reciprocal relation between subjects, in which each sees the other both as its equal and also as separate from it. This relation is constitutive for subjectivity: one becomes an individual subject only by virtue of recognizing, and being recognized

---

13 Lara Nettlefield & Sarah Wagner, *Srebrenica in the Aftermath of Genocide*, New York 2013.

14 Leydesdorff, *Surviving...*, *op. cit.*, chapter V.

15 Laurel Fletcher & Harvey Weinstein, "Violence and social repair: Rethinking the contribution of justice to reconciliation", *Human Rights Quarterly* 24 (2002): 601-603.

16 Nancy Fraser & Axel Honneth, *Redistribution or Recognition? A Political-Philosophical Exchange*, London 2003.

by, another subject. Recognition from others is thus essential to the development of a sense of self. To be denied recognition – or to be "misrecognised" – is to suffer both a distortion of one's relation to one's self and an injury to one's identity.[17]

And this happens, I would add, because it involves reconnection to a society and a world that seem to have been lost.

Money does not revalidate the right to exist as a human being, which is a crucial factor in being able to go on living. No juridical act or decision does either. Whoever looks at the survivors' wishes or reads the many psychological reports will see that the absolute central desire is to return to a normal daily life and to escape the legal and administrative web. These people are extremely poor; many still live in refugee camps. Money constitutes mere materialisation of their grief. But, in terms of psychological state and need, they are in a totally different place.

One could argue that Srebrenica was "only" less than thirty years ago, so the pain is still acute. Although the loss of loved ones is more important than anything else, poverty adds qualitatively to the misery. To live in a refugee camp, to exist in unimaginable destitution without any help, is another form of non-recognition. It permeates the entire personality; everything is experienced within a sense of total loss. Nezira, who in 2005 lived in a suburb of Sarajevo, no longer cared for life:

I can't help crying, I think that this is the end of my life. First, my father's remains were found and then my son's. My husband died; forty days had passed after his death, when I buried my son. I went with my only child. There was no one to lay him in the grave. Neighbours and people – somebody – put him in the grave; I don't really know what happened.

Zumra told one of my collaborators in an interview in Sarajevo:

Not one day passes that I haven't said something about it. That means it is on my mind all the time. I can't understand. Sometimes I visit a happy family, where all the members are there together, and they have problems buying a fridge or they need to change the curtains or something else in their house. I'm not interested in that. I don't, I don't have the power inside me to listen to that. I don't worry anymore about which dress I have on, what kind of shoes, which bag. All I worry about now is that I'm neat, that I'm not filthy, and I pray to dear Allah to keep me sane, to keep me aware and reasonable, so that I can communicate normally with people.

She felt that she should have done more:

I couldn't say anything more. I had the feeling that I was paralysed, and I cried rivers of tears. I didn't shriek or scream. I didn't say that they must not take him. I didn't ask: "Why him?" Nothing, nothing. I'm not saying now that, if I had said something, it might have saved him. But I couldn't help. They just told us to go along. I couldn't do anything, not a thing. And he was so gentle, worrying all the time. It was very hot that day. I felt a bit sick; he held my hand all the time, kept telling me everything is going to be all right. His arm on my shoulder was so heavy. I felt it so deep in my body. Heavy, wobbly, with fear of what will happen to us. Although he knew everything, was aware of everything; he kept saying everything would be all right. Five minutes before they separated us, I turned around to see his eyes. Now I can say it: He was looking at death. He was speechless. His eyes were focused at one point. He wasn't saying anything. He held his jacket in his hands. For a moment, I thought he has squeezed it so hard it screamed in his hands. The truck almost moved on with 15 men on it, and then on came my Omer. They said he has to stay. I couldn't say anything at that time. I just felt like I can't move, and I cried rivers of tears. I didn't yell or scream, didn't say don't take him or asked why him. Nothing, nothing. I say it today that maybe if I have said something that I could have saved him or help him somehow. But unfortunately, I couldn't help. So, I was pushed into the truck. I came to Bratunac without knowing it. I came to my sense in Bratunac, where I had a feeling like I've come to another world.

After this confusion, there is another layer: The feeling of being forsaken by the world in 1995 and even before in the years that Srebrenica was under siege. They believed that they would be protected, and promises of protection had kept them alive, but no one helped them.

It took me a long time to realise that the life stories of the survivors of Srebrenica are not only fragmented by the trauma of 1995, but also by the impossibility of telling the longer story. Because any narrative of the past is interwoven with a vision of the future, the confusion is aggravated. The women do remember the multicultural society they originally came from, and they still think it is important to live together. They were raised on a brand of communism that suppressed any expression of cultural differences, but at the same time they internalised positive feelings towards the members of the other group. Despite the current nationalist myth that the region has always been rife with war and hostility, even the most

---

17 Nancy Fraser, "Rethinking recognition", *New Left Review* 3 (2000): 108.

illiterate women are able to describe the alliance between nationalism and state politics that was the origin of all of the destruction and bloodshed. The loss of friendships mingles with a fundamental loss of trust in the world and the loss of loved ones. The survivors are left with unsettling grief, mourning, and conflicting emotions with no stable sense of normality to provide a counterbalance.

Bida could not talk about the death. Her husband committed suicide when he became aware that his daughter had been raped. Instead, she talked about her brother who was also killed, and she missed him greatly. In 2006, she said:

> I don't know, I tell you I can't; it's so hard for me. When I start talking about it, I can't go on, believe me, I lose my voice. We left the house. That moment was difficult for me; I just can't talk about it. Believe me. Everything till then, the children and worries, it was so hard for me to leave our home, it makes my hair stand on end, I lose my voice; that is that. I wish that all that was over and [that I'd] never talk about [it].
>
> You don't know how difficult it is for me. After this, I don't know how, but I know that I will get a headache, I will get ill, believe me. Whenever we sit somewhere, we talk about the war, about our survival, about fear. Somebody says: "Why do you talk about it?" I don't know, I wish we could avoid it. As soon as I start talking, I lose my voice. I wish we could avoid all this, but we can't, it stays inside us, it persists.
>
> But regardless of everything, we sit together and talk and cry; we can't do differently. But the worst thing with me is that I lose my voice, something happens. Most of us are like that, it can't be different, so accept it. I watch my children and I see that I'm tougher than they are, than any of them.

Lack of communication

People like Bida, who have lost their sense of place in the world, live in a chaotic nightmare. Context and connections have become blurred and one's position in society has dissolved. It feels as though nothing is left for them. All that remains is the story of grief and loss, and it is a story that others prefer not to hear. Societies do not know how to accommodate traumatic stories. Talking about one's past, and hence being able to present a meaningful identity, is difficult.

Bida made me aware of how many essential stories are behind what is being told in the offices of the organisations of survivors of Srebrenica. In some way, there the language of accusation has become the standard way of speaking; there is hardly room for other stories. A socially accepted language was always there. Which was the language of accusation?

Of course, the fact that rape is such a taboo aggravated the problem. However, because so many were raped, it would be much more helpful to be open about what happened. The groups of survivors have a uniform image of history, and a sadness that is not always understandable lingers in the rooms. Still, one can feel it. My feeling is that the real sadness centres on the inability to do anything against the slaughter. The women have some form of survivor's guilt, which has been described well by Judith Zur in relation to Guatemalan women. She described how it became impossible for widows in Guatemala to talk in a world where everyone knew women had been forced to look at the killing of their husbands while they were unable to stop it. Afterwards, for years, it was the official policy not to talk about what had happened. It was legally forbidden. Now, there is shame which constitutes a new hindrance to speak.[18]

During interviews, accounts of catastrophes are not immediately comprehensible. Narratives of trauma are not straightforwardly referential; rather, they are what Cathy Caruth refers to as expressions of "a crisis of witnessing." She has dealt extensively with the ways in which trauma becomes sedimented in language and literature, and she considers any eyewitness account to be rooted in dislocations of history, which are imperative.[19] Whoever has interviewed trauma cases knows that chronology fails, lapses occur, and confusion is normal. Talking about trauma often means reliving it in all of its pain, difficulty, fear, confusion, and shame. I have called the stories behind the interviews a second voice, but I should write it in plural, because we deal with polyphony. During the interviews, there are many identities who speak, many histories melt and adapt to existing discourses. The story about the self is interwoven with the story of other selves, told of and by other subjects. No speaker has the final representation at their disposal of all the perspectives and historical and political facts. No storyteller is capable of expressing the exact truth in words.

Stories are not easy, either for the narrator or those who listen. Dori Laub, the American psychiatrist, has written:

> I will propose there is a need for tremendous libidinal investment in those interview situations: There is so much destruction recounted, so much death, so much loss, so much hopelessness, that there has to be an abundance of holding and of emotional investment in the encounter.[20]

---

18 "Remembering and forgetting: Guatemalan war widows' forbidden memories", in Kim Lacy Rogers & Selma Leydesdorff (eds), *Trauma: Life Stories of Survivors*, New York 2002, p. 45-59.
19 *Unclaimed Experience: Trauma, Narrative and History*, Baltimore 2016.
20 "Bearing witness, or the vicissitudes of listening", in Shoshana Felman & Dori Laub (eds), *Testimony: Crises of Witnessing in Literature, Psychoanalysis, and History*, New York 1992, p. 77.

Absolute freedom of speech is required, and patience is obligatory. Clear answers are never given, but the desire to answer always leads to the beginnings of a new story, because one memory brings forth new memories. The narrator is often unaware of how much s/he has to tell. An emotional dynamic exists between the two who sit together, having committed themselves to the story. In this difficult process of remembering, the use of existing narration genres is a way to escape personal memories, and collective memories are redundant. This complicates any understanding of what is told. The interviewer has to continually question whether the story is indeed personal or whether the language of others is being used.

By narrowing down the desires of survivors to material compensation and juridical procedures, their life stories are also reduced to the demands, format, and language of the law. In preparation for the proceedings and in court, exact information is required, yet the victim struggles with something incomprehensible, something beyond any traditional concept of history. The significance of remembered life stories lies not in absolute truth, but in how one remembers, how one gives meaning and representation to events. Stories do not exist until they are told, and an adequate history can not be written without including the suffering of victims and the memories of survivors. Therefore, we should not dismiss them as constructions that lack factual authority, but rather regard them as being ontologically authentic.

This view of survivor subjectivity is not in line with how witness accounts are perceived in the public arena, where the "true" story of what "really" happened and the exact timeline are needed. The court proceedings of the ICTY are creating history based on eyewitness accounts, in a manner similar to how the Nuremberg trials and other post-Holocaust trials created history.

Images of chaos, chaotic images difficult to remember

The genocide in Srebrenica/Potočari was the conscious creation of chaos and panic through which the Serbs managed to dominate thousands of people. I want to think about that chaos. It was unlike other stories of mass killing, such as the Holocaust, where those who survived talk about organisation as part of a structure of domination. During the Srebrenica genocide, thousands of babies, children, the sick, and the old were herded into the compound of Potočari without sanitation and without food. During three days of aggression, over 30,000 people faced physical crimes: Killings, beatings, rape, and other atrocities that I resist talking about. They also faced psychological torture: They did not know if they were going to be killed, and they did not know where their men were. They were terrified. In truth, this situation in which one could only be scared was purposely staged by the Serbs. Remembering that situation seems impossible, although people have narrated about it, mostly in broken stories. There has hardly ever been a clear historical discourse, and the events in Potočari were clearly not integrated into personal life stories. These events stood apart, and were at the same time part of a more general confusion in memory. The trauma was the last element in a problematic interplay between not being able to remember and not wanting to remember.

From my interviews, I have concluded that the main problem is not how memories are constructed versus "reality". The main problem is what can not be remembered and put into words. To begin with, the women I have interviewed were reluctant to talk about the atrocities and the pain that they had gone through. At a deeper level, the survivors either did not wish to remember or, more frequently, certain episodes were too difficult to recall in the light of their present lives. I am referring not to traumatic episodes, but to their past peaceful co-existence with those who had lived in the same street and who eventually betrayed them. This past can hardly be understood now. The betrayal they witnessed – the participation of friends, neighbours, and loved ones in murder and genocide – also prevents them from developing any vision of the future; for such a vision can only be based on feelings about what was perceived as "good" in the past.

Problematic voices

Over the decades, voices of victims became an accepted and essential source for Holocaust historiography, but only after fierce historical debate. This is not yet the case with Srebrenica. The stories told to me, though fragmented and chaotic, still reveal what is not known and not presented by the official reports created by the various state actors that were involved. It has been difficult to obtain the narratives because the events were relatively recent, and it was only possible within the framework of life stories to understand the depth of the trauma and grief.[21]

The stories are also told by people who are confused about the disintegration of the former Yugoslavia, and the way various entities have become enemies after many years of what was called "unity". Often, the auxiliaries or perpetrators were people they had known for a very long time, people who had been their friends. War is presented as having come suddenly, although when one listens carefully it was not so sudden. In the nearly seventy interviews I have conducted with women of all ages, memories often manifested themselves in bitterness and in angry accusations of betrayal – by the Dutch Army in particular. The women I have spoken to recount the arrival of the Serb soldiers (known as the Chetniks), the

---

21 Leydesdorff, "When communities...", *op cit.*

disruption of previously good relations between the ethnic groups, and the mass murder. They also describe how they have tried to give meaning to what happened to them, how they have resumed their lives, and how they have attempted to incorporate their experiences into their life stories. These are traumatic fragments that reflect the women's truth about their subjective experience.

Listen to them

As I wrote, women survivors doubt whether they have told their own story when they do remember. I interviewed Nermina, a woman in her early forties, in Mihatovići, a nasty camp, but a camp considered not to be as bad as many others. She said:

> It is a dream, I mean a nightmare. But one moment stands out: My husband began to kiss our children. He took the eldest one and cried, and he wailed: "Armin, my son, maybe your father will never see you again." He cried. Then he took little Omer: "Omer, my son, your father will never see you again." The whole war, everything we went through, was not as terrible as this farewell, this saying good-bye. He came to the youngest one and only then stepped back. He went to the gate and stood there, crying.

That parting is a film that replays in Nermina's head. It is the story told by the surviving women again and again: There is always that last moment engraved in their memory. A husband, a son, a father, a member of the family. A man and a woman embrace for the last time, their faces distorted, their cheeks and eyes full of tears. A father embraces his daughter, and both know it is the last time. A child cries and calls the father, begging: "Daddy, please come back!" A mother begs: "Don't take my son away, he is so small!" She tries to free him from the hands of Serb soldiers, in vain. Her life seems to be over.

The genocide of Potočari was chaos and blood everywhere; there was a horrible stench. Men were deported to be murdered, but on the spot women and girls were raped, and incredible violence was used. We know now that 731 children are missing, and that more than five percent of the victims were under the age of fifteen. Thousands of women and children needed to be evacuated without too much protest and without too much questioning about where the men were. It had to look like a clean and smooth operation. It was not.

How can victims/survivors find words for the horror that unfolded before their eyes? Is it not better to be silent, as the task of remembering and speaking is so horrendous? Who is good? Who can be trusted? Good memories of coexistence with "the other" have become problematic. It is easier not to talk about them, to deny past feelings and replace them with stronger emotions of hatred and disappointment. Memories of their previous lives are eclipsed by feelings of loss. This is why the women I interviewed can hardly imagine positive feelings when they think about the past. Everything that was normal has been disrupted. The moment of disruption is clearly grafted onto their memory, but it is precisely that moment which also conceals all positive feelings about the time before. Cruelty is ubiquitous in their memories.

There are too many chaotic memories. The charitableness that has come slowly is astounding given the fact that all of them underwent the same fate, although in different ways. They lost husbands, sons, fathers, and brothers, and their lives will never return to what they once were. If legal language and the demands of law become the dominant narrative for framing eyewitness accounts of genocide, we risk erasing a representation of how deeply lives have been disrupted.[22] We erase the fragmentations, the silences, and the dislocations. By not allowing the full truth of the stories in all their layered and unfinished forms, by dismissing them as outbursts of emotion, we deny their mediated authenticity and the way they might reconfigure or even remake the world for those who have lost their place in it. In turn, we dislocate the meaning and place assigned to an event. In this entwinement between the legal truth and the victim's need to speak out, material compensation is merely one of many ways to reclaim a place in the world.

---

22 Michael Levine, *The Belated Witness: Literature, Testimony, and the Question of Holocaust Survival*, Stanford 2006.